Ellie Greenwild

PLANT BASED

COOKBOOK FOR BEGINNERS

**2000+ Days of Super Easy, Nourishing
Recipes for Breakfast, Lunch, and Dinner.
Includes a 30-Day No-Stress Meal Plan
for a Healthier Lifestyle**

Table of Contents

Chapter 4: Delicious Dinner 39

Chapter 5: Hearty Beans and Grains 54

Chapter 6: Yummy Smoothie 68

Chapter 7: Lively Salads 72

Introduction

Imagine a world where your meals do more than just satisfy hunger—they rejuvenate your body, protect the planet, and bring you closer to nature's bounty. This is not just a distant dream but a tangible reality you can embrace today. This book is your invitation to explore a world of culinary delights that are as nourishing as kind to the earth.

Embarking on a plant-based journey can seem daunting at first. Concerns about nutrition, flavor variety, meal satisfaction, and even the social aspects of dining can make the transition seem challenging. But what if you had someone to walk you through these challenges, offering practical advice, insightful solutions, and a plethora of delectable recipes that turn each meal into an exploration?

That's exactly what I aim to be for you. With years of experience and a deep passion for plant-based living, I've designed this cookbook to be more than a simple collection of recipes. It's a comprehensive guide to transforming your life, one delicious meal at a time.

My name is Ellie Greenwild, and I'm not just a chef — I'm someone who has personally experienced the transformative power of plant-based eating. I've navigated the journey you're about to embark on, and I've come to understand that food is more than sustenance; it's a source of joy, health, and harmony with our environment.

In this book, you'll discover a treasure trove of culinary delights: mouthwatering recipes, insights into your nutritional needs, and tips for preparing meals that will impress even the most discerning palates. My aim is to demystify plant-based cooking, making it accessible and enjoyable for you, regardless of your previous cooking experience.

But "Plant-Based Cookbook for Beginnings" Is more than a cookbook; it calls for a more conscious, healthful, and compassionate way of living. I'm here to guide you, share my passion, and provide you with innovative recipes that promise to make every meal a celebration of taste and well-being.

Let's follow this beautiful journey together. Your plant-based adventure starts now.

Thank You for Choosing My Book!

I sincerely appreciate your decision to explore the transformative principles of Plan-Based Diet through my book. To express my gratitude and to further assist you on your journey to better health, I am thrilled to offer you an exclusive bonus:

Alkaline Juices Recipe Book

Incorporating alkaline juices into your diet is more than just a trend—it's a pathway to enhanced health. These juices aim to balance the body's pH levels, which can often become overly acidic due to modern dietary habits that prioritize processed foods and sugars. By emphasizing alkaline-rich ingredients, these juices help neutralize excess acidity, fostering an environment where your body can thrive.

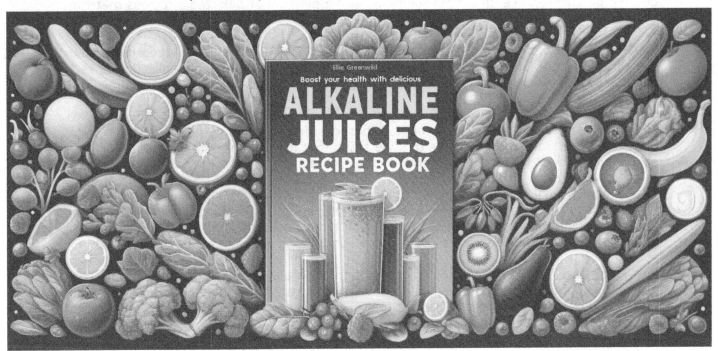

Here's how you can claim your free Alkaline Juices Recipe Book:

1. Simply scan the QR code with your smartphone.
2. Send me an email that pops up after you scan

   the QR code.
3. I will personally send you the Alkaline Juices Recipe

   Book directly to your inbox.

This is my way of saying thank you for starting this healthful adventure. Whether you are new to alkaline diets or looking to expand your current practices, these juice recipes will provide you with additional resources to invigorate your routine and enhance your nutritional intake.

Thank you once again for your support, and here's to your health and vitality!

Warm regards, Ellie.

Chapter 1: The Beginner's Guide

Understanding the Plant-Based Diet and Benefits for Your Health

Embarking on a plant-based journey opens up a new world of culinary adventures and health benefits. Fundamentally, a plant-centric eating plan emphasizes foods sourced from plants, encompassing vegetables, fruits, grains, nuts, seeds, and legumes, while limiting or eliminating animal-derived products. The beauty of this diet lies in its flexibility and inclusiveness, allowing for a spectrum of choices that can be tailored to individual ethical, health, or environmental motivations.

Plant-based foods, with their unique nutrient-dense composition, offer a plethora of health benefits. Their exceptional antioxidant content not only aids digestion but also provides a host of other advantages.

- **Heart Health Improvement**
- While diets rich in processed and animal-based foods have been associated with an increased risk of heart disease, a diet centered on whole, plant-based foods can be a game-changer. It not only provides essential nutrients but also enhances the heart's efficiency in circulating blood throughout the body.
- **Diabetes Prevention and Management**
- Eating various plant foods has been shown to decrease significantly blood sugar levels. Comparative studies between diets high in plant-based ingredients versus those dominated by meat indicate that a diet focused on plants can considerably reduce the chance of diabetes by 50%.
- **Cognitive Function Enhancement**
- Consuming fruits and vegetables boost the brain's metabolism due to their detoxifying properties and the abundance of plant compounds and antioxidants they contain. These nutrients contribute to slowing down cognitive decline and provide steady energy, which improves memory, language skills, thinking, and judgment.
- **Facilitates Weight Loss**
- Diets high in animal products are often associated with weight gain. Adopting a plant-based diet, on the other hand, can lead to more accessible and more rapid weight loss as the body more efficiently breaks down fat stores.

Principles and Guidelines of a Plant-Based Diet

The basis of a plant-centered diet is established upon several fundamental principles:
1. **Whole Foods:** Prioritize whole, unprocessed, or minimally processed plant foods to maximize nutritional intake.
2. **Variety:** Embrace a wide range of plant foods to ensure a rich intake of nutrients.
3. **Balance:** Seek a harmonious plate that includes carbohydrates sourced from whole grains, proteins derived from legumes and nuts, beneficial fats obtained from seeds and avocados, and a rich array of vitamins and minerals from fruits and vegetables.
4. **Limit Animal Products:** Whether you choose to exclude animal products entirely or significantly reduce their intake, the focus is on plant-derived foods.
5. **Mindful Eating:** Listen to your body, eat with intention, and choose foods that are both nourishing and enjoyable.

Myth-Busting Points for Plant-Based Eating

Shifting towards a plant-based diet may cause misunderstandings and falsehoods that could discourage newcomers. Let's address and debunk some common myths to clear the path for your plant-based journey.

Myth 1: Plant-Based Diets Are Protein Deficient

Truth: Plant-based diets can provide all the necessary protein your body needs. Legumes, lentils, chickpeas, tofu, tempeh, seitan, nuts, and seeds are excellent protein sources. Quinoa and soy products offer complete proteins containing all nine essential amino acids.

Myth 2: Plant-Based Eating Is Expensive
Truth: Plant-based eating can be incredibly cost-effective. Staples like beans, lentils, rice, and seasonal vegetables often cost less than meat and dairy products. Planning your meals and buying in bulk can reduce expenses, making plant-based eating affordable for any budget.

Myth 3: You'll Feel Hungry All the Time
Truth: A well-planned plant-based diet is filling and satisfying. Nutrient-rich foods such as whole grains, veggies, and legumes, packed with fiber, can help you stay satiated for extended periods. Incorporating various foods ensures you receive a balance of essential nutrients, keeping hunger at bay.

Myth 4: Plant-Based Food Lacks Flavor
Truth: Plant-based cuisine bursts with natural flavors. Fruits, vegetables, herbs, and spices provide various tastes and aromas. Exploring international cuisines and experimenting with seasoning can turn plant-based meals into a delightful culinary adventure.

Myth 5: It's All or Nothing
Truth: Plant-based eating doesn't have to be an all-or-nothing approach. Many people find success and health benefits by starting with "Meatless Mondays" or incorporating more plant-based meals throughout the week. Each plant-centered meal represents progress toward improved health and ecological sustainability.

Myth 6: Plant-Based Diets Are Not Suitable for Athletes
Truth: Many athletes thrive on plant-based diets, enjoying improved recovery times, increased energy levels, and strong performances. Proper planning ensures athletes receive adequate calories, proteins, and nutrients to fuel their activities and recovery.

Myth 7: Cooking Plant-Based Meals Is Time-Consuming
Truth: Like all culinary styles, plant-based cuisine can vary from swift and uncomplicated to intricate and time-intensive.
Many plant-based recipes are straightforward and require no more time than cooking with meat. Preparing batches of grains, legumes, and vegetables in advance can make daily cooking even more convenient.

Myth 8: Plant-Based Diets Lack Calcium and Iron
Truth: Calcium and iron are abundant in plants. Leafy greens, fortified plant milk, tofu, and tahini are rich in calcium. Iron can be found in legumes, grains, nuts, seeds, and green vegetables. Consuming vitamin C-rich foods alongside iron-rich foods enhances iron absorption.

Myth 9: Plant-Based Diets Are Automatically Healthy
Truth: Like any diet, plant-based eating requires balance and variety to be genuinely healthy. Processed plant-based foods, such as vegan junk food, can be high in sugar, salt, and unhealthy fats. Focusing on whole, minimally processed foods and a variety of fruits, vegetables, whole grains, nuts, and seeds ensures you receive comprehensive nutrition and health benefits.

Myth 10: Plant-Based Eating Means Giving Up All Your Favorite Foods
Truth: Transitioning to a plant-based diet doesn't mean you must forsake the flavors and dishes you love. Many traditional favorites can be adapted to plant-based versions that are just as delicious, if not more so. Ingredients like mushrooms, lentils, and jackfruit can be used to recreate the textures and tastes of meat, while cashews and nutritional yeast can mimic cheesy flavors. Creativity and suitable recipes allow you to enjoy plant-based versions of your favorite meals without feeling deprived.

These myth-busting points illuminate the truth about plant-based eating: it's nutritious, versatile, affordable, and suitable for everyone, including athletes. Plant-based cooking offers a world of flavorful, satisfying meals that support your health and the planet. Let these truths guide you as you embark on your plant-based culinary journey.

How to Start Plant-Based Eating

Welcome to the exciting transition towards a plant-based lifestyle! Whether your motivation stems from health, ethical, or environmental reasons, beginning a plant-based diet is a rewarding and transformative journey. Here's a step-by-step guide to help you navigate this new culinary landscape with ease and enjoyment.

Step 1: Understand Your Why
Clarifying your reasons for moving towards a plant-based diet can provide motivation and direction. Understanding your ' why ' will keep you anchored on this journey, whether it's to improve your health, reduce your carbon footprint, or align with your ethical beliefs.

Step 2: Educate Yourself
Knowledge is power. Familiarize yourself with the basics of nutrition to ensure a balanced diet, learn about the myriad of plant-based ingredients available, and understand how to substitute traditional animal-based products with plant-based alternatives. Resources like this cookbook, nutritional blogs, documentaries, and scientific articles can offer valuable insights.

Step 3: Start Slow

If the idea of a full transition seems daunting, begin with small, manageable steps. Incorporate "Meatless Mondays," switch to plant-based milk, or dedicate one meal daily to be entirely plant-based. Gradual changes allow you to adjust without feeling overwhelmed.

Step 4: Master a Few Go-To Recipes

Begin by mastering a handful of simple plant-based recipes that you enjoy. Having a repertoire of 5-10 go-to dishes makes meal planning easier and helps build confidence in your cooking skills. Choose recipes that excite you and meet your nutritional needs, from hearty breakfasts to satisfying dinners.

Step 5: Stock Your Pantry

Transforming your pantry is key to a seamless transition. Stock up on plant-based staples such as legumes, whole grains, nuts, seeds, spices, and various canned and fresh produce. Having these ingredients on hand makes it easier to whip up nutritious meals on the fly.

Step 6: Experiment with Plant-Based Alternatives

Explore the world of plant-based alternatives for meat, dairy, and eggs. Products like tofu, tempeh, nut cheeses, and plant-based yogurts can open up new culinary possibilities and add interesting textures and flavors to your meals.

Step 7: Plan Your Meals

Meal planning can significantly simplify your plant-based journey. Spend some time each week planning your meals, ensuring variety and nutritional balance. This not only helps in grocery shopping but also reduces food waste and last-minute dining dilemmas.

Step 8: Connect with the Community

Joining plant-based groups, online forums, or local meetups can provide support, inspiration, and friendship. Sharing experiences, challenges, and successes with others on a similar path can be incredibly motivating.

Step 9: Be Patient and Kind to Yourself

Transitioning to a plant-based diet is a journey, not a race. There may be challenges and learning curves along the way. Remember to be patient and kind to yourself, celebrating each small victory and learning from setbacks.

Step 10: Enjoy the Journey

Lastly, enjoy the process! Discovering new foods, experimenting with recipes, and feeling the positive changes in your body and mind can be deeply rewarding. Embrace the adventure of plant-based eating as a continuous journey of growth and discovery.

By following these steps, you'll find that adopting a plant-based diet can be a joyful, enriching experience that benefits not only your health but also the planet and its inhabitants. Welcome to your plant-based beginning—let the adventure begin!

Meal Planning and Preparation

Embarking on a plant-based lifestyle brings excitement and novelty to your meals but also requires some planning and preparation to ensure success. This short guide is designed to help beginners navigate meal planning and preparation, making the process enjoyable and stress-free.

Embrace the Basics of Meal Planning

1. Start with a Template: Begin each week with a simple meal planning template that includes slots for breakfast, lunch, dinner, and snacks for each day. This visual aid helps you organize and balance your meals.

2. Build Around Plant-Based Proteins: Center your meals around plant-based protein sources like beans, lentils, tofu, and tempeh. These will keep you satisfied and ensure you're getting essential nutrients.

3. Incorporate Variety: Aim for diversity in your meals to cover a broad spectrum of nutrients. A diverse array of colorful vegetables and fruits, an assortment of grains, and a selection of nuts and seeds will enhance the nutritional value of your meals.

4. Plan for Leftovers: Cooking once and eating twice (or more) saves time and energy. Plan to make larger batches of meals that can easily be repurposed into future dishes.

5. Keep Snacks in Mind: Healthy plant-based snacks, such as cut vegetables with hummus, fruit with nut butter, or homemade granola bars, are great to include in your meal plan.

Tips for Efficient Meal Preparation

1. Batch Cooking: Dedicate a few hours each week to cook large quantities of basics like grains, legumes, and roasted vegetables. Place them in the refrigerator or freezer to simplify meal preparation over the course of the week.

2. Pre-Chop Vegetables: Wash and chop veggies right after shopping so they're ready to use. This reduces meal prep time and makes it more likely you'll reach for healthy options.

3. Use Your Appliances: Slow cookers, pressure cookers, and blenders can be plant-based eaters' best friends, making it easier to prepare complex dishes with minimal effort.

4. Create a Prep Routine: Find a meal prep rhythm that works for you. Some prefer a big prep day once a week, while others do a little each day. Experiment to find your ideal routine.

5. Embrace Simple Meals: Not every meal needs to be a culinary masterpiece. Simple, whole food-based meals are often the most satisfying. A quick stir-fry, salad, or bowl can be nutritious and fulfilling.

6. Explore Meal Themes: To keep things interesting without becoming overwhelming, consider theme nights, like Taco Tuesday or Stir-Fry Saturday. This gives a structure to your planning while allowing for creativity.

Remember, meal planning and preparation are not about strict adherence to a schedule but about making your life easier and your meals healthier. Be open to swapping out ingredients based on what's in season or on sale, and don't be afraid to experiment with new recipes or flavors.

With these strategies, meal planning and preparation become less of a chore and more of a joyful exploration of plant-based eating. Let this guide to spark your creativity in crafting flavorful and nutritious dishes that complement your fresh lifestyle, establishing the groundwork for a fulfilling and gratifying journey into plant-based eating.

30-Day No Stress Meal Plan

Embarking on a 30-day plant-based menu plan is an opportunity to nourish your body with a diverse array of whole foods. This diet emphasizes vegetables, fruits, whole grains, legumes, seeds, and nuts, offering a plethora of flavors and nutritional benefits. With snacks and desserts like energy bites and dairy-free treats, variety is abundant. ***The variety of recipes presented in this book can provide more than 2000 days of healthy eating.***

The dietary recommendations provided serve as a universal guideline for maintaining a healthy lifestyle, though it's crucial to adjust these based on individual health goals, conditions, and cultural dietary practices. Below is a general overview of the daily nutritional requirements for the average adult:

Calories: The typical adult requires approximately 2,000 to 2,500 calories daily. The exact amount varies, with women generally needing fewer calories than men, and active individuals requiring more.

Protein: It is recommended that adults consume about 0.8 grams of protein per kilogram of body weight daily. This equates to roughly 56 grams for an average sedentary man and 46 grams for an average sedentary woman.

Carbohydrates: Carbohydrates should constitute about 45% to 65% of your total daily caloric intake. For someone on a 2,000-calorie diet, this would be approximately 225 to 325 grams per day.

Fat: Dietary fat should make up 20% to 35% of your total daily calories. On a 2,000-calorie diet, this translates to around 44 to 77 grams per day.

Fiber: An intake of 25 grams per day for women and 38 grams for men is recommended to promote digestive health and prevent chronic diseases.

Cholesterol: Although specific recommendations can vary, it's generally suggested to limit cholesterol intake to less than 300 milligrams per day, focusing instead on consuming healthier fats.

Sodium: Limiting sodium intake to no more than 2,300 milligrams a day, with an ideal target of no more than 1,500 mg per day for most adults, is recommended to support heart health.

Potassium: Adults are advised to consume 2,600 mg (for women) to 3,400 mg (for men) of potassium daily to maintain proper cellular function and counteract the effects of sodium on blood pressure.

Remember, these guidelines serve as a starting point. Individual needs may vary based on factors like age, sex, physical activity level, and existing health conditions. Consulting with healthcare professionals can provide personalized advice to meet your specific dietary needs and health objectives. Add to your menu the dish options that are necessary for an optimally balanced diet specifically for you.

Day	Breakfast	First Snack	Lunch	Second Snack	Dinner
1	Avocado Toast with Tomato Slices	Carrot Sticks and Hummus	Quinoa Salad with Black Beans and Corn	Apple Slices with Almond Butter	Vegetable Stir-Fry with Tofu
2	Berry Banana Smoothie	Cucumber Slices with Guacamole	Lentil Soup with Spinach	Orange Segments	Chickpea Curry with Brown Rice
3	Oatmeal with Fresh Berries and Flaxseed	Bell Pepper Strips with Salsa	Vegan Sushi Rolls	Mixed Nuts	Spaghetti with Marinara Sauce and Meatless Meatballs
4	Whole Wheat Chocolate Waffle	Green Smoothie (Spinach, Pineapple, Banana)	Falafel Salad with Tahini Dressing	Chili Lime Edamame	Vegan Chili with Avocado and Cornbread
5	Spelt Berry Hot Breakfast Cereal	Rice Cakes with Avocado	Sweet Potato and Black Bean Burrito	Sliced Apple with Peanut Butter	Stuffed Bell Peppers
6	Chia Pudding with Mango	Cherry Tomatoes and Vegan Cheese	Vegan Caesar Salad with Chickpea Croutons	Kale Chips	Mushroom Stroganoff
7	Vegan Pancakes with Maple Syrup	Avocado and Tomato Sandwich on Whole Grain Bread	Vegetable and Bean Soup	Dried Apricots	Roasted Vegetable Pizza with Vegan Cheese
8	Tropical Fruit Salad with a Squeeze of Lime	Snap Peas with Hummus	Tofu Teriyaki Stir-Fry	Almonds and Walnuts	Butternut Squash Risotto
9	Blueberry Lemon Breakfast Quinoa	Cocoa with Coconut Milk	Vegan Tacos with Lentil Walnut Meat	Sliced Cucumber and Carrots with Bean Dip	Eggplant Parmesan with Cashew Cheese
10	Muesli with Plant-Based Yogurt and Fresh Fruit	Roasted Chickpeas	Quinoa and Roasted Vegetable Salad with Lemon Tahini Dressing	Mixed Berry and Banana Fruit Salad	Vegan Pad Thai with Tofu
11	Toasted Whole Grain Bread with Avocado and Radish Slices	Pitted Dates	Vegan Caesar Wrap with Smoky Tempeh	Carrot and Cucumber Sticks with Beet Hummus	Stuffed Acorn Squash with Wild Rice and Cranberries
12	Vegan Blueberry Muffins	Kiwi and Strawberry Skewers	Spinach and Avocado Pasta Salad	Almond Protein Bars	Moroccan Vegetable Tagine with Couscous
13	Overnight Oats with Chia Seeds, Almond Milk, and Mango	Orange and Grapefruit Citrus Salad	Vegan Minestrone Soup	Guacamole with Whole Grain Crackers	Black Bean and Sweet Potato Enchiladas
14	Vegan French Toast with Berry Compote	Baked Apple with Cinnamon and Nutmeg	Chickpea Salad Sandwich	Cashews and Dried Cranberries	Vegan Paella with Artichokes and Bell Peppers
15	Banana and Walnut Oatmeal	Veggie Sticks with Cashew Cheese Dip	Mediterranean Chickpea and Quinoa Salad	Fresh Fig Halves	Vegan Mushroom Bourguignon
16	Avocado and Spinach Smoothie	Chilled Creamy Tofu Cheese	Pesto Pasta with Cherry Tomatoes	Sliced Cucumber with Lime and Chili Powder	Vegan Jambalaya

Day	Breakfast	First Snack	Lunch	Second Snack	Dinner
17	Toast with Almond Butter and Sliced Banana	Baked Sweet Potato Fries	Vegan Cobb Salad with Coconut Bacon	Fresh Pineapple Chunks	Lentil Sloppy Joes
18	Chia and Berry Parfait	Dark Chocolate and Almonds	Vegan Sushi Bowl with Avocado and Cucumber	Olives and Pickles	Stuffed Zucchini Boats
19	Green Tea Smoothie Bowl with Kiwi and Coconut	Rice Cakes with Tahini and Honey	Vegan Pho with Tofu and Mushrooms	Spiced Roasted Nuts	Vegan Shepherd's Pie
20	Pear and Ginger Oatmeal	Mixed Berries	Vegan Greek Salad with Tofu Feta	Hummus with Bell Pepper Strips	Cauliflower Tacos with Avocado Crema
21	Vegan Banana Bread	Apple with Cinnamon	Curried Lentil Soup	Edamame with Sea Salt	Vegan Gnocchi with Spinach and Tomatoes
22	Raspberry and Almond Butter Smoothie	Air-Popped Popcorn with Nutritional Yeast	Vegan Quiche with Spinach and Mushrooms	Carrot Sticks with Almond Dip	Vegan Bolognese with Lentils over Whole Wheat Pasta
23	Vegan Protein Pancakes topped with Fresh Berries	Orange Slices	Vegan Caesar Salad with Crispy Chickpeas	Roasted Seaweed Snacks	Vegan Fajitas with Portobello Mushrooms and Bell Peppers
24	Golden Milk Spice Smoothie with Pear and Fig Tart	Sliced Peaches	Chickpea Avocado Salad Sandwich	Vegan Cheese and Whole Grain Crackers	Stuffed Sweet Potatoes with Black Beans and Salsa
25	Coconut Yogurt with Granola and Kiwi	Balsamic Avocado	Vegan Burrito Bowls with Quinoa, Beans, and Veggies	Trail Mix with Nuts and Dried Fruit	Vegan Thai Green Curry with Tofu and Vegetables
26	Peanut Butter and Jelly Oatmeal	Baked Apple Chips	Vegan Niçoise Salad	Veggie Spring Rolls with Peanut Dipping Sauce	Eggplant Lasagna with Cashew Ricotta
27	Avocado, Kale, and Tomato on Toast	Banana with Peanut Butter	Vegan Miso Soup with Tofu and Seaweed	Dark Chocolate Squares	Pizza with Artichokes, Olives, and Cashew Cheese
28	Chia Seed Pudding with Coconut Milk and Mango	Homemade Granola Bars	Waldorf Salad with Apples, Walnuts, and Tofu	Cucumber and Jicama with Lime Juice	Moroccan Lentil Stew with Apricots and Spinach
29	Toasted Bagel with Vegan Cream Cheese and Sliced Tomato	A Bowl of Fresh Watermelon Cubes	Cold Pasta Salad with Cherry Tomatoes, Cucumbers, Olives, and Vegan Feta	A Cup of Mixed Berries with a Dollop of Vegan Yogurt	Vegan Sloppy Joes served with a Side of Baked Sweet Potato Fries
30	Fruit Salad with a Drizzle of Agave and a Sprinkle of Chia Seeds	Cocoa with Banana Milk	Grilled Vegetable Wrap with Hummus and Arugula	Steamed Edamame Pods sprinkled with Sea Salt	Vegan Mushroom Risotto with a Side of Steamed Green Beans

Chapter 2:
Energizing Breakfast

Avocado Toast with Tomato Slices

Yield: 2 servings | **Prep time**: 5 minutes | **Cook time**: 3 minutes

Ingredients:
- 4 slices of whole grain bread
- 1 ripe avocado
- 1 medium tomato, sliced
- Salt and pepper, to taste
- Optional: Red pepper flakes or fresh herbs for garnish

Directions:
1. Toast the slices of bread to your preferred level of crispiness.
2. While the bread is toasting, halve the avocado, remove the pit, and scoop the flesh into a bowl. Mash the avocado with a fork until it reaches your desired consistency. Season with salt and pepper to taste.
3. Spread the mashed avocado evenly onto the toasted bread slices. Top each slice with tomato slices. If desired, add a sprinkle of red pepper flakes or fresh herbs for extra flavor.
4. Serve immediately for the best taste and texture.

Nutritional Information: 320 calories, 9g protein, 37g carbohydrates, 17g fat, 13g fiber, 0mg cholesterol, 300mg sodium, 970mg potassium.

Vegan Pancakes with Maple Syrup

Yield: 4 servings | **Prep time:** 10 minutes | **Cook time:** 15 minutes

Ingredients:
- 1 cup all-purpose flour
- 1 tablespoon sugar (or maple syrup)
- 2 tablespoons baking powder
- 1/8 teaspoon salt
- 1 cup almond milk
- 2 tablespoons vegetable oil
- Maple syrup for serving

Directions:
1. In a large bowl, whisk together the flour, sugar, baking powder, and salt.
2. In another bowl, mix the almond milk and vegetable oil. Pour the wet ingredients into the dry ingredients and stir until just combined; some lumps are okay.
3. Heat a non-stick skillet over medium heat. Pour 1/4 cup of batter for each pancake. Cook until bubbles form on the surface, then flip and cook until golden brown on the other side.
4. Serve hot with maple syrup.

Nutritional Information: 230 calories, 4g protein, 38g carbohydrates, 7g fat, 1g fiber, 0mg cholesterol, 590mg sodium, 50mg potassium.

Oatmeal with Fresh Berries and Flaxseed

Yield: 4 servings | **Prep time**: 5 minutes | **Cook time**: 5 minutes

Ingredients:
- 2 cups water or almond milk
- 1 cup old-fashioned oats
- 1 cup fresh berries (such as blueberries, raspberries, and sliced strawberries)
- 2 tablespoons ground flaxseed
- 1-2 tablespoons maple syrup or honey, to taste
- Optional: A pinch of salt

Directions:
1. In a medium saucepan, bring the water or almond milk to a boil. Add a pinch of salt if desired.
2. Stir in the oats and reduce the heat to medium. Cook for 5 minutes, stirring occasionally, until the oats are soft and have absorbed most of the liquid.
3. Remove from heat and let the oatmeal sit for 2 minutes to thicken further.
4. Serve the oatmeal in bowls, topped with fresh berries and a sprinkle of ground flaxseed. Drizzle with maple syrup or honey to taste.

Nutritional Information: 190 calories, 6g protein, 33g carbohydrates, 4g fat, 7g fiber, 0mg cholesterol, 30mg sodium, 200mg potassium.

Chia Pudding with Mango

Yield: 4 servings | **Prep time:** 10 minutes | **Cook time:** 0 minutes (plus 4 hours for chilling)

Ingredients:
- 1/4 cup chia seeds
- 1 cup almond milk
- 2 tablespoons maple syrup
- 1 teaspoon vanilla extract
- 1 large mango, peeled and cubed

Directions:
1. In a mixing bowl, combine the chia seeds, almond milk, maple syrup, and vanilla extract. Stir well to combine.
2. Divide the mixture evenly among four glasses or bowls. Cover and refrigerate for at least 4 hours, or overnight, until the pudding has thickened.
3. Before serving, top each serving of chia pudding with cubed mango.

Nutritional Information: 150 calories, 3g protein, 24g carbohydrates, 5g fat, 8g fiber, 0mg cholesterol, 40mg sodium, 200mg potassium.

Whole Wheat Chocolate Waffle

Yield: 4 servings | **Prep time:** 10 minutes | **Cook time:** 5 minutes

Ingredients:
- 1 1/2 cups whole wheat flour
- 1/4 cup unsweetened cocoa powder
- 2 teaspoons baking powder
- 1/4 teaspoon salt
- 2 tablespoons maple syrup or honey
- 1 1/4 cups almond milk
- 1/4 cup unsweetened applesauce
- 1 teaspoon vanilla extract
- Cooking spray for waffle iron

Directions:
1. In a large bowl, whisk together the whole wheat flour, cocoa powder, baking powder, and salt.
2. In another bowl, mix the maple syrup, almond milk, applesauce, and vanilla extract until well combined.
3. Pour the wet ingredients into the dry ingredients and stir until just combined, being careful not to overmix.
4. Preheat your waffle iron according to the manufacturer's instructions and lightly coat with cooking spray. Pour enough batter to just cover the waffle grid, close the lid, and cook until the waffle is crisp and browned, usually about 5 minutes.
5. Serve the waffles warm with your choice of toppings, such as fresh berries, banana slices, or a drizzle of maple syrup.

Nutritional Information: 210 calories, 6g protein, 44g carbohydrates, 2g fat, 8g fiber, 0mg cholesterol, 380mg sodium, 300mg potassium.

Toasted Whole Grain Bread with Avocado and Radish Slices

Yield: 4 servings | **Prep time:** 5 minutes | **Cook time:** 3 minutes

Ingredients:
- 4 slices of whole grain bread
- 2 ripe avocados
- 8 radishes, thinly sliced
- Salt and pepper to taste
- Optional: A drizzle of olive oil and a sprinkle of crushed red pepper flakes for garnish

Directions:
1. Toast the whole grain bread slices to your preferred level of crispiness.
2. Halve and pit the avocados. Scoop out the flesh and mash it with a fork. Season with salt and pepper.
3. Spread the mashed avocado evenly over the toasted bread slices.
4. Arrange the thinly sliced radishes on top of the avocado. If desired, drizzle with olive oil and sprinkle with red pepper flakes for extra flavor.

5. Serve immediately, enjoying the blend of creamy avocado with the crisp bite of radish.

Nutritional Information: 300 calories, 7g protein, 34g carbohydrates, 17g fat, 10g fiber, 0mg cholesterol, 200mg sodium, 800mg potassium.

Tropical Fruit Salad with a Squeeze of Lime

Yield: 4 servings | **Prep time:** 15 minutes

Ingredients:
- 1 mango, peeled and cubed
- 1 cup pineapple, cubed
- 1 cup papaya, cubed
- 2 kiwis, peeled and sliced
- Juice of 1 lime
- 1 tablespoon honey (optional for sweetness)

Directions:
1. In a large bowl, combine the mango, pineapple, papaya, and kiwi slices.
2. Squeeze the juice of one lime over the fruit. Drizzle with honey if using and gently toss to combine.
3. Let the salad sit for 5-10 minutes to allow the flavors to meld together before serving.

Nutritional Information: 120 calories, 1g protein, 30g carbohydrates, 0.5g fat, 3g fiber, 0mg cholesterol, 5mg sodium, 400mg potassium.

Muesli with Plant-Based Yogurt and Fresh Fruit

Yield: 4 servings | **Prep time:** 10 minutes

Ingredients:
- 2 cups unsweetened plant-based yogurt (such as almond, soy, or coconut yogurt)
- 1 cup muesli
- 1/2 cup fresh berries (strawberries, blueberries, raspberries)
- 1 apple, cored and chopped
- 1 banana, sliced
- Optional: honey or maple syrup for sweetness

Directions:
1. In four serving bowls, layer the plant-based yogurt at the bottom.
2. Sprinkle muesli over the yogurt evenly among the bowls.
3. Top with a mix of fresh berries, chopped apple, and banana slices.
4. Drizzle with a little honey or maple syrup if desired for added sweetness.

Nutritional Information: 250 calories, 8g protein, 42g carbohydrates, 6g fat, 5g fiber, 0mg cholesterol, 55mg sodium, 350mg potassium.

Overnight Oats with Chia Seeds, Almond Milk, and Mango

Yield: 4 servings | **Prep time:** 5 minutes |
Cook time: 0 minutes (plus overnight soaking)
Ingredients:
- 2 cups rolled oats
- 4 tablespoons chia seeds
- 2 cups unsweetened almond milk
- 1 large mango, peeled and cubed
- 2 tablespoons maple syrup (optional)
- Optional toppings: additional mango cubes or a sprinkle of shredded coconut

Directions:
1. In a large bowl, mix together the rolled oats, chia seeds, and almond milk. Stir in the maple syrup if using for added sweetness.
2. Divide the mixture evenly between four jars or bowls. Cover and refrigerate overnight.
3. In the morning, stir the oats and top with fresh mango cubes. Add additional toppings if desired.

Nutritional Information: 350 calories, 10g protein, 55g carbohydrates, 9g fat, 12g fiber, 0mg cholesterol, 30mg sodium, 400mg potassium.

Chia and Berry Parfait

Yield: 4 servings | **Prep time:** 15 minutes |
Cook time: 0 min. (+at least 4 hours for chilling)
Ingredients:
- 1/3 cup chia seeds
- 2 cups unsweetened almond milk
- 2 tablespoons maple syrup
- 1 teaspoon vanilla extract
- 2 cups mixed berries
- Optional: granola for layering

Directions:
1. Mix chia seeds, almond milk, maple syrup, and vanilla in a bowl. Let it sit for about 5 minutes, then stir again to prevent clumping. Cover and refrigerate for at least 4 hours or overnight.
2. To assemble the parfaits, layer the chia pudding with mixed berries and optional granola in glasses or jars.
3. Serve chilled, layered with additional berries and granola if desired.

Nutritional Information: 220 calories, 6g protein, 30g carbohydrates, 9g fat, 13g fiber, 0mg cholesterol, 80mg sodium, 350mg potassium.

Vegan French Toast with Berry Compote

Yield: 4 servings | **Prep time:** 10 minutes | **Cook time:** 20 minutes
Ingredients:
- 8 slices of whole grain bread
- 1 cup unsweetened almond milk
- 1/4 cup chickpea flour
- 1 tablespoon maple syrup, plus more for serving
- 1 teaspoon vanilla extract
- 2 cups mixed berries (fresh or frozen)
- 1 tablespoon sugar (optional for compote)

Directions:
1. In a shallow dish, whisk together almond milk, chickpea flour, maple syrup, and vanilla extract.
2. Dip each slice of bread into the mixture, allowing it to soak for a few seconds on each side.
3. Cook the soaked bread slices on a nonstick skillet over medium heat until golden brown on both sides.
4. For the berry compote, cook mixed berries with sugar (if using) in a saucepan over medium heat until the berries are soft and the sauce is thickened.
5. Serve the French toast warm, topped with berry compote and additional maple syrup if desired.

Nutritional Information: 280 calories, 9g protein, 50g carbohydrates, 3g fat, 8g fiber, 0mg cholesterol, 200mg sodium, 300mg potassium.

Green Tea Smoothie Bowl with Kiwi and Coconut

Yield: 2 servings | **Prep time:** 10 minutes |
Cook time: 0 minutes
Ingredients:
- 1 cup brewed green tea, cooled
- 2 ripe bananas, frozen
- 1 kiwi, peeled and sliced
- 1/2 cup spinach leaves
- 2 tablespoons shredded coconut
- Optional toppings: sliced kiwi, coconut flakes, chia seeds

Directions:
1. In a blender, combine green tea, frozen bananas, kiwi, and spinach. Blend until smooth.
2. Pour the smoothie mixture into bowls and garnish with shredded coconut and optional toppings such as more kiwi slices, coconut flakes, and chia seeds.
3. Serve immediately.

Nutritional Information: 180 calories, 3g protein, 38g carbohydrates, 4g fat, 6g fiber, 0mg cholesterol, 20mg sodium, 600mg potassium.

Vegan Banana Bread

Yield: 6 servings | **Prep time:** 10 minutes | **Cook time:** 60 minutes

Ingredients:
- 3 ripe bananas, mashed
- 1/3 cup melted coconut oil
- 1/2 cup maple syrup
- 2 cups whole wheat flour
- 1/4 cup almond milk
- 1 teaspoon baking soda

Directions:
1. Preheat oven to 350°F (175°C). In a large bowl, mix the mashed bananas with melted coconut oil and maple syrup.
2. Add the whole wheat flour, almond milk, and baking soda to the banana mixture. Stir until combined.
3. Pour the batter into a greased loaf pan. Bake for 60 minutes, or until a toothpick inserted into the center comes out clean.
4. Let the bread cool before slicing and serving.

Nutritional Information: 330 calories, 5g protein, 58g carbohydrates, 10g fat, 6g fiber, 0mg cholesterol, 210mg sodium, 400mg potassium.

Coconut Yogurt with Granola and Kiwi

Yield: 4 servings | **Prep time:** 5 minutes | **Cook time:** 0 minutes

Ingredients:
- 2 cups coconut yogurt
- 1 cup granola
- 4 kiwis, peeled and sliced
- Optional: honey or agave syrup for drizzling

Directions:
1. Spoon the coconut yogurt into 4 serving bowls.
2. Top each bowl of yogurt with granola and kiwi slices.
3. Optionally, drizzle with honey or agave syrup for added sweetness.

Nutritional Information: 320 calories, 6g protein, 38g carbohydrates, 16g fat, 5g fiber, 0mg cholesterol, 60mg sodium, 500mg potassium.

Vegan Protein Pancakes topped with Fresh Berries

Yield: 4 servings | **Prep time:** 10 minutes | **Cook time:** 15 minutes

Ingredients:
- 1 cup whole wheat flour
- 1/2 cup plant-based protein powder
- 2 teaspoons baking powder
- 1 1/4 cups almond milk
- 1 ripe banana, mashed
- 2 cups fresh berries for topping

Directions:
1. In a large bowl, mix together flour, protein powder, and baking powder. Add in almond milk and mashed banana, stirring until well combined.
2. Heat a non-stick skillet over medium heat. Pour 1/4 cup of batter for each pancake, cooking until bubbles form on the surface, then flip and cook until golden brown.
3. Serve the pancakes topped with fresh berries.

Nutritional Information: 280 calories, 15g protein, 49g carbohydrates, 3g fat, 8g fiber, 0mg cholesterol, 200mg sodium, 300mg potassium.

Homemade Coconut Yogurt

Yield: 4 servings | **Prep time:** 10 minutes | **Cook time:** 24 hours for fermentation

Ingredients:
- 2 cans (13.5 ounces each) full-fat coconut milk
- 2 probiotic capsules (ensure they are dairy-free if you want the yogurt to be vegan)

Directions:
1. Shake the cans of coconut milk well. Pour the coconut milk into a clean glass bowl or jar.
2. Open the probiotic capsules and sprinkle the powder over the coconut milk. Stir the mixture with a wooden or plastic spoon (metal can react with the probiotics).
3. Cover the mixture with a clean cloth and secure it with a rubber band or string. Let the bowl sit in a warm place for 24-48 hours. The time needed can vary depending on the room temperature; warmer environments accelerate fermentation.
4. After 24-48 hours, the yogurt should have thickened and have a tangy flavor. If not, let it ferment for a few more hours. Once ready, stir the yogurt well. If any liquid has separated on top, you can either stir it back in or pour it off if you prefer thicker yogurt.
5. Transfer the yogurt to an airtight container and refrigerate. The yogurt will continue to thicken in the fridge.

Nutritional Information: (per serving, based on the average content of coconut milk and probiotics) 450 calories, 5g protein, 8g carbohydrates, 48g fat, 0g fiber, 0mg cholesterol, 30mg sodium, 500mg potassium.

Peanut Butter and Jelly Oatmeal

Yield: 4 servings | **Prep time:** 5 minutes | **Cook time:** 10 minutes

Ingredients:
- 2 cups rolled oats
- 4 cups water or almond milk
- 4 tablespoons peanut butter
- 4 tablespoons jelly or jam of choice
- Optional: sliced bananas or strawberries for topping

Directions:
1. In a medium saucepan, bring the water or almond milk to a boil. Add the oats and reduce heat to simmer, cooking for 5-10 minutes until thickened, stirring occasionally.
2. Serve the oatmeal into bowls, swirling in a tablespoon of peanut butter and a tablespoon of jelly into each serving.
3. Optionally, top with sliced bananas or strawberries.

Nutritional Information: 360 calories, 10g protein, 50g carbohydrates, 14g fat, 7g fiber, 0mg cholesterol, 100mg sodium, 300mg potassium.

Chia Seed Pudding with Coconut Milk and Mango

Yield: 4 servings | **Prep time:** 5 minutes |
Cook time: 0 minutes (plus 4 hours for chilling)
Ingredients:
- 1/4 cup chia seeds
- 1 cup coconut milk
- 2 tablespoons maple syrup
- 1 teaspoon vanilla extract
- 1 mango, peeled and cubed

Directions:
1. In a bowl, mix together chia seeds, coconut milk, maple syrup, and vanilla extract. Let sit for 5 minutes, then stir again to prevent clumping.
2. Cover and refrigerate for at least 4 hours or overnight until it thickens into a pudding consistency.
3. Serve the chia pudding topped with cubed mango.

Nutritional Information: 250 calories, 4g protein, 35g carbohydrates, 12g fat, 10g fiber, 0mg cholesterol, 15mg sodium, 350mg potassium.

Fruit Salad with a Drizzle of Agave and a Sprinkle of Chia Seeds

Yield: 4 servings | **Prep time:** 15 minutes |
Ingredients:
- 1 cup strawberries, hulled and halved
- 1 cup blueberries
- 1 cup sliced kiwi
- 1 cup cubed pineapple
- 2 tablespoons agave syrup
- 1 tablespoon chia seeds

Directions:
1. In a large bowl, combine strawberries, blueberries, kiwi, and pineapple.
2. Drizzle the agave syrup over the fruit and gently toss to coat.
3. Sprinkle chia seeds over the salad before serving.

Nutritional Information: 150 calories, 2g protein, 35g carbohydrates, 1g fat, 5g fiber, 0mg cholesterol, 5mg sodium, 300mg potassium.

Banana Almond Muffins

Yield: 6 servings | **Prep time:** 10 minutes |
Cook time: 20 minutes
Ingredients:
- 2 ripe bananas, mashed
- 1 cup almond flour
- 3 tablespoons maple syrup
- 1 teaspoon baking soda
- 2 eggs
- 1/2 cup chopped almonds

Directions:
1. Preheat the oven to 350°F (175°C). Line a muffin tin with paper liners.
2. In a bowl, combine mashed bananas, almond flour, maple syrup, baking soda, and eggs. Mix until well combined.
3. Fold in the chopped almonds.
4. Divide the batter evenly among the muffin cups.
5. Bake for 20 minutes or until a toothpick inserted into the center comes out clean.

Nutritional Information: 240 calories, 8g protein, 20g carbohydrates, 16g fat, 4g fiber, 62mg cholesterol, 240mg sodium, 300mg potassium.

Apple Cinnamon Overnight Oats

Yield: 4 servings | **Prep time:** 5 minutes |
Cook time: 0 minutes (plus overnight soaking)
Ingredients:
- 2 cups rolled oats
- 2 cups almond milk
- 1 large apple, grated
- 2 teaspoons cinnamon
- 2 tablespoons maple syrup
- Optional: chopped nuts for topping

Directions:
1. In a bowl, mix together the oats, almond milk, grated apple, cinnamon, and maple syrup.
2. Divide the mixture into serving bowls or jars, cover, and refrigerate overnight.
3. Before serving, stir the oats and add more almond milk if needed. Top with chopped nuts if desired.

Nutritional Information: 280 calories, 6g protein, 53g carbohydrates, 5g fat, 8g fiber, 0mg cholesterol, 80mg sodium, 250mg potassium.

Berry Almond Smoothie

Yield: 2 servings | **Prep time:** 5 minutes | **Cook time:** 0 minutes

Ingredients:
- 1 cup almond milk
- 1 cup mixed berries (fresh or frozen)
- 1 banana
- 2 tablespoons almond butter
- Optional: 1 tablespoon honey or maple syrup for sweetness

Directions:
1. In a blender, combine almond milk, mixed berries, banana, and almond butter. Blend until smooth.
2. Taste and add honey or maple syrup if additional sweetness is desired. Blend again to incorporate.
3. Serve immediately.

Nutritional Information: 280 calories, 6g protein, 40g carbohydrates, 14g fat, 7g fiber, 0mg cholesterol, 100mg sodium, 400mg potassium.

Sweet Potato Hash Browns

Yield: 4 servings | **Prep time:** 10 minutes | **Cook time:** 15 minutes

Ingredients:
- 2 large sweet potatoes, peeled and grated
- 2 tablespoons olive oil
- Salt and pepper to taste

Directions:
1. Squeeze the grated sweet potatoes with a clean towel to remove excess moisture.
2. Heat olive oil in a large skillet over medium-high heat.
3. Form small patties with the grated sweet potatoes and place them in the skillet. Flatten them with a spatula and season with salt and pepper.
4. Cook until crispy and browned on both sides, about 5-7 minutes per side.

Nutritional Information: 220 calories, 2g protein, 30g carbohydrates, 10g fat, 4g fiber, 0mg cholesterol, 150mg sodium, 440mg potassium.

Mushroom Avocado Toast

Yield: 4 servings | **Prep time:** 10 minutes | **Cook time:** 10 minutes

Ingredients:
- 4 slices of whole grain bread, toasted
- 1 ripe avocado
- 1 cup sliced mushrooms
- 1 tablespoon olive oil
- Salt and pepper to taste
- Optional: red pepper flakes for garnish

Directions:
1. Heat olive oil in a skillet over medium heat. Add mushrooms, season with salt and pepper, and sauté until tender, about 5-7 minutes.
2. Mash the avocado with a fork and spread it evenly on the toasted bread slices.
3. Top each slice with cooked mushrooms and sprinkle with red pepper flakes if desired.

Nutritional Information: 230 calories, 6g protein, 27g carbohydrates, 12g fat, 8g fiber, 0mg cholesterol, 200mg sodium, 500mg potassium.

Pumpkin Spice Porridge

Yield: 4 servings | **Prep time:** 5 minutes | **Cook time:** 15 minutes

Ingredients:
- 2 cups rolled oats
- 3 cups almond milk
- 1 cup pumpkin puree
- 2 tablespoons maple syrup
- 1 teaspoon pumpkin pie spice
- Optional: chopped nuts for topping

Directions:
1. In a saucepan, combine oats and almond milk. Bring to a simmer over medium heat.
2. Stir in pumpkin puree, maple syrup, and pumpkin pie spice. Cook until thickened, about 10-15 minutes.
3. Serve hot, topped with chopped nuts if desired.

Nutritional Information: 280 calories, 6g protein, 53g carbohydrates, 5g fat, 8g fiber, 0mg cholesterol, 80mg sodium, 250mg potassium.

Crispy Tofu Scramble

Yield: 4 servings | **Prep time:** 10 minutes | **Cook time:** 20 minutes

Ingredients:
- 1 block (14 ounces) firm tofu, drained and crumbled
- 2 tablespoons nutritional yeast
- 1 teaspoon turmeric
- 1/2 teaspoon garlic powder
- Salt and pepper to taste
- 2 tablespoons olive oil
- Optional: diced vegetables (onion, bell pepper, spinach)

Directions:
1. In a bowl, combine crumbled tofu, nutritional yeast, turmeric, garlic powder, salt, and pepper.
2. Heat olive oil in a skillet over medium heat. Add optional vegetables and sauté until soft.
3. Add the tofu mixture to the skillet. Cook, stirring occasionally, until the tofu is crispy and golden, about 15-20 minutes.

Nutritional Information: 180 calories, 12g protein, 4g carbohydrates, 14g fat, 2g fiber, 0mg cholesterol, 200mg sodium, 300mg potassium.

Berry Quinoa Breakfast Bowl

Yield: 4 servings | **Prep time:** 5 minutes |
Cook time: 20 minutes
Ingredients:

- 1 cup quinoa, rinsed
- 2 cups water
- 2 cups mixed berries (fresh or frozen)
- 1/4 cup maple syrup
- 1/2 teaspoon vanilla extract
- Optional toppings: sliced almonds, coconut flakes

Directions:

1. In a medium saucepan, bring the quinoa and water to a boil. Reduce heat to low, cover, and simmer for 15 minutes or until the quinoa is cooked and the water is absorbed.
2. Remove from heat and stir in the maple syrup and vanilla extract.
3. Serve the quinoa in bowls, topped with mixed berries and optional toppings like sliced almonds and coconut flakes.

Nutritional Information: 280 calories, 8g protein, 55g carbohydrates, 2g fat, 6g fiber, 0mg cholesterol, 10mg sodium, 320mg potassium.

Spinach and Tomato Breakfast Wraps

Yield: 4 servings | **Prep time:** 10 minutes |
Cook time: 5 minutes
Ingredients:

- 4 whole grain tortillas
- 2 cups fresh spinach
- 1 cup cherry tomatoes, halved
- 1/2 cup hummus
- Salt and pepper to taste
- Optional: avocado slices

Directions:

1. Warm the tortillas in a skillet over medium heat for about 30 seconds on each side.
2. Spread each tortilla with hummus, then top with fresh spinach, cherry tomatoes, and optional avocado slices. Season with salt and pepper.
3. Roll up the tortillas tightly and serve immediately.

Nutritional Information: 220 calories, 7g protein, 35g carbohydrates, 7g fat, 6g fiber, 0mg cholesterol, 400mg sodium, 300mg potassium.

Coconut Rice Pudding

Yield: 4 servings | **Prep time:** 5 minutes |
Cook time: 25 minutes
Ingredients:

- 1 cup Arborio rice or short-grain rice
- 1 can (13.5 ounces) coconut milk
- 2 cups water
- 1/4 cup sugar
- 1/2 teaspoon vanilla extract
- Pinch of salt

Directions:

1. In a large saucepan, combine rice, coconut milk, water, sugar, and a pinch of salt. Bring to a boil, then reduce heat to low, cover, and simmer for 20-25 minutes, stirring occasionally, until the rice is tender and the mixture has thickened.
2. Remove from heat and stir in vanilla extract.
3. Serve warm or chilled, as preferred.

Nutritional Information: 350 calories, 5g protein, 45g carbohydrates, 18g fat, 1g fiber, 0mg cholesterol, 15mg sodium, 200mg potassium.

Peanut Butter Banana Smoothie

Yield: 2 servings | **Prep time:** 5 minutes |
Cook time: 0 minutes
Ingredients:

- 2 bananas, frozen
- 2 tablespoons peanut butter
- 1 cup almond milk
- 1 tablespoon honey or maple syrup (optional)

Directions:

1. Combine the bananas, peanut butter, almond milk, and honey (if using) in a blender.
2. Blend until smooth and creamy.
3. Serve immediately, optionally garnished with a drizzle of peanut butter or a few banana slices.

Nutritional Information: 300 calories, 8g protein, 50g carbohydrates, 11g fat, 5g fiber, 0mg cholesterol, 150mg sodium, 700mg potassium.

Zucchini Bread Oatmeal

Yield: 4 servings | **Prep time:** 5 minutes |
Cook time: 15 minutes
Ingredients:

- 2 cups rolled oats
- 3 1/2 cups water or almond milk
- 1 cup grated zucchini
- 1 teaspoon cinnamon
- 2 tablespoons maple syrup
- Optional: walnuts or pecans for topping

Directions:

1. In a large saucepan, bring the water or almond milk to a boil. Add the oats and grated zucchini, reduce heat to low, and simmer for 10-15 minutes, stirring occasionally, until the oats are cooked and creamy.
2. Stir in cinnamon and maple syrup. Adjust sweetness to taste.
3. Serve hot, garnished with nuts if desired.

Nutritional Information: 220 calories, 6g protein, 40g carbohydrates, 3g fat, 5g fiber, 0mg cholesterol, 30mg sodium, 250mg potassium.

Simple Mango Freeze

Yield: 4 servings | **Prep time:** 5 minutes |
Cook time: 0 minutes (plus freezing time)
Ingredients:
- 3 cups mango chunks, frozen
- 1/2 cup coconut milk
- 2 tablespoons honey or agave syrup (optional)

Directions:
1. Place the frozen mango chunks, coconut milk, and honey (if using) in a blender.
2. Blend until smooth and creamy, scraping down the sides as necessary.
3. Serve immediately for a soft-serve texture, or freeze for 1-2 hours for a firmer consistency.

Nutritional Information: 160 calories, 1g protein, 28g carbohydrates, 5g fat, 3g fiber, 0mg cholesterol, 5mg sodium, 200mg potassium.

Baked Avocado Eggs

Yield: 2 servings | **Prep time:** 5 minutes |
Cook time: 15 minutes
Ingredients:
- 2 ripe avocados
- 4 eggs
- Salt and pepper to taste
- Optional toppings: chopped chives, shredded cheese

Directions:
1. Preheat the oven to 425°F (220°C). Halve the avocados and remove the pits. Scoop out a little more flesh to make room for the eggs.
2. Place the avocado halves in a baking dish to prevent them from tipping over. Crack an egg into each avocado half. Season with salt and pepper.
3. Bake for 14-16 minutes, or until the eggs are set to your liking.
4. Garnish with optional toppings before serving.

Nutritional Information: 320 calories, 14g protein, 12g carbohydrates, 26g fat, 10g fiber, 372mg cholesterol, 120mg sodium, 800mg potassium.

Savory Chickpea Pancakes

Yield: 4 servings | **Prep time:** 10 minutes |
Cook time: 20 minutes
Ingredients:
- 1 cup chickpea flour
- 1 1/4 cups water
- 1/2 teaspoon salt
- 1/2 teaspoon ground turmeric
- 1/4 cup chopped onions
- 1/4 cup chopped tomatoes
- 2 tablespoons chopped cilantro
- Olive oil for cooking

Directions:
1. Whisk together chickpea flour, water, salt, and turmeric in a bowl until smooth. Stir in onions, tomatoes, and cilantro.
2. Heat a non-stick skillet over medium heat and lightly oil it. Pour 1/4 of the batter into the skillet, spreading it to form a pancake.
3. Cook until the edges are dry and the bottom is golden brown, about 3-4 minutes. Flip and cook the other side. Repeat with the remaining batter.
4. Serve hot.

Nutritional Information: 180 calories, 8g protein, 20g carbohydrates, 6g fat, 5g fiber, 0mg cholesterol, 300mg sodium, 400mg potassium.

Golden Turmeric Latte

Yield: 2 servings | **Prep time:** 5 minutes |
Cook time: 5 minutes
Ingredients:
- 2 cups almond milk
- 1 teaspoon ground turmeric
- 1/2 teaspoon ground cinnamon
- 1/4 teaspoon ground ginger
- 1 tablespoon honey or maple syrup

Directions:
1. In a small saucepan, heat the almond milk until just simmering.
2. Whisk in the turmeric, cinnamon, ginger, and honey/maple syrup until fully combined.
3. Pour into mugs and serve warm.

Nutritional Information: 120 calories, 2g protein, 20g carbohydrates, 4g fat, 1g fiber, 0mg cholesterol, 80mg sodium, 300mg potassium.

Raspberry Coconut Chia Pudding

Yield: 4 servings | **Prep time:** 10 minutes |
Cook time: 0 minutes (plus chilling)
Ingredients:
- 1/4 cup chia seeds
- 1 cup coconut milk
- 1 cup raspberries (fresh or thawed from frozen)
- 2 tablespoons maple syrup
- Optional: shredded coconut for topping

Directions:
1. In a bowl, mix together chia seeds, coconut milk, and maple syrup. Let sit for 5 minutes, then stir again to prevent clumping.
2. Gently fold in the raspberries.
3. Cover and refrigerate for at least 2 hours, or overnight, until it has thickened to a pudding consistency.
4. Serve with optional shredded coconut on top.

Nutritional Information: 250 calories, 4g protein, 25g carbohydrates, 15g fat, 8g fiber, 0mg cholesterol, 15mg sodium, 250mg potassium.

Pear and Walnut Toast

Yield: 4 servings | **Prep time:** 5 minutes |
Cook time: 5 minutes
Ingredients:
- 4 slices of whole grain bread, toasted
- 2 pears, thinly sliced
- 1/4 cup walnut pieces, toasted
- Honey or maple syrup for drizzling
- Optional: soft cheese like ricotta or goat cheese

Directions:
1. Spread a thin layer of soft cheese on each slice of toasted bread, if using.
2. Arrange pear slices over the cheese or directly on the toast.
3. Sprinkle with toasted walnut pieces and drizzle with honey or maple syrup.
4. Serve immediately.

Nutritional Information: 220 calories, 6g protein, 35g carbohydrates, 8g fat, 5g fiber, 0mg cholesterol, 200mg sodium, 250mg potassium.

Citrus Berry Salad

Yield: 4 servings | **Prep time:** 10 minutes |
Cook time: 0 minutes
Ingredients:
- 2 oranges, peeled and sectioned
- 1 grapefruit, peeled and sectioned
- 1 cup sliced strawberries
- 1 cup blueberries
- 1 tablespoon honey or agave syrup
- Fresh mint leaves for garnish

Directions:
1. In a large bowl, combine the orange and grapefruit sections, strawberries, and blueberries.
2. Drizzle with honey or agave syrup and gently toss to coat.
3. Garnish with fresh mint leaves before serving.

Nutritional Information: 120 calories, 2g protein, 30g carbohydrates, 0.5g fat, 4g fiber, 0mg cholesterol, 2mg sodium, 350mg potassium.

Grapefruit Brûlée

Yield: 4 servings | **Prep time:** 5 minutes |
Cook time: 5 minutes (plus cooling)
Ingredients:
- 2 grapefruits, halved
- 4 teaspoons sugar

Directions:
1. Preheat the broiler. Sprinkle 1 teaspoon of sugar over each grapefruit half.
2. Place grapefruit halves sugar-side up on a baking sheet and broil until the sugar is caramelized, about 3-5 minutes.
3. Allow to cool slightly before serving.

Nutritional Information: 100 calories, 1g protein, 25g carbohydrates, 0g fat, 2g fiber, 0mg cholesterol, 0mg sodium, 250mg potassium.

Vegan Breakfast Burrito

Yield: 4 servings | **Prep time:** 15 minutes |
Cook time: 10 minutes
Ingredients:
- 4 large whole wheat tortillas
- 1 cup tofu scramble (crumbled tofu, turmeric, nutritional yeast, salt, pepper)
- 1 avocado, sliced
- 1 cup black beans, rinsed and drained
- 1 cup diced tomatoes
- 1/2 cup red onion, finely chopped
- Optional: salsa, vegan cheese

Directions:
1. Prepare the tofu scramble by sautéing crumbled tofu with turmeric, nutritional yeast, salt, and pepper until cooked through.
2. Warm the tortillas in a dry skillet over medium heat for about 30 seconds on each side.
3. On each tortilla, layer the tofu scramble, avocado slices, black beans, diced tomatoes, and red onion. Add salsa and vegan cheese if desired.
4. Fold the bottom of the tortilla up over the filling, then fold in the sides and roll up tightly.
5. Serve immediately or heat through in the skillet for a crispy exterior.

Nutritional Information: 350 calories, 15g protein, 45g carbohydrates, 15g fat, 10g fiber, 0mg cholesterol, 300mg sodium, 600mg potassium.

Kiwi Spinach Smoothie Bowl

Yield: 2 servings | **Prep time:** 10 minutes |
Cook time: 0 minutes
Ingredients:
- 2 ripe kiwis, peeled and sliced
- 2 cups fresh spinach
- 1 banana, frozen
- 1/2 cup almond milk
- Toppings: sliced kiwi, granola, coconut flakes, chia seeds

Directions:
1. In a blender, combine kiwi slices, fresh spinach, frozen banana, and almond milk. Blend until smooth.
2. Pour the smoothie into bowls and top with sliced kiwi, granola, coconut flakes, and chia seeds.
3. Serve immediately.

Nutritional Information: 180 calories, 4g protein, 38g carbohydrates, 2g fat, 6g fiber, 0mg cholesterol, 55mg sodium, 600mg potassium.

Avocado Chocolate Smoothie

Yield: 2 servings | **Prep time:** 5 minutes |
Cook time: 0 minutes
Ingredients:
- 1 ripe avocado
- 2 tablespoons cocoa powder
- 1 banana, frozen
- 1 1/2 cups almond milk
- 2 tablespoons maple syrup
- Ice cubes (optional)

Directions:
1. Combine avocado, cocoa powder, frozen banana, almond milk, maple syrup, and ice cubes (if using) in a blender.
2. Blend until smooth and creamy.
3. Serve immediately, optionally topped with a sprinkle of cocoa powder.

Nutritional Information: 300 calories, 4g protein, 40g carbohydrates, 16g fat, 9g fiber, 0mg cholesterol, 100mg sodium, 700mg potassium.

Blueberry Lemon Breakfast Quinoa

Yield: 4 servings | **Prep time:** 5 minutes |
Cook time: 20 minutes
Ingredients:
- 1 cup quinoa, rinsed
- 2 cups water
- 1 cup fresh blueberries
- Zest and juice of 1 lemon
- 2 tablespoons maple syrup
- Optional: almond slivers, extra blueberries for garnish

Directions:
1. In a medium saucepan, combine quinoa and water. Bring to a boil, then reduce heat to low, cover, and simmer for 15 minutes, or until water is absorbed.
2. Stir in blueberries, lemon zest, lemon juice, and maple syrup.
3. Serve warm, garnished with almond slivers and additional blueberries if desired.

Nutritional Information: 220 calories, 6g protein, 40g carbohydrates, 3g fat, 5g fiber, 0mg cholesterol, 10mg sodium, 320mg potassium.

Sweet Corn Fritters

Yield: 4 servings | **Prep time:** 10 minutes |
Cook time: 10 minutes
Ingredients:
- 2 cups corn kernels (fresh or thawed from frozen)
- 1/2 cup all-purpose flour
- 1/4 cup almond milk
- 1 green onion, finely chopped
- Salt and pepper to taste
- Olive oil for frying

Directions:
1. In a bowl, mix together corn kernels, flour, almond milk, green onion, salt, and pepper until well combined.
2. Heat a thin layer of olive oil in a skillet over medium heat. Drop spoonfuls of the batter into the skillet, flattening them slightly.
3. Fry until golden brown on both sides, about 2-3 minutes per side.
4. Serve hot.

Nutritional Information: 180 calories, 4g protein, 30g carbohydrates, 7g fat, 3g fiber, 0mg cholesterol, 150mg sodium, 250mg potassium.

Almond Joy Oatmeal

Yield: 4 servings | **Prep time:** 5 minutes |
Cook time: 10 minutes
Ingredients:
- 2 cups rolled oats
- 3 1/2 cups almond milk
- 1/4 cup shredded coconut
- 1/4 cup sliced almonds
- 1/4 cup chocolate chips
- Optional: sweetener to taste

Directions:
1. In a medium saucepan, bring almond milk to a boil. Add oats and reduce heat to simmer. Cook for 5-7 minutes, stirring occasionally, until thickened.
2. Stir in shredded coconut and sliced almonds. Sweeten if desired.
3. Serve topped with chocolate chips.

Nutritional Information: 350 calories, 10g protein, 45g carbohydrates, 16g fat, 7g fiber, 0mg cholesterol, 100mg sodium, 300mg potassium.

Pineapple Coconut Overnight Oats

Yield: 4 servings | **Prep time:** 10 minutes |
Cook time: 0 minutes (plus overnight chilling)
Ingredients:
- 2 cups rolled oats
- 1 1/2 cups coconut milk
- 1 cup chopped pineapple
- 1 tablespoon chia seeds
- 2 tablespoons shredded coconut
- Optional: honey or maple syrup to taste

Directions:
1. In a bowl, combine oats, coconut milk, pineapple, chia seeds, and shredded coconut. Mix well.
2. Cover and refrigerate overnight.
3. Stir before serving and sweeten with honey or maple syrup if desired.

Nutritional Information: 300 calories, 7g protein, 45g carbohydrates, 12g fat, 9g fiber, 0mg cholesterol, 30mg sodium, 350mg potassium.

Olive Oil Granola

Yield: 6 servings | **Prep time:** 10 minutes | **Cook time:** 20 minutes

Ingredients:
- 3 cups rolled oats
- 1 cup mixed nuts, chopped
- 1/2 cup pumpkin seeds
- 1/4 cup olive oil
- 1/4 cup maple syrup
- 1/2 teaspoon salt
- 1 teaspoon cinnamon
- 1/2 cup dried fruit (such as cranberries or raisins), optional

Directions:
1. Preheat the oven to 300°F. In a large bowl, mix together oats, nuts, and pumpkin seeds.
2. Whisk together olive oil, maple syrup, salt, and cinnamon. Pour over the oat mixture and stir until well coated.
3. Spread the mixture evenly on a baking sheet and bake for 20 minutes, stirring halfway through, until golden brown.
4. Let cool completely, then stir in dried fruit if using.

Nutritional Information: 380 calories, 10g protein, 40g carbohydrates, 20g fat, 6g fiber, 0mg cholesterol, 200mg sodium, 300mg potassium.

Spelt Berry Hot Breakfast Cereal

Yield: 4 servings | **Prep time:** 5 minutes | **Cook time:** 60 minutes

Ingredients:
- 1 cup spelt berries
- 3 cups water
- 1 cinnamon stick
- Pinch of salt
- Optional toppings: maple syrup, almond milk, fresh fruit

Directions:
1. Rinse spelt berries under cold water. Combine spelt berries, water, cinnamon stick, and salt in a saucepan. Bring to a boil, then reduce heat to low, cover, and simmer for 60 minutes or until berries are tender.
2. Remove the cinnamon stick. Serve hot with optional toppings like maple syrup, almond milk, and fresh fruit.

Nutritional Information: 160 calories, 5g protein, 34g carbohydrates, 1g fat, 5g fiber, 0mg cholesterol, 60mg sodium, 200mg potassium.

Olive Tapenade Crostini

Yield: 4 servings | **Prep time:** 10 minutes | **Cook time:** 5 minutes

Ingredients:
- 1 baguette, sliced into 1/2-inch pieces
- 1 cup pitted mixed olives
- 2 tablespoons capers
- 2 cloves garlic
- 1/4 cup olive oil
- 1 tablespoon lemon juice

Directions:
1. Preheat oven to 400°F (200°C). Arrange baguette slices on a baking sheet and toast for 5 minutes until lightly golden.
2. In a food processor, blend olives, capers, garlic, olive oil, and lemon juice until smooth.

Nutritional Information: 310 calories, 5g protein, 35g carbohydrates, 16g fat, 2g fiber, 0mg cholesterol, 700mg sodium, 100mg potassium.

Green Breakfast Soup

Yield: 4 servings | **Prep time:** 10 minutes | **Cook time:** 15 minutes

Ingredients:
- 4 cups vegetable broth
- 2 cups spinach
- 1 cup broccoli florets
- 1 avocado
- Salt and pepper to taste
- Optional toppings: pumpkin seeds, croutons

Directions:
1. In a large pot, bring the vegetable broth to a simmer. Add spinach and broccoli, cooking until the broccoli is tender.
2. Transfer to a blender, add the avocado, and blend until smooth. Season with salt and pepper.
3. Serve hot with optional toppings.

Nutritional Information: 150 calories, 4g protein, 12g carbohydrates, 10g fat, 6g fiber, 0mg cholesterol, 500mg sodium, 500mg potassium.

Tomato Basil Socca

Yield: 4 servings | **Prep time:** 10 minutes | **Cook time:** 10 minutes

Ingredients:
- 1 cup chickpea flour
- 1 1/4 cups water
- 2 tablespoons olive oil, divided
- 1/2 teaspoon salt
- 1 tomato, sliced
- A handful of fresh basil leaves

Directions:
1. Whisk together chickpea flour, water, 1 tablespoon olive oil, and salt. Let sit for 30 minutes.
2. Heat the remaining tablespoon of olive oil in a skillet. Pour the batter to form pancakes. Cook for about 3-4 minutes on each side.
3. Top with tomato slices and basil leaves before serving.

Nutritional Information: 220 calories, 8g protein, 24g carbohydrates, 10g fat, 5g fiber, 0mg cholesterol, 300mg sodium, 400mg potassium.

Chapter 3:
Nutritious Lunch

Vegan Caesar Salad with Chickpea Croutons

Yield: 4 servings | **Prep time:** 15 minutes | **Cook time:** 30 minutes

Ingredients:
- 2 heads of romaine lettuce, chopped
- 1 can (15 oz) chickpeas, drained and rinsed
- 2 tablespoons olive oil (1 for chickpeas, 1 for dressing)
- 1/2 cup vegan Caesar dressing
- 1/4 cup nutritional yeast
- Salt and pepper to taste

Directions:
1. Preheat oven to 400°F. Coat chickpeas with 1 tablespoon of olive oil, salt, and pepper. Place them on a baking sheet and bake for 25-30 minutes until they achieve a crispy texture.
2. Toss the chopped romaine lettuce with vegan Caesar dressing until well coated. Divide among plates.
3. Top the salad with baked chickpea croutons and a sprinkle of nutritional yeast before serving.

Nutritional Information: 220 calories, 8g protein, 20g carbohydrates, 12g fat, 7g fiber, 0mg cholesterol, 300mg sodium, 400mg potassium.

Quinoa Salad with Black Beans and Corn

Yield: 4 servings | **Prep time:** 10 minutes | **Cook time:** 15 minutes

Ingredients:
- 1 cup quinoa
- 2 cups water
- 1 can (15 oz) black beans, drained and rinsed
- 1 cup corn kernels (fresh or frozen)
- 1/2 red onion, finely chopped
- 1/4 cup lime juice
- Salt and pepper to taste

Directions:
1. Rinse quinoa under cold water. In a medium-sized pot, let quinoa and water come to a boil. Subsequently, reduce the heat, cover the pot, and allow it to simmer for a duration of 15 minutes. Fluff with a fork and cool slightly.
2. Combine the prepared quinoa, black beans, corn, and red onion in a sizable mixing bowl.
3. Dress with lime juice, salt, and pepper. Toss well before serving.

Nutritional Information: 270 calories, 11g protein, 49g carbohydrates, 3g fat, 8g fiber, 0mg cholesterol, 200mg sodium, 700mg potassium.

Quinoa and Roasted Vegetable Salad with Lemon Tahini Dressing

Yield: 4 servings | **Prep time:** 15 minutes | **Cook time:** 25 minutes

Ingredients:
- 1 cup quinoa
- 2 cups vegetable broth
- 2 cups mixed vegetables (e.g., bell peppers, zucchini, cherry tomatoes), chopped
- 1/4 cup tahini
- 2 tablespoons lemon juice
- Salt and pepper to taste

Directions:
1. Preheat the oven to 425°F. Toss chopped vegetables with salt, pepper, and a bit of olive oil. Roast for 20-25 minutes until tender and slightly charred.
2. Meanwhile, cook quinoa in vegetable broth according to package instructions. Fluff and let cool.
3. Whisk tahini and lemon juice in a small bowl, adding water if necessary to achieve desired consistency. Season with salt and pepper.
4. Combine quinoa and roasted vegetables in a large bowl. Drizzle with lemon tahini dressing and toss to combine before serving.

Nutritional Information: 310 calories, 10g protein, 45g carbohydrates, 10g fat, 7g fiber, 0mg cholesterol, 300mg sodium, 600mg potassium.

Falafel Salad with Tahini Dressing

Yield: 4 servings | **Prep time:** 20 minutes | **Cook time:** 10 minutes (if using pre-made falafel)

Ingredients:
- 8 pre-made falafel balls
- 4 cups mixed greens
- 1/2 cup cherry tomatoes, halved
- 1/2 cucumber, sliced
- 1/4 cup tahini
- 2 tablespoons lemon juice
- Water to thin the dressing

Directions:
1. In a small bowl combine tahini, lemon juice, and sufficient water in a small bowl until the mixture achieves a smooth, pourable dressing consistency
2. Arrange mixed greens on plates, top with falafel balls, cherry tomatoes, and cucumber slices.
3. Drizzle tahini dressing over the salad before serving.

Nutritional Information: 320 calories, 13g protein, 33g carbohydrates, 16g fat, 9g fiber, 0mg cholesterol, 400mg sodium, 500mg potassium.

Vegan Greek Salad with Tofu Feta

Yield: 4 servings | **Prep time:** 15 minutes |
Cook time: 0 minutes
Ingredients:
- 2 cups cucumbers, diced
- 2 cups cherry tomatoes, halved
- 1 cup red onion, thinly sliced
- 1 cup tofu feta (tofu marinated in lemon juice, olive oil, and herbs)
- 1/4 cup Kalamata olives
- 2 tablespoons olive oil
- Juice of 1 lemon
- Salt and pepper to taste

Directions:
1. In a large bowl, combine cucumbers, cherry tomatoes, red onion, tofu feta, and Kalamata olives.
2. Drizzle with olive oil and lemon juice. Season with salt and pepper.
3. Toss to combine and serve chilled.

Nutritional Information: 220 calories, 8g protein, 18g carbohydrates, 14g fat, 4g fiber, 0mg cholesterol, 400mg sodium, 300mg potassium.

Waldorf Salad with Apples, Walnuts, and Tofu

Yield: 4 servings | **Prep time:** 15 minutes |
Cook time: 0 minutes
Ingredients:
- 2 apples, cored and chopped
- 1/2 cup walnuts, chopped
- 1/2 cup celery, sliced
- 1/2 cup firm tofu, cubed
- 1/4 cup vegan mayonnaise
- 1 tablespoon lemon juice

Directions:
1. In a large bowl, combine apples, walnuts, celery, and tofu.
2. In a small bowl, whisk together vegan mayonnaise and lemon juice. Pour over the apple mixture and toss to coat evenly.
3. Chill in the refrigerator for at least 30 minutes before serving.

Nutritional Information: 250 calories, 6g protein, 20g carbohydrates, 18g fat, 4g fiber, 0mg cholesterol, 150mg sodium, 300mg potassium.

Cold Pasta Salad with Cherry Tomatoes, Cucumbers, Olives, and Vegan Feta

Yield: 4 servings | **Prep time:** 15 minutes |
Cook time: 10 minutes
Ingredients:
- 8 oz whole wheat pasta
- 1 cup cherry tomatoes, halved
- 1 cucumber, diced
- 1/2 cup olives, sliced
- 1/2 cup vegan feta, crumbled
- 2 tablespoons olive oil
- Salt and pepper to taste

Directions:
1. Prepare the pasta following the instructions on the package until it reaches an al dente texture. Rinse under cold water and drain.
2. In a spacious bowl, mix together the cooked pasta, cherry tomatoes, cucumber, olives, and vegan feta.
3. Drizzle a bit of olive oil over the mixture, then lightly season with salt and pepper, gently stirring until everything is well combined.
4. Refrigerate for a minimum of 1 hour prior to serving.

Nutritional Information: 330 calories, 10g protein, 55g carbohydrates, 9g fat, 8g fiber, 0mg cholesterol, 400mg sodium, 350mg potassium.

Spinach and Avocado Pasta Salad

Yield: 4 servings | **Prep time:** 10 minutes |
Cook time: 10 minutes
Ingredients:
- 8 oz whole wheat pasta
- 2 cups spinach leaves
- 1 ripe avocado, diced
- 1/2 cup cherry tomatoes, halved
- 1/4 cup pine nuts
- 2 tablespoons olive oil
- Salt and pepper to taste

Directions:
1. Cook pasta according to package instructions. Drain and rinse under cold water to cool.
2. In a large bowl, combine the cooked pasta, spinach leaves, avocado, cherry tomatoes, and pine nuts.
3. Drizzle with olive oil and season with salt and pepper. Toss gently to combine.

Nutritional Information: 360 calories, 10g protein, 52g carbohydrates, 16g fat, 8g fiber, 0mg cholesterol, 10mg sodium, 450mg potassium.

Mediterranean Chickpea and Quinoa Salad

Yield: 4 servings | **Prep time:** 15 minutes |
Cook time: 15 minutes
Ingredients:
- 1 cup quinoa
- 2 cups water
- 1 can (15 oz) chickpeas, drained and rinsed
- 1 cup cherry tomatoes, halved
- 1 cucumber, diced
- 1/4 cup red onion, finely chopped
- 1/4 cup olive oil
- Juice of 1 lemon
- Salt and pepper to taste

Directions:

1. Rinse quinoa under cold water. In a sauce-pan, combine quinoa with water and bring to a boil. Reduce heat to low, cover, and simmer for 15 minutes. Fluff with a fork and let cool.
2. In a large bowl, combine cooked quinoa, chickpeas, cherry tomatoes, cucumber, and red onion.
3. Whisk together olive oil, lemon juice, salt, and pepper. Pour over the salad and toss to combine.

Nutritional Information: 330 calories, 10g protein, 45g carbohydrates, 14g fat, 8g fiber, 0mg cholesterol, 200mg sodium, 400mg potassium.

Vegan Caesar Wrap with Smoky Tempeh

Yield: 4 servings | **Prep time:** 15 minutes | **Cook time:** 10 minutes

Ingredients:
- 4 whole wheat wraps
- 1 cup smoky tempeh, cooked and sliced
- 2 cups romaine lettuce, chopped
- 1/2 cup vegan Caesar dressing
- 1/4 cup nutritional yeast
- Salt and pepper to taste

Directions:

1. Lay out the wraps on a flat surface. Spread each wrap with vegan Caesar dressing.
2. Top with romaine lettuce, sliced smoky tempeh, and a sprinkle of nutritional yeast.
3. Season with salt and pepper, roll up the wraps tightly, and cut in half before serving.

Nutritional Information: 350 calories, 18g protein, 35g carbohydrates, 18g fat, 6g fiber, 0mg cholesterol, 600mg sodium, 400mg potassium.

Vegan Nicoise Salad

Yield: 4 servings | **Prep time:** 20 minutes | **Cook time:** 0 minutes

Ingredients:
- 6 cups mixed greens
- 1 cup green beans, blanched and cooled
- 1 cup small potatoes, boiled and sliced
- 1/2 cup cherry tomatoes, halved
- 1/4 cup olives
- 1 cup chickpeas, drained and rinsed
- 1/4 cup vegan Dijon dressing

Directions:

1. Arrange mixed greens on a large platter.
2. Top with arranged rows of green beans, potatoes, cherry tomatoes, olives, and chickpeas.
3. Drizzle with vegan Dijon dressing before serving.

Nutritional Information: 260 calories, 8g protein, 38g carbohydrates, 10g fat, 10g fiber, 0mg cholesterol, 300mg sodium, 800mg potassium.

Vegan Sushi Rolls

Yield: 4 servings | **Prep time:** 30 minutes | **Cook time:** 20 minutes

Ingredients:
- 2 cups sushi rice
- 3 cups water
- 1/4 cup rice vinegar
- 2 tablespoons sugar
- 1/2 teaspoon salt
- 4 nori sheets
- 1 cucumber, julienned
- 1 avocado, sliced
- 1 carrot, julienned
- Soy sauce for serving

Directions:

1. Rinse the sushi rice under cold water until the water runs clear. Combine with water in a rice cooker and cook according to the manufacturer's instructions.
2. Once cooked, mix the rice vinegar, sugar, and salt and fold into the rice. Let cool to room temperature.
3. Place a nori sheet on a bamboo mat, spread a layer of rice on the nori, leaving a small margin at the top. Place cucumber, avocado, and carrot on the rice.
4. Roll the sushi tightly using the bamboo mat. Wet the top edge of the nori to seal the roll. Slice into pieces.
5. Serve with soy sauce.

Nutritional Information: 410 calories, 7g protein, 83g carbohydrates, 5g fat, 6g fiber, 0mg cholesterol, 300mg sodium, 400mg potassium.

Vegan Caesar Salad with Crispy Chickpeas

Yield: 4 servings | **Prep time:** 10 minutes | **Cook time:** 30 minutes

Ingredients:
- 2 cans (15 oz each) chickpeas, rinsed and drained
- 2 tablespoons olive oil
- 1 teaspoon garlic powder
- 6 cups romaine lettuce, chopped
- 1/2 cup vegan Caesar dressing
- 1/4 cup nutritional yeast

Directions:

1. Preheat oven to 400°F. Toss chickpeas with olive oil and garlic powder, spread on a baking sheet, and bake for 25-30 minutes until crispy.
2. Toss chopped romaine with vegan Caesar dressing and top with crispy chickpeas and nutritional yeast.

Nutritional Information: 350 calories, 15g protein, 45g carbohydrates, 15g fat, 12g fiber, 0mg cholesterol, 400mg sodium, 600mg potassium.

Vegan Pho with Tofu and Mushrooms

Yield: 4 servings | **Prep time:** 15 minutes | **Cook time**: 30 minutes

Ingredients:
- 8 cups vegetable broth
- 1 onion, sliced
- 4 garlic cloves, minced
- 2 tablespoons soy sauce
- 1-inch piece ginger, sliced
- 1 cup mushrooms, sliced
- 14 oz firm tofu, cubed
- 8 oz rice noodles
- Optional garnishes: basil, lime wedges, jalapeños, bean sprouts

Directions:
1. In a large pot, combine vegetable broth, onion, garlic, soy sauce, and ginger. Bring to a boil, then reduce heat and simmer for 20 minutes.
2. Add mushrooms and tofu, simmering for an additional 10 minutes.
3. Cook rice noodles according to package instructions. Divide noodles among bowls.
4. Pour hot soup over noodles and serve with optional garnishes.

Nutritional Information: 350 calories, 20g protein, 65g carbohydrates, 5g fat, 3g fiber, 0mg cholesterol, 700mg sodium, 400mg potassium.

Vegetable and Bean Soup

Yield: 4 servings | **Prep time:** 15 minutes | **Cook time:** 30 minutes

Ingredients:
- 1 tablespoon olive oil
- 1 onion, diced
- 2 carrots, diced
- 2 celery stalks, diced
- 1 can (15 oz) diced tomatoes
- 1 can (15 oz) white beans, rinsed and drained
- 4 cups vegetable broth
- Salt and pepper to taste

Directions:
1. Heat olive oil in a large pot over medium heat. Add onion, carrots, and celery; sauté until softened.
2. Add diced tomatoes, white beans, and vegetable broth. Bring to a boil, then reduce heat and simmer for 20 minutes.
3. Season with salt and pepper to taste. Serve hot.

Nutritional Information: 220 calories, 10g protein, 40g carbohydrates, 4g fat, 10g fiber, 0mg cholesterol, 700mg sodium, 800mg potassium.

Vegan Minestrone Soup

Yield: 4 servings | **Prep time:** 15 minutes | **Cook time:** 30 minutes

Ingredients:
- 1 tablespoon olive oil
- 1 onion, diced
- 2 carrots, diced
- 2 celery stalks, diced
- 1 zucchini, diced
- 1 can (15 oz) diced tomatoes
- 1 can (15 oz) kidney beans, rinsed and drained
- 4 cups vegetable broth
- 1/2 cup small pasta, uncooked
- Salt and pepper to taste

Directions:
1. Heat olive oil in a large pot over medium heat. Add onion, carrots, and celery; sauté until softened.
2. Add zucchini, diced tomatoes, kidney beans, and vegetable broth. Bring to a boil, then add pasta and simmer for 10 minutes.
3. Season with salt and pepper. Serve hot.

Nutritional Information: 280 calories, 12g protein, 52g carbohydrates, 4g fat, 12g fiber, 0mg cholesterol, 400mg sodium, 700mg potassium.

Zucchini Lasagna with Cashew Cheese

Yield: 6 servings | **Prep time:** 20 minutes | **Cook time:** 45 minutes

Ingredients:
- 4 large zucchinis, sliced lengthwise
- 1 cup raw cashews, soaked for 4 hours and drained
- 1 lemon, juiced
- 1 garlic clove
- 1 can (28 oz) crushed tomatoes
- 2 tablespoons nutritional yeast
- Salt and pepper to taste

Directions:
1. Preheat oven to 375°F. Lay zucchini slices on paper towels and sprinkle with salt to draw out moisture.
2. In a blender, combine cashews, lemon juice, garlic, nutritional yeast, salt, and pepper until smooth.
3. Spread a layer of crushed tomatoes in the bottom of a baking dish. Layer zucchini slices, cashew cheese, and repeat, finishing with a layer of cashew cheese.
4. Bake for 45 minutes or until bubbly and golden. Let cool before slicing.

Nutritional Information: 220 calories, 10g protein, 24g carbohydrates, 12g fat, 6g fiber, 0mg cholesterol, 200mg sodium, 800mg potassium.

Curried Lentil Soup

Yield: 4 servings | **Prep time:** 10 minutes | **Cook time:** 30 minutes

Ingredients:
- 1 tablespoon coconut oil
- 1 onion, diced
- 1 tablespoon curry powder
- 1 cup red lentils, rinsed
- 4 cups vegetable broth
- 1 can (15 oz) coconut milk
- Salt to taste

Directions:
1. Heat coconut oil in a pot over medium heat. Add onion and curry powder; sauté until onion is soft.
2. Add lentils, vegetable broth, and coconut milk. Bring to a boil, then simmer for 25 minutes or until lentils are soft.
3. Season with salt. Serve hot.

Nutritional Information: 350 calories, 18g protein, 45g carbohydrates, 14g fat, 15g fiber, 0mg cholesterol, 200mg sodium, 800mg potassium.

Lentil Soup with Spinach

Yield: 4 servings | **Prep time:** 10 minutes | **Cook time:** 40 minutes

Ingredients:
- 1 tablespoon olive oil
- 1 onion, chopped
- 2 garlic cloves, minced
- 1 cup dried lentils, rinsed
- 4 cups vegetable broth
- 2 cups spinach leaves
- Salt and pepper to taste

Directions:
1. Heat olive oil in a large pot over medium heat. Add onion and garlic; sauté until softened.
2. Add lentils and vegetable broth. Bring to a boil, then reduce heat, cover, and simmer for 30 minutes.
3. Stir in spinach until wilted. Season with salt and pepper.

Nutritional Information: 250 calories, 18g protein, 38g carbohydrates, 4g fat, 19g fiber, 0mg cholesterol, 300mg sodium, 700mg potassium.

Vegan Miso Soup with Tofu and Seaweed

Yield: 4 servings | **Prep time:** 5 minutes | **Cook time:** 10 minutes

Ingredients:
- 4 cups water
- 2 tablespoons miso paste
- 1/2 block tofu, cubed
- 1/4 cup dried seaweed, rehydrated
- 2 green onions, sliced

Directions:
1. Heat water in a pot over medium heat. Just before boiling, reduce heat and dissolve miso paste in the water.
2. Add tofu and seaweed. Simmer for 5 minutes.
3. Garnish with green onions before serving.

Nutritional Information: 80 calories, 6g protein, 8g carbohydrates, 3g fat, 2g fiber, 0mg cholesterol, 600mg sodium, 200mg potassium.

Pesto Pasta with Cherry Tomatoes

Yield: 4 servings | **Prep time:** 10 minutes | **Cook time:** 10 minutes

Ingredients:
- 8 oz whole wheat pasta
- 1 cup basil pesto
- 2 cups cherry tomatoes, halved
- Salt and pepper to taste

Directions:
1. Cook pasta according to package instructions. Drain and return to pot.
2. Stir in basil pesto and cherry tomatoes. Season with salt and pepper.
3. Serve warm or at room temperature.

Nutritional Information: 450 calories, 12g protein, 56g carbohydrates, 22g fat, 6g fiber, 0mg cholesterol, 300mg sodium, 400mg potassium.

Pumpkin Soup with Coconut Milk

Yield: 4 servings | **Prep time:** 15 minutes | **Cook time:** 30 minutes

Ingredients:
- 1 tablespoon olive oil
- 1 onion, chopped
- 2 cloves garlic, minced
- 4 cups pumpkin puree
- 3 cups vegetable broth
- 1 can (14 oz) coconut milk
- 1 teaspoon curry powder
- Salt and pepper to taste
- Pumpkin seeds, for garnish

Directions:
1. In a large pot, heat olive oil over medium heat. Add onion and garlic; cook until soft.
2. Add pumpkin puree, vegetable broth, coconut milk, and curry powder. Bring to a simmer and cook for 25 minutes.
3. Puree the soup with an immersion blender until smooth. Season with salt and pepper.
4. Serve garnished with pumpkin seeds.

Nutritional Information: 300 calories, 6g protein, 28g carbohydrates, 20g fat, 7g fiber, 0mg cholesterol, 480mg sodium, 750mg potassium.

Chickpea Avocado Salad Sandwich

Yield: 4 servings | **Prep time:** 10 minutes
Ingredients:
- 1 can (15 oz) chickpeas, drained and mashed
- 1 ripe avocado, mashed
- 2 tablespoons lemon juice
- Salt and pepper to taste
- 8 slices whole grain bread
- Optional: lettuce, tomato slices

Directions:
1. In a bowl, mix together mashed chickpeas, avocado, lemon juice, salt, and pepper.
2. Spread the mixture on 4 slices of bread. Add optional lettuce and tomato if desired.
3. Top with remaining bread slices.

Nutritional Information: 400 calories, 15g protein, 60g carbohydrates, 12g fat, 15g fiber, 0mg cholesterol, 600mg sodium, 700mg potassium.

Vegan Alfredo Pasta with Broccoli

Yield: 4 servings | **Prep time:** 10 minutes |
Cook time: 20 minutes
Ingredients:
- 8 oz fettuccine
- 2 cups broccoli florets
- 1 cup cashews, soaked and drained
- 1 garlic clove
- 1 tablespoon lemon juice
- 1 cup water
- Salt and pepper to taste

Directions:
1. Cook fettuccine according to package instructions, adding broccoli in the last 3 minutes of cooking. Drain and set aside.
2. In a blender, combine cashews, garlic, lemon juice, water, salt, and pepper until smooth.
3. Toss the pasta and broccoli with the Alfredo sauce. Heat gently if needed.

Nutritional Information: 420 calories, 15g protein, 60g carbohydrates, 16g fat, 6g fiber, 0mg cholesterol, 150mg sodium, 500mg potassium.

Vegan Bolognese with Lentils

Yield: 4 servings | **Prep time:** 10 minutes |
Cook time: 30 minutes
Ingredients:
- 1 tablespoon olive oil
- 1 onion, diced
- 2 garlic cloves, minced
- 1 cup dried lentils
- 1 can (28 oz) crushed tomatoes
- 1 teaspoon Italian seasoning
- Salt and pepper to taste

Directions:
1. Heat olive oil in a large skillet over medium heat. Add onion and garlic, sauté until softened.
2. Add lentils, crushed tomatoes, Italian seasoning, salt, and pepper. Bring to a boil, then simmer for 25-30 minutes, until lentils are tender.
3. Serve over cooked whole wheat pasta or spaghetti squash.

Nutritional Information: 330 calories, 18g protein, 60g carbohydrates, 4g fat, 15g fiber, 0mg cholesterol, 300mg sodium, 800mg potassium.

Vegan Sushi Bowl with Avocado and Cucumber

Yield: 4 servings | **Prep time:** 10 minutes |
Cook time: 20 minutes
Ingredients:
- 2 cups sushi rice
- 1 cucumber, diced
- 1 avocado, diced
- 2 tablespoons rice vinegar
- 1 tablespoon soy sauce
- 1 teaspoon sesame seeds
- Optional: seaweed, pickled ginger

Directions:
1. Cook sushi rice according to package instructions. Let cool slightly and then season with rice vinegar.
2. In serving bowls, arrange the cooked rice, cucumber, and avocado.
3. Drizzle soy sauce over the bowls and sprinkle with sesame seeds. Add optional seaweed and pickled ginger if desired.

Nutritional Information: 380 calories, 6g protein, 70g carbohydrates, 9g fat, 7g fiber, 0mg cholesterol, 200mg sodium, 500mg potassium.

Tofu Teriyaki Stir-Fry

Yield: 4 servings | **Prep time:** 15 minutes |
Cook time: 20 minutes
Ingredients:
- 14 oz firm tofu, pressed and cubed
- 2 tablespoons olive oil
- 1 bell pepper, sliced
- 1 cup broccoli florets
- 1/2 cup teriyaki sauce
- 2 cups cooked brown rice

Directions:
1. Heat olive oil in a large skillet over medium-high heat. Add tofu cubes and fry until golden on all sides.
2. Add bell pepper and broccoli to the skillet and stir-fry for about 5 minutes, or until vegetables are tender-crisp.
3. Pour teriyaki sauce over the tofu and vegetables, stir well to coat.
4. Serve the stir-fry over cooked brown rice.

Nutritional Information: 350 calories, 15g protein, 45g carbohydrates, 12g fat, 4g fiber, 0mg cholesterol, 700mg sodium, 400mg potassium.

Vegan Burrito Bowls with Quinoa, Beans, and Veggies

Yield: 4 servings | **Prep time:** 15 minutes | **Cook time:** 20 minutes

Ingredients:
- 1 cup quinoa
- 2 cups water
- 1 can (15 oz) black beans, drained and rinsed
- 1 bell pepper, diced
- 1 cup corn kernels (fresh or frozen)
- 1 avocado, diced
- 1/4 cup fresh cilantro, chopped
- Salt and lime juice to taste

Directions:
1. Rinse quinoa under cold water. In a medium pot, combine quinoa and water; bring to a boil. Reduce heat to low, cover, and simmer for 15 minutes, or until water is absorbed. Fluff with a fork.
2. In a large bowl, mix cooked quinoa, black beans, bell pepper, corn, and avocado. Season with salt and lime juice.
3. Serve in bowls and garnish with fresh cilantro.

Nutritional Information: 360 calories, 14g protein, 60g carbohydrates, 9g fat, 15g fiber, 0mg cholesterol, 200mg sodium, 900mg potassium.

Stuffed Bell Peppers with Quinoa and Black Beans

Yield: 4 servings | **Prep time:** 20 minutes | **Cook time:** 40 minutes

Ingredients:
- 4 large bell peppers, tops removed and seeded
- 1 cup quinoa, cooked
- 1 can (15 oz) black beans, drained and rinsed
- 1 cup corn kernels (fresh or frozen)
- 1 teaspoon chili powder
- 1 cup salsa
- Salt and pepper to taste

Directions:
1. Preheat oven to 350°F. Place bell peppers in a baking dish, cut-side up.
2. In a bowl, mix together quinoa, black beans, corn, chili powder, and salsa. Season with salt and pepper.
3. Stuff the mixture into the bell peppers. Cover with foil and bake for 30 minutes. Uncover and bake for an additional 10 minutes.
4. Serve hot, topped with more salsa or avocado slices if desired.

Nutritional Information: 280 calories, 12g protein, 50g carbohydrates, 3g fat, 10g fiber, 0mg cholesterol, 400mg sodium, 800mg potassium.

Vegan Quiche with Spinach and Mushrooms

Yield: 6 servings | **Prep time:** 15 minutes | **Cook time:** 45 minutes

Ingredients:
- 1 vegan pie crust
- 14 oz silken tofu
- 2 cups spinach, chopped
- 1 cup mushrooms, sliced
- 1/4 cup nutritional yeast
- Salt and pepper to taste

Directions:
1. Preheat oven to 375°F. Press the vegan pie crust into a pie dish.
2. Blend silken tofu in a blender until smooth. Mix tofu, spinach, mushrooms, and nutritional yeast in a bowl. Season with salt and pepper.
3. Pour the filling into the pie crust and bake for 45 minutes, or until set.
4. Let cool for 10 minutes before slicing and serving.

Nutritional Information: 260 calories, 12g protein, 20g carbohydrates, 16g fat, 3g fiber, 0mg cholesterol, 300mg sodium, 400mg potassium.

Vegan Tacos with Lentil Walnut Meat

Yield: 4 servings | **Prep time:** 15 minutes | **Cook time:** 15 minutes

Ingredients:
- 1 cup lentils, cooked
- 1/2 cup walnuts, chopped
- 1 tablespoon taco seasoning
- 8 corn tortillas
- 1 avocado, sliced
- 1/2 cup salsa

Directions:
1. Pulse lentils and walnuts in a food processor until the mixture resembles ground meat. Transfer to a skillet, add taco seasoning, and cook for 5 minutes.
2. Warm the tortillas in a skillet or microwave.
3. Assemble the tacos by filling tortillas with the lentil walnut mixture, avocado slices, and salsa.

Nutritional Information: 320 calories, 12g protein, 38g carbohydrates, 15g fat, 9g fiber, 0mg cholesterol, 200mg sodium, 600mg potassium.

Roasted Cauliflower Tacos with Avocado Lime Crema

Yield: 4 servings | **Prep time:** 20 minutes | **Cook time:** 25 minutes

Ingredients:
- 1 head cauliflower, cut into florets
- 2 tablespoons olive oil
- 1 teaspoon chili powder
- 1 avocado
- Juice of 1 lime
- 8 corn tortillas
- Salt to taste

Directions:
1. Preheat oven to 425°F. Toss cauliflower florets with olive oil, chili powder, and salt. Roast for 25 minutes, or until tender and browned.
2. Mash the avocado and mix with lime juice and salt to make the crema.
3. Warm tortillas in the oven or on a skillet. Fill each tortilla with roasted cauliflower and top with avocado lime crema.

Nutritional Information: 300 calories, 8g protein, 40g carbohydrates, 15g fat, 12g fiber, 0mg cholesterol, 200mg sodium, 800mg potassium.

Vegan Shepherd's Pie with Lentils and Sweet Potato

Yield: 6 servings | **Prep time:** 30 minutes | **Cook time:** 30 minutes

Ingredients:
- 2 sweet potatoes, peeled and cubed
- 1 tablespoon olive oil
- 1 onion, diced
- 2 carrots, diced
- 1 cup lentils, cooked
- 1 cup vegetable broth
- Salt and pepper to taste

Directions:
1. Boil sweet potatoes until tender, then mash and set aside.
2. In a skillet, heat olive oil over medium heat. Add onion and carrots, and sauté until softened. Stir in lentils and vegetable broth. Season with salt and pepper.
3. Transfer lentil mixture to a baking dish. Top with mashed sweet potatoes.
4. Bake at 375°F for 30 minutes, or until the top is slightly browned.

Nutritional Information: 280 calories, 12g protein, 50g carbohydrates, 3g fat, 15g fiber, 0mg cholesterol, 300mg sodium, 800mg potassium.

Spicy Peanut Noodles with Stir-Grilled Vegetable Wrap with Hummus and Arugula

Yield: 4 servings | **Prep time:** 10 minutes | **Cook time:** 10 minutes

Ingredients:
- 4 large whole wheat wraps
- 1 cup hummus
- 2 cups arugula
- 1 zucchini, sliced and grilled
- 1 red bell pepper, sliced and grilled
- Salt and pepper to taste

Directions:
1. Spread hummus evenly over each wrap.
2. Layer grilled zucchini, bell pepper, and arugula on top of the hummus. Season with salt and pepper.
3. Roll up the wraps tightly, cut in half, and serve.

Nutritional Information: 320 calories, 12g protein, 45g carbohydrates, 12g fat, 8g fiber, 0mg cholesterol, 400mg sodium, 600mg potassium.

Pumpkin and White Bean Chili with Cornbread Muffins

Yield: 4 servings | **Prep time:** 15 minutes | **Cook time:** 30 minutes

Ingredients:
- For the chili:
  - 1 tablespoon olive oil
  - 1 onion, diced
  - 2 cloves garlic, minced
  - 1 can (15 oz) pumpkin puree
  - 1 can (15 oz) white beans, drained and rinsed
  - 2 cups vegetable broth
  - 1 can (14.5 oz) diced tomatoes
  - 1 tablespoon chili powder
  - 1 teaspoon cumin
  - Salt and pepper to taste
- For the cornbread muffins:
  - 1 cup cornmeal
  - 1 cup all-purpose flour
  - 1/4 cup sugar
  - 1 tablespoon baking powder
  - 1 cup non-dairy milk
  - 1/3 cup vegetable oil

Directions:
1. For the chili, heat olive oil in a large pot over medium heat. Add onion and garlic; sauté until softened. Stir in pumpkin puree, white beans, vegetable broth, diced tomatoes, chili powder, and cumin. Simmer for 25 minutes. Season with salt and pepper.
2. For the cornbread muffins, preheat oven to 400°F (200°C). Mix cornmeal, flour, sugar, and baking powder in a bowl. Stir in non-dairy milk and vegetable oil until just combined. Pour into greased muffin tins and bake for 20 minutes.

3. Serve chili with warm cornbread muffins on the side.

Nutritional Information: 450 calories, 14g protein, 75g carbohydrates, 12g fat, 15g fiber, 0mg cholesterol, 700mg sodium, 800mg potassium.

Sweet Potato and Black Bean Burrito

Yield: 4 servings | **Prep time:** 15 minutes | **Cook time:** 25 minutes

Ingredients:
- 2 sweet potatoes, cubed and roasted
- 1 can (15 oz) black beans, rinsed and drained
- 1 teaspoon cumin
- 4 large whole wheat tortillas
- 1/2 cup salsa
- 1 avocado, sliced

Directions:
1. Preheat the oven to 425°F. Toss sweet potato cubes with oil and cumin, roast until tender, about 20 minutes.
2. Warm tortillas according to package instructions.
3. Divide roasted sweet potato, black beans, salsa, and avocado slices among tortillas. Roll up burritos.
4. Serve immediately, with extra salsa if desired.

Nutritional Information: 390 calories, 11g protein, 65g carbohydrates, 9g fat, 15g fiber, 0mg cholesterol, 600mg sodium, 1000mg potassium.

Fried Vegetables

Yield: 4 servings | **Prep time:** 15 minutes | **Cook time:** 15 minutes

Ingredients:
- 8 oz whole wheat spaghetti
- 2 tablespoons peanut butter
- 2 tablespoons soy sauce
- 1 tablespoon sriracha sauce
- 2 cups mixed vegetables (carrots, bell peppers, broccoli), sliced
- 1 tablespoon olive oil

Directions:
1. Cook spaghetti according to package instructions. Drain and set aside.
2. In a small bowl, mix peanut butter, soy sauce, and sriracha to make the sauce.
3. In a large skillet, heat olive oil. Add vegetables and stir-fry until just tender.
4. Add the spaghetti and peanut sauce to the skillet. Toss everything together until well coated.

Nutritional Information: 350 calories, 12g protein, 55g carbohydrates, 10g fat, 8g fiber, 0mg cholesterol, 600mg sodium, 400mg potassium.

Red Lentil and Spinach Dal

Yield: 4 servings | **Prep time:** 10 minutes | **Cook time:** 25 minutes

Ingredients:
- 1 cup red lentils
- 4 cups water
- 1 teaspoon turmeric
- 1 tablespoon coconut oil
- 1 onion, finely chopped
- 2 cloves garlic, minced
- 2 cups spinach, chopped
- Salt to taste

Directions:
1. Rinse lentils and cook with water and turmeric until soft, about 20 minutes.
2. In another pan, heat coconut oil and sauté onion and garlic until golden.
3. Add cooked lentils to the onion mixture, add spinach, and cook until wilted. Season with salt.
4. Serve hot, accompanied by rice or naan.

Nutritional Information: 250 calories, 18g protein, 40g carbohydrates, 5g fat, 19g fiber, 0mg cholesterol, 300mg sodium, 800mg potassium.

Portobello Mushroom Steaks with Garlic Mashed Potatoes

Yield: 4 servings | **Prep time:** 20 minutes | **Cook time:** 30 minutes

Ingredients:
- 4 large Portobello mushrooms, stems removed
- 2 tablespoons soy sauce
- 2 tablespoons olive oil, divided
- 4 potatoes, peeled and cubed
- 2 cloves garlic, minced
- 1/4 cup almond milk
- Salt and pepper to taste

Directions:
1. Marinate mushrooms in soy sauce and 1 tablespoon olive oil for 15 minutes.
2. Grill or pan-fry mushrooms over medium heat for 5 minutes per side.
3. Boil potatoes until tender, then mash with garlic, almond milk, and remaining olive oil. Season with salt and pepper.
4. Serve mushrooms on top of the garlic mashed potatoes.

Nutritional Information: 290 calories, 8g protein, 45g carbohydrates, 10g fat, 7g fiber, 0mg cholesterol, 400mg sodium, 900mg potassium.

Butternut Squash and Chickpea Curry

Yield: 4 servings | **Prep time:** 15 minutes | **Cook time:** 30 minutes

Ingredients:
- 1 tablespoon coconut oil
- 1 small onion, diced
- 2 cloves garlic, minced
- 1 tablespoon curry powder
- 1 small butternut squash, peeled and cubed
- 1 can (15 oz) chickpeas, drained and rinsed
- 1 can (14 oz) coconut milk
- Salt to taste

Directions:
1. In a large pot, heat coconut oil over medium heat. Add onion and garlic, sauté until softened.
2. Stir in curry powder, then add butternut squash and chickpeas. Cook for 2 minutes.
3. Pour in coconut milk and bring to a simmer. Cover and cook until squash is tender, about 20 minutes. Season with salt.
4. Serve with rice or naan bread.

Nutritional Information: 350 calories, 10g protein, 45g carbohydrates, 18g fat, 10g fiber, 0mg cholesterol, 300mg sodium, 700mg potassium.

Barbecue Jackfruit Sandwiches with Coleslaw

Yield: 4 servings | **Prep time:** 15 minutes | **Cook time:** 25 minutes

Ingredients:
- 2 cans (20 oz each) young green jackfruit in brine, drained and rinsed
- 1 tablespoon olive oil
- 1 small onion, thinly sliced
- 1 cup barbecue sauce
- 4 whole wheat hamburger buns
- 2 cups coleslaw mix
- 1/4 cup vegan mayonnaise
- 1 tablespoon apple cider vinegar
- Salt and pepper to taste

Directions:
1. Shred the jackfruit with a fork. Heat olive oil in a skillet over medium heat, add onion, and sauté until translucent. Add jackfruit and barbecue sauce, cover, and simmer for 20 minutes.
2. In a bowl, mix coleslaw mix with vegan mayonnaise and apple cider vinegar. Season with salt and pepper.
3. Toast the hamburger buns, place a generous amount of barbecue jackfruit on each bun, and top with coleslaw.
4. Serve immediately.

Nutritional Information: 450 calories, 8g protein, 75g carbohydrates, 10g fat, 10g fiber, 0mg cholesterol, 1050mg sodium, 500mg potassium.

Korean BBQ Tofu Bowls with Kimchi and Vegetables

Yield: 4 servings | **Prep time:** 20 minutes | **Cook time:** 15 minutes

Ingredients:
- 14 oz firm tofu, pressed and cubed
- 2 tablespoons sesame oil
- 1/4 cup Korean BBQ sauce
- 2 cups cooked brown rice
- 1 cup kimchi
- 1 cucumber, sliced
- 1 carrot, julienned
- 1 tablespoon sesame seeds

Directions:
1. Marinate tofu cubes in Korean BBQ sauce for 15 minutes. Heat sesame oil in a skillet over medium-high heat and fry tofu until crispy on all sides.
2. Divide cooked brown rice among bowls. Top with BBQ tofu, kimchi, cucumber, and carrot.
3. Garnish with sesame seeds and serve immediately.

Nutritional Information: 400 calories, 15g protein, 50g carbohydrates, 18g fat, 6g fiber, 0mg cholesterol, 700mg sodium, 600mg potassium.

Moroccan Stew with Sweet Potatoes and Kale

Yield: 4 servings | **Prep time**: 15 minutes | **Cook time**: 30 minutes

Ingredients:
- 2 tablespoons olive oil
- 1 onion, chopped
- 2 garlic cloves, minced
- 1 teaspoon ground cumin
- 1/2 teaspoon ground cinnamon
- 2 sweet potatoes, cubed
- 4 cups vegetable broth
- 1 can (14 oz) diced tomatoes
- 4 cups kale, chopped
- Salt and pepper to taste

Directions:
1. Heat olive oil in a large pot over medium heat. Add onion and garlic, sauté until soft.
2. Stir in cumin and cinnamon, then add sweet potatoes, vegetable broth, and diced tomatoes. Bring to a simmer.
3. Cover and cook until sweet potatoes are tender, about 20 minutes.
4. Add kale and cook until wilted. Season with salt and pepper.
5. Serve hot, with crusty bread if desired.

Nutritional Information: 220 calories, 6g protein, 40g carbohydrates, 5g fat, 7g fiber, 0mg cholesterol, 500mg sodium, 900mg potassium.

Chapter 4:
Delicious Dinner

Chickpea Curry with Brown Rice

Yield: 4 servings | **Prep time:** 15 minutes | **Cook time:** 35 minutes

Ingredients:
- 1 cup brown rice, uncooked
- 2 tablespoons olive oil
- 1 onion, finely chopped
- 3 cloves garlic, minced
- 1 tablespoon ginger, grated
- 1 1/2 tablespoons curry powder
- 1 teaspoon ground cumin
- 1 can (14 oz) diced tomatoes
- 1 can (14 oz) chickpeas, drained and rinsed
- 1 can (14 oz) coconut milk
- Salt and pepper to taste
- Fresh cilantro, for garnish

Directions:
1. Cook brown rice according to package instructions; set aside.
2. In a large skillet, heat olive oil over medium heat. Add onion, garlic, and ginger, sautéing until the onion is translucent, about 5 minutes. Stir in curry powder and cumin, cooking for another minute until fragrant.
3. Add diced tomatoes (with juices), chickpeas, and coconut milk to the skillet. Bring to a simmer, reduce heat, and cook for 25 minutes, stirring occasionally. Season with salt and pepper.
4. Serve the curry over the cooked brown rice and garnish with fresh cilantro.

Nutritional Information: 575 calories, 15g protein, 75g carbohydrates, 27g fat, 10g fiber, 0mg cholesterol, 430mg sodium, 950mg potassium.

Vegan Pumpkin Curry with Basmati Rice

Yield: 4 servings | **Prep time:** 15 minutes | **Cook time:** 25 minutes

Ingredients:
- 1 tablespoon coconut oil
- 1 onion, diced
- 2 cloves garlic, minced
- 1 tablespoon grated ginger
- 1 can (15 oz) pumpkin puree
- 1 can (14 oz) coconut milk
- 1 tablespoon curry powder
- 1 teaspoon turmeric
- 1/2 teaspoon cayenne pepper (optional)
- Salt to taste
- 2 cups cooked basmati rice

Directions:
1. Heat coconut oil in a large skillet over medium heat. Add onion, garlic, and ginger; sauté until onion is translucent.
2. Stir in pumpkin puree, coconut milk, curry powder, turmeric, and cayenne pepper. Simmer for 20 minutes. Season with salt.
3. Serve the curry over cooked basmati rice.

Nutritional Information: 410 calories, 6g protein, 50g carbohydrates, 20g fat, 5g fiber, 0mg cholesterol, 300mg sodium, 600mg potassium.

Stuffed Sweet Potatoes with Black Beans and Salsa

Yield: 4 servings | **Prep time:** 10 minutes | **Cook time:** 45 minutes

Ingredients:
- 4 medium sweet potatoes
- 1 can (15 oz) black beans, drained and rinsed
- 1 cup salsa
- 1 avocado, diced
- 1/4 cup fresh cilantro, chopped
- Lime wedges, for serving

Directions:
1. Preheat oven to 400°F (200°C). Prick sweet potatoes with a fork and bake for 45 minutes, until tender.
2. Split the sweet potatoes open and fluff the insides with a fork. Top with black beans, salsa, and diced avocado.
3. Garnish with fresh cilantro and serve with lime wedges on the side.

Nutritional Information: 350 calories, 10g protein, 65g carbohydrates, 7g fat, 15g fiber, 0mg cholesterol, 300mg sodium, 1070mg potassium.

Pizza with Artichokes, Olives, and Cashew Cheese

Yield: 4 servings | **Prep time:** 20 minutes | **Cook time:** 20 minutes

Ingredients:
- 1 pre-made pizza crust
- 1/2 cup marinara sauce
- 1 cup cashew cheese (prepared similar to cashew ricotta)
- 1 can (14 oz) artichoke hearts, drained and quartered
- 1/2 cup black olives, sliced
- 2 tablespoons capers
- 1 teaspoon dried Italian herbs

Directions:
1. Preheat oven to 450°F (230°C). Spread marinara sauce over the pizza crust.
2. Top with cashew cheese, artichoke hearts, black olives, capers, and Italian herbs.
3. Bake for 18-20 minutes, until the crust is golden and toppings are heated through.
4. Slice and serve immediately.

Nutritional Information: 410 calories, 13g protein, 58g carbohydrates, 16g fat, 7g fiber, 0mg cholesterol, 870mg sodium, 400mg potassium.

Butternut Squash Risotto

Yield: 4 servings | **Prep time:** 20 minutes | **Cook time:** 40 minutes

Ingredients:
- 4 cups vegetable broth
- 2 tablespoons olive oil
- 1 small butternut squash, peeled and diced
- 1 onion, finely chopped
- 2 cloves garlic, minced
- 1 cup Arborio rice
- 1/2 cup dry white wine
- Salt and pepper to taste
- 1/4 cup grated Parmesan cheese (optional, use vegan Parmesan for a vegan version)
- Fresh sage leaves, for garnish

Directions:
1. Heat vegetable broth in a saucepan over low heat. Keep warm.
2. In a large skillet, heat 1 tablespoon olive oil over medium heat. Add butternut squash and cook until tender and lightly browned, about 15 minutes. Remove from skillet and set aside.
3. In the same skillet, add remaining olive oil, onion, and garlic. Sauté until onion is translucent. Add Arborio rice, stirring to coat with oil. Cook for 2 minutes.
4. Pour in white wine, stirring constantly, until the wine has been absorbed. Add 1 cup of warm broth, stirring frequently, until the broth is absorbed. Continue adding broth 1 cup at a time, allowing each addition to be absorbed before adding the next, until the rice is tender and creamy.
5. Stir in the cooked butternut squash. Season with salt and pepper. Garnish with Parmesan and fresh sage.

Nutritional Information: 410 calories, 8g protein, 75g carbohydrates, 10g fat, 5g fiber, 2mg cholesterol, 870mg sodium, 500mg potassium.

Pumpkin and Sage Risotto with Toasted Pine Nuts

Yield: 4 servings | **Prep time:** 10 minutes | **Cook time:** 30 minutes

Ingredients:
- 1 tablespoon olive oil
- 1 small onion, finely chopped
- 2 cloves garlic, minced
- 1 cup Arborio rice
- 1/2 cup dry white wine
- 4 cups vegetable broth, warmed
- 1 cup pumpkin puree
- 1 tablespoon fresh sage, chopped
- 1/4 cup pine nuts, toasted
- Salt and pepper to taste

Directions:
1. Heat olive oil in a large saucepan over medium heat.

2. Add onion and garlic; cook until softened. Stir in Arborio rice until coated with oil.
3. Pour in white wine; stir until absorbed. Add vegetable broth 1/2 cup at a time, stirring constantly, until each addition is absorbed before adding the next.
4. Once rice is tender and creamy, stir in pumpkin puree and sage. Season with salt and pepper.
5. Serve topped with toasted pine nuts.

Nutritional Information: 380 calories, 8g protein, 62g carbohydrates, 10g fat, 4g fiber, 0mg cholesterol, 700mg sodium, 250mg potassium.

Spaghetti with Marinara Sauce and Meatless Meatballs

Yield: 4 servings | **Prep time:** 20 minutes | **Cook time:** 20 minutes

Ingredients:
- 12 oz spaghetti
- 2 tablespoons olive oil
- 1 jar (24 oz) marinara sauce
- 1 package (12 oz) meatless meatballs
- Fresh basil leaves, for garnish
- Grated Parmesan cheese (optional, for serving)

Directions:
1. Cook spaghetti according to package instructions; drain and set aside.
2. In a large skillet, heat olive oil over medium heat. Add meatless meatballs and cook until browned and heated through, about 8 minutes.
3. Pour marinara sauce into the skillet with meatballs; simmer for 10 minutes, stirring occasionally.
4. Serve the spaghetti topped with the marinara sauce and meatless meatballs. Garnish with fresh basil and grated Parmesan cheese if desired.

Nutritional Information: 610 calories, 25g protein, 92g carbohydrates, 18g fat, 8g fiber, 0mg cholesterol, 780mg sodium, 1250mg potassium.

Vegan Chili with Avocado and Cornbread

Yield: 4 servings | **Prep time:** 15 minutes |
Cook time: 40 minutes
Ingredients:
- For the chili:
    - 2 tablespoons olive oil
    - 1 onion, chopped
    - 2 cloves garlic, minced
    - 1 bell pepper, diced
    - 2 cans (14 oz each) diced tomatoes
    - 1 can (14 oz) black beans, drained and rinsed
    - 1 can (14 oz) kidney beans, drained and rinsed
    - 2 teaspoons chili powder
    - 1 teaspoon cumin
    - Salt and pepper to taste
- For serving:
    - 1 avocado, sliced
    - Cornbread (prepare according to package instructions)

Directions:
1. In a large pot, heat olive oil over medium heat. Add onion, garlic, and bell pepper, sautéing until softened, about 5 minutes.
2. Stir in diced tomatoes, black beans, kidney beans, chili powder, and cumin. Bring to a simmer and cook for 35 minutes, stirring occasionally. Season with salt and pepper.
3. Serve the chili with sliced avocado on top and a side of cornbread.

Nutritional Information: 450 calories, 18g protein, 68g carbohydrates, 14g fat, 15g fiber, 0mg cholesterol, 890mg sodium, 1200mg potassium.

Mushroom Stroganoff

Yield: 4 servings | **Prep time:** 10 minutes |
Cook time: 20 minutes
Ingredients:
- 12 oz fettuccine
- 2 tablespoons olive oil
- 1 onion, thinly sliced
- 3 cloves garlic, minced
- 16 oz mushrooms, sliced
- 1 tablespoon soy sauce
- 1 teaspoon thyme
- 1 cup vegetable broth
- 1 cup vegan sour cream
- Salt and pepper to taste
- Fresh parsley, for garnish

Directions:
1. Cook fettuccine according to package instructions; drain and set aside.
2. In a large skillet, heat olive oil over medium heat. Add onion and garlic; sauté until softened. Add mushrooms, soy sauce, and thyme; cook until mushrooms are browned and tender.
3. Stir in vegetable broth and bring to a simmer. Reduce heat and stir in vegan sour cream; season with salt and pepper. Cook until heated through.
4. Serve the mushroom stroganoff over cooked fettuccine. Garnish with fresh parsley.

Nutritional Information: 480 calories, 14g protein, 72g carbohydrates, 16g fat, 6g fiber, 0mg cholesterol, 640mg sodium, 950mg potassium.

Vegetable Stir-Fry with Tofu

Yield: 4 servings | **Prep time:** 15 minutes |
Cook time: 20 minutes
Ingredients:
- 1 block (14 oz) firm tofu, pressed and cubed
- 2 tablespoons sesame oil
- 2 cups broccoli florets
- 1 red bell pepper, sliced
- 1 cup snap peas
- 2 carrots, sliced
- 2 cloves garlic, minced
- 1 tablespoon ginger, minced
- 1/4 cup soy sauce
- 2 tablespoons maple syrup
- 1 tablespoon rice vinegar
- 1 teaspoon cornstarch dissolved in 2 tablespoons water
- Sesame seeds, for garnish
- Cooked rice for serving

Directions:
1. In a large skillet or wok, heat 1 tablespoon sesame oil over medium-high heat. Add tofu and fry until golden on all sides. Remove tofu and set aside.
2. In the same skillet, add the remaining sesame oil, broccoli, bell pepper, snap peas, carrots, garlic, and ginger. Stir-fry for 5-7 minutes until vegetables are tender but still crisp.
3. In a small bowl, whisk together soy sauce, maple syrup, rice vinegar, and dissolved cornstarch. Pour over the vegetables in the skillet. Add the tofu back in and cook for an additional 2-3 minutes, until the sauce has thickened.
4. Serve over cooked rice and garnish with sesame seeds.

Nutritional Information: 320 calories, 20g protein, 38g carbohydrates, 12g fat, 6g fiber, 0mg cholesterol, 880mg sodium, 650mg potassium.

Roasted Vegetable Pizza with Vegan Cheese

Yield: 4 servings | **Prep time:** 20 minutes | **Cook time:** 20 minutes

Ingredients:
- 1 pre-made pizza crust
- 2 tablespoons olive oil
- 2 cups assorted vegetables (zucchini, bell peppers, onions), thinly sliced
- 1/2 cup tomato sauce
- 1 teaspoon Italian seasoning
- 1 cup shredded vegan cheese
- Fresh basil leaves, for garnish

Directions:
1. Preheat oven according to pizza crust package instructions.
2. On a baking sheet, toss the sliced vegetables with olive oil and roast for 10 minutes, until slightly softened.
3. Spread tomato sauce over the pizza crust. Sprinkle with Italian seasoning. Arrange the roasted vegetables on top and sprinkle with shredded vegan cheese.
4. Bake according to pizza crust instructions, until the crust is golden and cheese is melted, about 10-15 minutes.
5. Garnish with fresh basil before serving.

Nutritional Information: 410 calories, 12g protein, 52g carbohydrates, 18g fat, 8g fiber, 0mg cholesterol, 580mg sodium, 450mg potassium.

Eggplant Parmesan with Cashew Cheese

Yield: 4 servings | **Prep time:** 25 minutes | **Cook time:** 30 minutes

Ingredients:
- 2 large eggplants, sliced into 1/2-inch thick rounds
- 2 cups marinara sauce
- 1 cup cashews, soaked for 4 hours and drained
- 2 cloves garlic
- Juice of 1 lemon
- 2 tablespoons nutritional yeast
- Salt and pepper to taste
- 1/4 cup fresh basil leaves for garnish

Directions:
1. Preheat oven to 400°F (200°C). Place eggplant rounds on a baking sheet, lightly salt, and let sit for 15 minutes. Pat dry and bake for 20 minutes, until slightly golden.
2. For the cashew cheese, blend soaked cashews, garlic, lemon juice, nutritional yeast, salt, and pepper in a food processor until smooth.
3. Spread a thin layer of marinara sauce on the bottom of a baking dish. Layer baked eggplant rounds, top with a spoonful of cashew cheese, and repeat, ending with marinara sauce.

4. Bake for 30 minutes. Garnish with fresh basil before serving.

Nutritional Information: 330 calories, 13g protein, 42g carbohydrates, 15g fat, 12g fiber, 0mg cholesterol, 640mg sodium, 950mg potassium.

Moroccan Vegetable Tagine with Couscous

Yield: 4 servings | **Prep time:** 20 minutes | **Cook time:** 40 minutes

Ingredients:
- 1 tablespoon olive oil
- 1 onion, chopped
- 2 cloves garlic, minced
- 2 carrots, sliced
- 2 zucchinis, sliced
- 1 bell pepper, chopped
- 1 sweet potato, peeled and cubed
- 2 teaspoons ground cumin
- 1 teaspoon ground cinnamon
- 1/2 teaspoon ground ginger
- 1 can (14 oz) diced tomatoes
- 1/2 cup vegetable broth
- 1 can (15 oz) chickpeas, drained and rinsed
- 1 cup dried couscous
- Fresh cilantro, for garnish

Directions:
1. In a large pot or tagine, heat olive oil over medium heat. Add onion and garlic, sautéing until soft. Add carrots, zucchinis, bell pepper, and sweet potato. Cook for 5 minutes.
2. Stir in cumin, cinnamon, and ginger. Add diced tomatoes and vegetable broth. Bring to a simmer, cover, and cook for 30 minutes.
3. Stir in chickpeas and cook for an additional 10 minutes. Prepare couscous according to package instructions.
4. Serve the vegetable tagine over couscous, garnished with fresh cilantro.

Nutritional Information: 420 calories, 13g protein, 85g carbohydrates, 5g fat, 15g fiber, 0mg cholesterol, 300mg sodium, 890mg potassium.

Vegan Pad Thai with Tofu

Yield: 4 servings | **Prep time:** 20 minutes | **Cook time:** 15 minutes

Ingredients:
- 8 oz rice noodles
- 2 tablespoons vegetable oil
- 1 block (14 oz) firm tofu, pressed and cubed
- 2 cloves garlic, minced
- 1 cup bean sprouts
- 1 red bell pepper, thinly sliced
- 3 green onions, chopped
- 1/4 cup peanuts, crushed
- For the sauce:
  - 2 tablespoons tamarind paste
  - 2 tablespoons soy sauce
  - 2 tablespoons brown sugar
  - 1 tablespoon lime juice
  - 1 teaspoon chili powder

Directions:
1. Cook rice noodles according to package instructions; drain and set aside.
2. In a large skillet or wok, heat vegetable oil over medium-high heat. Add tofu and cook until golden brown on all sides. Remove tofu and set aside.
3. In the same skillet, add garlic, bean sprouts, bell pepper, and green onions. Stir-fry for 3-5 minutes.
4. Whisk together all sauce ingredients in a bowl. Add cooked noodles, tofu, and sauce to the skillet. Toss well to combine.
5. Serve garnished with crushed peanuts.

Nutritional Information: 420 calories, 18g protein, 58g carbohydrates, 14g fat, 4g fiber, 0mg cholesterol, 720mg sodium, 300mg potassium.

Vegan Thai Green Curry with Tofu and Vegetables

Yield: 4 servings | **Prep time:** 15 minutes | **Cook time:** 25 minutes

Ingredients:
- 1 tablespoon coconut oil
- 2 tablespoons green curry paste
- 1 can (14 oz) coconut milk
- 1 block (14 oz) firm tofu, pressed and cubed
- 1 zucchini, sliced
- 1 red bell pepper, sliced
- 1 cup snap peas
- 1/2 cup bamboo shoots
- 1 tablespoon soy sauce
- 1 tablespoon maple syrup
- Juice of 1 lime
- Cooked jasmine rice for serving
- Fresh basil leaves for garnish

Directions:
1. In a large skillet, heat coconut oil over medium heat. Add green curry paste and stir for 1 minute until fragrant.
2. Stir in coconut milk, bringing to a simmer. Add tofu, zucchini, bell pepper, snap peas, and bamboo shoots. Cook for 15-20 minutes, until vegetables are tender and tofu is heated through.
3. Stir in soy sauce, maple syrup, and lime juice. Adjust seasoning to taste.
4. Serve over jasmine rice, garnished with fresh basil leaves.

Nutritional Information: 400 calories, 18g protein, 28g carbohydrates, 26g fat, 4g fiber, 0mg cholesterol, 630mg sodium, 550mg potassium.

Stuffed Acorn Squash with Wild Rice and Cranberries

Yield: 4 servings | **Prep time:** 20 minutes | **Cook time:** 60 minutes

Ingredients:
- 2 acorn squash, halved and seeded
- 2 tablespoons olive oil
- 1 cup wild rice blend, cooked
- 1/2 cup dried cranberries
- 1/2 cup pecans, chopped
- 1 onion, diced
- 2 cloves garlic, minced
- 2 stalks celery, diced
- 1 teaspoon thyme
- Salt and pepper to taste
- 2 cups vegetable broth

Directions:
1. Preheat oven to 400°F (200°C). Brush acorn squash halves with 1 tablespoon olive oil and season with salt and pepper. Place cut-side down on a baking sheet and roast for 40 minutes, until tender.
2. In a frying pan, warm up the leftover olive oil on medium flame. Add onion, garlic, and celery; sauté until softened. Stir in cooked wild rice, cranberries, pecans, thyme, and season with salt and pepper.
3. Stuff the baked acorn squash halves with the wild rice blend. Pour vegetable broth into the baking sheet (around the squash, not over it) to keep them moist.
4. Return to the oven and bake for an additional 20 minutes.
5. Serve warm.

Nutritional Information: 350 calories, 6g protein, 60g carbohydrates, 12g fat, 8g fiber, 0mg cholesterol, 480mg sodium, 890mg potassium.

Black Bean and Sweet Potato Enchiladas

Yield: 4 servings | **Prep time:** 25 minutes |
Cook time: 20 minutes
Ingredients:
- 2 sweet potatoes, cubed
- 1 tablespoon olive oil
- 1 teaspoon cumin
- Salt and pepper to taste
- 1 can (15 oz) black beans, drained and rinsed
- 8 corn tortillas
- 1 jar (16 oz) enchilada sauce
- 1 cup shredded vegan cheese
- Fresh cilantro, for garnish

Directions:
1. Preheat oven to 375°F (190°C). Toss sweet potatoes with olive oil, cumin, salt, and pepper. Roast for 20 minutes, until tender.
2. In a bowl, mix roasted sweet potatoes with black beans. Fill tortillas with the mixture, roll up, and place in a baking dish.
3. Pour enchilada sauce over the filled tortillas and sprinkle with vegan cheese.
4. Bake for 20 minutes, until the cheese is melted and the enchiladas are heated through. Garnish with fresh cilantro before serving.

Nutritional Information: 450 calories, 15g protein, 75g carbohydrates, 10g fat, 15g fiber, 0mg cholesterol, 700mg sodium, 950mg potassium.

Vegan Mushroom Bourguignon

Yield: 4 servings | **Prep time:** 20 minutes |
Cook time: 30 minutes
Ingredients:
- 2 tablespoons olive oil
- 1 pound mushrooms, sliced
- 1 onion, diced
- 2 carrots, sliced
- 2 cloves garlic, minced
- 1 cup red wine
- 2 cups vegetable broth
- 2 tablespoons tomato paste
- 1 teaspoon thyme
- 2 tablespoons flour
- Salt and pepper to taste
- Cooked pasta or mashed potatoes, for serving

Directions:
1. In a large pot, heat olive oil over medium heat. Add mushrooms, cooking until browned. Remove and set aside.
2. In the same pot, add onion, carrots, and garlic. Cook until softened. Stir in red wine, scraping any bits off the bottom of the pot.
3. Add vegetable broth, tomato paste, thyme, and mushrooms back to the pot. Sprinkle flour over the mixture and stir well. Simmer for 20 minutes.
4. Season with salt and pepper. Serve over cooked pasta or mashed potatoes.

Nutritional Information: 290 calories, 6g protein, 35g carbohydrates, 8g fat, 5g fiber, 0mg cholesterol, 480mg sodium, 650mg potassium.

Vegan Shepherd's Pie

Yield: 4 servings | **Prep time:** 20 minutes |
Cook time: 30 minutes
Ingredients:
- For the filling:
  - 2 tablespoons olive oil
  - 1 onion, diced
  - 2 carrots, diced
  - 2 cloves garlic, minced
  - 1 cup green peas
  - 1 cup corn kernels
  - 1 can (15 oz) lentils, drained and rinsed
  - 2 tablespoons tomato paste
  - 1 cup vegetable broth
  - 1 teaspoon thyme
  - Salt and pepper to taste
- For the mashed potato topping:
  - 2 pounds potatoes, peeled and cubed
  - 1/4 cup almond milk
  - 2 tablespoons vegan butter
  - Salt and pepper to taste

Directions:
1. Preheat oven to 400°F (200°C). Boil potatoes in salted water until tender, about 15 minutes. Drain and mash with almond milk, vegan butter, salt, and pepper. Set aside.
2. In a skillet, heat olive oil over medium heat. Add onion, carrots, and garlic; cook until softened. Add peas, corn, lentils, tomato paste, vegetable broth, thyme, salt, and pepper. Simmer until thickened, about 10 minutes.
3. Transfer the filling to a baking dish. Spread mashed potatoes over the top. Bake for 20 minutes, until the top is golden.
4. Let cool slightly before serving.

Nutritional Information: 410 calories, 14g protein, 75g carbohydrates, 8g fat, 15g fiber, 0mg cholesterol, 410mg sodium, 1200mg potassium.

Vegan Jambalaya

Yield: 4 servings | **Prep time:** 15 minutes |
Cook time: 35 minutes
Ingredients:
- 2 tablespoons olive oil
- 1 onion, diced
- 2 cloves garlic, minced
- 1 bell pepper, diced
- 2 celery stalks, diced
- 1 cup rice
- 1 can (14 oz) diced tomatoes, with juice
- 2 cups vegetable broth
- 1 teaspoon paprika
- 1 teaspoon thyme
- 1/2 teaspoon cayenne pepper
- 1 cup okra, sliced
- 1 can (15 oz) red beans, drained and rinsed
- Salt and pepper to taste
- Green onions, sliced for garnish

Directions:
1. In a large skillet or pot, heat olive oil over medium heat. Add onion, garlic, bell pepper, and celery; sauté until softened.
2. Stir in rice, diced tomatoes, vegetable broth, paprika, thyme, and cayenne pepper. Bring to a boil, then reduce heat to low. Cover and simmer for 25 minutes.
3. Add okra and red beans to the pot. Cook for an additional 10 minutes, until rice is tender and most of the liquid is absorbed. Season with salt and pepper.
4. Serve garnished with sliced green onions.

Nutritional Information: 380 calories, 10g protein, 70g carbohydrates, 7g fat, 10g fiber, 0mg cholesterol, 500mg sodium, 800mg potassium.

Vegan Sloppy Joes served with a Side of Baked Sweet Potato Fries

Yield: 4 servings | **Prep time:** 15 minutes |
Cook time: 30 minutes
Ingredients:
- For the Sloppy Joes:
    - 1 tablespoon olive oil
    - 1 onion, diced
    - 2 cloves garlic, minced
    - 1 bell pepper, diced
    - 1 can (15 oz) lentils, drained and rinsed
    - 1 can (15 oz) tomato sauce
    - 2 tablespoons tomato paste
    - 1 tablespoon maple syrup
    - 1 tablespoon soy sauce
    - 1 teaspoon smoked paprika
    - 4 whole wheat burger buns
- For the Sweet Potato Fries:
    - 2 large sweet potatoes, cut into fries
    - 2 tablespoons olive oil
    - Salt and pepper to taste

Directions:
1. Preheat oven to 425°F (220°C). Toss sweet potato fries with olive oil, salt, and pepper. Bake for 25-30 minutes, turning once, until crispy.
2. Meanwhile, heat olive oil in a skillet over medium heat. Add onion, garlic, and bell pepper; cook until softened. Stir in lentils, tomato sauce, tomato paste, maple syrup, soy sauce, and smoked paprika; simmer for 15 minutes until thickened.
3. Serve the Sloppy Joe mixture on burger buns with a side of baked sweet potato fries.

Nutritional Information: 540 calories, 18g protein, 92g carbohydrates, 14g fat, 18g fiber, 0mg cholesterol, 760mg sodium, 1200mg potassium.

Lentil Sloppy Joes

Yield: 4 servings | **Prep time:** 10 minutes |
Cook time: 25 minutes
Ingredients:
- 1 tablespoon olive oil
- 1 onion, diced
- 1 bell pepper, diced
- 2 cloves garlic, minced
- 1 cup dried lentils, rinsed
- 2 cups vegetable broth
- 1 can (15 oz) tomato sauce
- 2 tablespoons tomato paste
- 1 tablespoon mustard
- 1 tablespoon maple syrup
- 1 tablespoon soy sauce
- 4 whole wheat hamburger buns
- Salt and pepper to taste

Directions:
1. In a large skillet, heat olive oil over medium heat. Add onion, bell pepper, and garlic; sauté until softened.
2. Add lentils and vegetable broth; bring to a boil. Reduce heat and simmer until lentils are tender, about 20 minutes.
3. Stir in tomato sauce, tomato paste, mustard, maple syrup, and soy sauce. Cook for an additional 5 minutes. Season with salt and pepper.
4. Serve the lentil mixture on whole wheat hamburger buns.

Nutritional Information: 410 calories, 20g protein, 75g carbohydrates, 5g fat, 20g fiber, 0mg cholesterol, 680mg sodium, 1010mg potassium.

Stuffed Zucchini Boats

Yield: 4 servings | **Prep time:** 15 minutes | **Cook time:** 25 minutes

Ingredients:
- 4 medium zucchinis, halved lengthwise
- 1 tablespoon olive oil
- 1 onion, diced
- 2 cloves garlic, minced
- 1 tomato, diced
- 1 cup cooked quinoa
- 1 can (15 oz) black beans, drained and rinsed
- 1 teaspoon cumin
- Salt and pepper to taste
- 1/2 cup shredded vegan cheese
- Fresh cilantro, for garnish

Directions:
1. Preheat oven to 375°F (190°C). Scoop out the center of each zucchini half to create a boat. Chop the scooped-out zucchini flesh.
2. In a skillet, heat olive oil over medium heat. Add onion, garlic, and the chopped zucchini flesh; cook until softened.
3. Stir in tomato, cooked quinoa, black beans, and cumin. Season with salt and pepper.
4. Fill zucchini boats with the quinoa mixture. Top with shredded vegan cheese.
5. Bake for 20 minutes, until zucchini is tender and cheese is melted. Garnish with fresh cilantro before serving.

Nutritional Information: 270 calories, 12g protein, 45g carbohydrates, 7g fat, 12g fiber, 0mg cholesterol, 300mg sodium, 960mg potassium.

Roasted Red Pepper Hummus Wraps

Yield: 4 servings | **Prep time:** 10 minutes | **Cook time:** 0 minutes

Ingredients:
- 4 large whole wheat tortillas
- 1 cup roasted red pepper hummus
- 2 cups mixed greens
- 1 cucumber, thinly sliced
- 1 carrot, julienned
- 1 avocado, sliced
- 1/4 cup red onion, thinly sliced

Directions:
1. Spread roasted red pepper hummus on each tortilla.
2. Top with mixed greens, cucumber, carrot, avocado, and red onion.
3. Roll up the tortillas tightly, slice in half, and serve.

Nutritional Information: 320 calories, 10g protein, 45g carbohydrates, 14g fat, 10g fiber, 0mg cholesterol, 580mg sodium, 750mg potassium.

Vegan Gnocchi with Spinach and Tomatoes

Yield: 4 servings | **Prep time:** 10 minutes | **Cook time:** 20 minutes

Ingredients:
- 1 package (16 oz) vegan gnocchi
- 2 tablespoons olive oil
- 2 cloves garlic, minced
- 2 cups cherry tomatoes, halved
- 4 cups baby spinach
- Salt and pepper to taste
- Fresh basil, for garnish
- Vegan Parmesan cheese, for serving (optional)

Directions:
1. Cook gnocchi according to package instructions; drain and set aside.
2. In a large skillet, heat olive oil over medium heat. Add garlic and cherry tomatoes; cook until tomatoes are soft, about 5 minutes.
3. Add spinach to the skillet; cook until wilted. Stir in cooked gnocchi, season with salt and pepper.
4. Serve garnished with fresh basil and vegan Parmesan cheese if desired.

Nutritional Information: 380 calories, 8g protein, 62g carbohydrates, 12g fat, 4g fiber, 0mg cholesterol, 450mg sodium, 400mg potassium.

Vegan Bolognese with Lentils over Whole Wheat Pasta

Yield: 4 servings | **Prep time:** 15 minutes | **Cook time:** 25 minutes

Ingredients:
- 1 tablespoon olive oil
- 1 onion, chopped
- 2 carrots, chopped
- 2 stalks celery, chopped
- 2 cloves garlic, minced
- 1 cup brown lentils, rinsed
- 1 can (28 oz) crushed tomatoes
- 1 teaspoon thyme
- Salt and pepper to taste
- 12 oz whole wheat pasta

Directions:
1. In a large pot, heat olive oil over medium heat. Add onion, carrots, celery, and garlic; cook until softened.
2. Add lentils, crushed tomatoes, thyme, salt, and pepper. Bring to a boil, then simmer for 20 minutes, until lentils are tender.
3. Cook pasta according to package instructions; drain. Serve the Bolognese sauce over pasta.

Nutritional Information: 480 calories, 21g protein, 90g carbohydrates, 5g fat, 19g fiber, 0mg cholesterol, 300mg sodium, 1000mg potassium.

Cauliflower Tacos with Avocado Crema

Yield: 4 servings | **Prep time:** 15 minutes | **Cook time:** 20 minutes

Ingredients:
- For the tacos:
    - 1 head cauliflower, cut into florets
    - 2 tablespoons olive oil
    - 1 teaspoon chili powder
    - 1/2 teaspoon cumin
    - 1/4 teaspoon garlic powder
    - Salt and pepper to taste
    - 8 corn tortillas
- For the avocado crema:
    - 1 ripe avocado
    - 1/4 cup coconut yogurt
    - Juice of 1 lime
    - Salt to taste
- Cabbage slaw, for topping
- Fresh cilantro, for garnish

Directions:
1. Preheat oven to 425°F (220°C). Toss cauliflower florets with olive oil, chili powder, cumin, garlic powder, salt, and pepper. Roast for 20 minutes, until tender and slightly charred.
2. For the avocado crema, blend avocado, coconut yogurt, lime juice, and salt until smooth.
3. Warm tortillas in the oven or on a skillet. Assemble tacos with roasted cauliflower, cabbage slaw, and a dollop of avocado crema. Garnish with fresh cilantro.

Nutritional Information: 350 calories, 9g protein, 45g carbohydrates, 18g fat, 12g fiber, 0mg cholesterol, 200mg sodium, 800mg potassium.

Eggplant Lasagna with Cashew Ricotta

Yield: 4 servings | **Prep time:** 30 minutes | **Cook time:** 45 minutes

Ingredients:
- 2 large eggplants, sliced lengthwise
- 2 tablespoons olive oil
- Salt and pepper to taste
- For the cashew ricotta:
    - 1 cup raw cashews, soaked for 4 hours and drained
    - 1 clove garlic
    - Juice of 1 lemon
    - 1/4 cup nutritional yeast
    - Salt to taste
- 1 jar (24 oz) marinara sauce
- 2 cups fresh spinach
- 1 teaspoon dried oregano

Directions:
1. Preheat oven to 375°F (190°C). Brush eggplant slices with olive oil and season with salt and pepper. Bake on a lined baking sheet for 25 minutes until tender.
2. Blend cashews, garlic, lemon juice, nutritional yeast, and salt in a food processor until smooth to make cashew ricotta.
3. In a baking dish, layer marinara sauce, baked eggplant slices, cashew ricotta, and spinach. Repeat layers and top with dried oregano.
4. Bake for 20 minutes. Let cool for 5 minutes before serving.

Nutritional Information: 380 calories, 14g protein, 40g carbohydrates, 20g fat, 12g fiber, 0mg cholesterol, 580mg sodium, 950mg potassium.

Pumpkin and Spinach Lasagna with Cashew Cream Sauce

Yield: 6 servings | **Prep time:** 30 minutes | **Cook time:** 45 minutes

Ingredients:
- For the lasagna:
    - 9 lasagna noodles, cooked
    - 1 tablespoon olive oil
    - 1 onion, diced
    - 3 cloves garlic, minced
    - 2 cups pumpkin puree
    - 4 cups fresh spinach
    - Salt and pepper to taste
- For the cashew cream sauce:
    - 1 cup cashews, soaked for 4 hours and drained
    - 1 cup water
    - 2 tablespoons nutritional yeast
    - 1 clove garlic
    - Juice of 1 lemon
    - Salt to taste

Directions:
1. Preheat oven to 375°F (190°C). For the sauce, blend cashews, water, nutritional yeast, garlic, lemon juice, and salt until smooth.
2. In a skillet, heat olive oil over medium heat. Add onion and garlic; sauté until softened. Stir in pumpkin puree and spinach; cook until spinach is wilted. Season with salt and pepper.
3. Spread a layer of pumpkin mixture in the bottom of a baking dish. Top with a layer of noodles, then cashew cream sauce. Repeat layers, finishing with cashew cream on top.
4. Bake for 45 minutes, until golden and bubbly.

Nutritional Information: 520 calories, 18g protein, 82g carbohydrates, 18g fat, 8g fiber, 0mg cholesterol, 300mg sodium, 900mg potassium.

Moroccan Lentil Stew with Apricots and Spinach

Yield: 4 servings | **Prep time:** 15 minutes | **Cook time:** 35 minutes

Ingredients:
- 2 tablespoons olive oil
- 1 onion, diced
- 2 cloves garlic, minced
- 1 teaspoon ground cumin
- 1 teaspoon ground coriander
- 1/2 teaspoon ground cinnamon
- 1 cup dried lentils
- 4 cups vegetable broth
- 1 can (14 oz) diced tomatoes
- 1 cup dried apricots, chopped
- 2 cups fresh spinach
- Salt and pepper to taste

Directions:
1. In a large pot, heat olive oil over medium heat. Add onion and garlic; cook until softened.
2. Stir in cumin, coriander, and cinnamon; cook for 1 minute. Add lentils, vegetable broth, diced tomatoes, and apricots. Bring to a boil, then simmer for 30 minutes, until lentils are tender.
3. Stir in spinach until wilted. Season with salt and pepper.
4. Serve warm.

Nutritional Information: 360 calories, 18g protein, 65g carbohydrates, 5g fat, 18g fiber, 0mg cholesterol, 480mg sodium, 1010mg potassium.

Smoky BBQ Tofu Bowls with Quinoa

Yield: 4 servings | **Prep time:** 15 minutes | **Cook time:** 30 minutes

Ingredients:
- 1 cup quinoa, rinsed
- 2 cups vegetable broth
- 1 block (14 oz) firm tofu, pressed and cubed
- 2 tablespoons olive oil
- 1/4 cup BBQ sauce
- 1 teaspoon smoked paprika
- 1 cup corn kernels
- 1 avocado, sliced
- 1/4 cup fresh cilantro, chopped

Directions:
1. Cook quinoa in vegetable broth according to package instructions.
2. Toss tofu with olive oil, BBQ sauce, and smoked paprika. Bake at 375°F (190°C) for 25 minutes, turning once, until crispy.
3. Divide quinoa among bowls. Top with BBQ tofu, corn, avocado slices, and cilantro.
4. Serve immediately.

Nutritional Information: 410 calories, 16g protein, 55g carbohydrates, 16g fat, 9g fiber, 0mg cholesterol, 480mg sodium, 890mg potassium.

Creamy Avocado Pasta with Cherry Tomatoes

Yield: 4 servings | **Prep time:** 10 minutes | **Cook time:** 10 minutes

Ingredients:
- 12 oz whole wheat spaghetti
- 2 ripe avocados, pitted and peeled
- 2 cloves garlic
- Juice of 1 lemon
- 1/4 cup olive oil
- Salt and pepper to taste
- 1 cup cherry tomatoes, halved
- Fresh basil, for garnish

Directions:
1. Cook spaghetti according to package instructions; drain and return to pot.
2. In a food processor, blend avocados, garlic, lemon juice, olive oil, salt, and pepper until smooth.
3. Toss pasta with avocado sauce and cherry tomatoes.
4. Serve garnished with fresh basil.

Nutritional Information: 520 calories, 14g protein, 72g carbohydrates, 24g fat, 12g fiber, 0mg cholesterol, 10mg sodium, 800mg potassium.

Zucchini Noodles (Zoodles) with Avocado Pesto

Yield: 4 servings | **Prep time:** 15 minutes | **Cook time:** 0 minutes

Ingredients:
- 4 large zucchinis, spiralized
- For the avocado pesto:
    - 1 ripe avocado
    - 1/2 cup fresh basil leaves
    - 2 cloves garlic
    - 2 tablespoons pine nuts
    - Juice of 1 lemon
    - 1/4 cup olive oil
    - Salt and pepper to taste

Directions:
1. Blend avocado, basil, garlic, pine nuts, lemon juice, and olive oil in a food processor until smooth. Season with salt and pepper.
2. Toss zucchini noodles with avocado pesto until well coated.
3. Serve immediately, garnished with extra pine nuts and basil leaves if desired.

Nutritional Information: 290 calories, 6g protein, 20g carbohydrates, 22g fat, 7g fiber, 0mg cholesterol, 20mg sodium, 890mg potassium.

Sweet Potato Chickpea Buddha Bowls

Yield: 4 servings | **Prep time:** 15 minutes | **Cook time:** 30 minutes

Ingredients:
- 2 large sweet potatoes, peeled and cubed
- 1 can (15 oz) chickpeas, drained, rinsed, and dried
- 2 tablespoons olive oil, divided
- 1 teaspoon smoked paprika
- Salt and pepper to taste
- 2 cups cooked quinoa
- 1 avocado, sliced
- 1 cup baby spinach
- 1/4 cup tahini
- Juice of 1 lemon

Directions:
1. Preheat oven to 400°F (200°C). Toss sweet potatoes and chickpeas with 1 tablespoon olive oil, smoked paprika, salt, and pepper. Spread on a baking sheet and roast for 25-30 minutes, until sweet potatoes are tender.
2. Divide cooked quinoa among bowls. Top with roasted sweet potatoes, chickpeas, avocado slices, and baby spinach.
3. Whisk together tahini, lemon juice, remaining olive oil, and water (as needed) to drizzle consistency; season with salt. Drizzle over each bowl.

Nutritional Information: 530 calories, 15g protein, 75g carbohydrates, 20g fat, 15g fiber, 0mg cholesterol, 300mg sodium, 900mg potassium.

Vegan "Tuna" Salad Sandwiches (made with chickpeas)

Yield: 4 servings | **Prep time:** 10 minutes | **Cook time:** 0 minutes

Ingredients:
- 1 can (15 oz) chickpeas, drained and mashed
- 1/4 cup vegan mayonnaise
- 1 tablespoon Dijon mustard
- 1/4 cup diced celery
- 1/4 cup diced red onion
- 2 tablespoons chopped dill pickles
- Salt and pepper to taste
- 8 slices whole wheat bread
- Lettuce and tomato slices, for serving

Directions:
1. In a bowl, combine mashed chickpeas, vegan mayonnaise, Dijon mustard, celery, red onion, and dill pickles. Season with salt and pepper.
2. Spread the chickpea mixture onto 4 slices of bread. Top with lettuce, tomato, and remaining bread slices.

Nutritional Information: 380 calories, 12g protein, 60g carbohydrates, 10g fat, 12g fiber, 0mg cholesterol, 580mg sodium, 400mg potassium.

Crispy Baked Tofu with Honey-Sriracha Sauce

Yield: 4 servings | **Prep time:** 15 minutes (plus marinating) | **Cook time:** 25 minutes

Ingredients:
- 1 block (14 oz) extra-firm tofu, pressed and cubed
- 2 tablespoons soy sauce
- 1 tablespoon olive oil
- 1 tablespoon cornstarch
- For the sauce:
    - 1/4 cup honey (use maple syrup for a vegan version)
    - 1/4 cup sriracha sauce
    - 2 tablespoons lime juice

Directions:
1. Marinate tofu cubes in soy sauce for at least 15 minutes. Preheat oven to 400°F (200°C).
2. Toss marinated tofu with olive oil and cornstarch. Spread on a baking sheet and bake for 25 minutes, until crispy.
3. Whisk together honey (or maple syrup), sriracha, and lime juice. Toss baked tofu in the sauce before serving.

Nutritional Information: 210 calories, 12g protein, 24g carbohydrates, 8g fat, 1g fiber, 0mg cholesterol, 630mg sodium, 300mg potassium.

Maple Glazed Carrot and Quinoa Salad

Yield: 4 servings | **Prep time:** 15 minutes | **Cook time:** 25 minutes

Ingredients:
- 1 cup quinoa
- 2 cups vegetable broth
- 4 large carrots, peeled and sliced
- 2 tablespoons olive oil
- 2 tablespoons maple syrup
- 1 teaspoon thyme
- Salt and pepper to taste
- 1/4 cup dried cranberries
- 1/4 cup chopped walnuts
- 2 tablespoons fresh parsley, chopped

Directions:
1. Cook quinoa in vegetable broth according to package instructions; set aside to cool.
2. Preheat oven to 400°F (200°C). Toss carrots with olive oil, maple syrup, thyme, salt, and pepper. Roast for 20 minutes until tender and caramelized.
3. In a large bowl, mix the cooled quinoa with roasted carrots, dried cranberries, walnuts, and parsley.
4. Serve at room temperature or chilled.

Nutritional Information: 410 calories, 10g protein, 65g carbohydrates, 14g fat, 8g fiber, 0mg cholesterol, 300mg sodium, 750mg potassium.

Garlic Roasted Brussels Sprouts with Balsamic Glaze

Yield: 4 servings | **Prep time:** 10 minutes | **Cook time:** 25 minutes

Ingredients:
- 1.5 pounds Brussels sprouts, halved
- 2 tablespoons olive oil
- 3 cloves garlic, minced
- Salt and pepper to taste
- 2 tablespoons balsamic vinegar
- 1 tablespoon honey (use maple syrup for a vegan version)

Directions:
1. Preheat oven to 400°F (200°C). Toss Brussels sprouts with olive oil, garlic, salt, and pepper. Spread on a baking sheet.
2. Roast for 25 minutes, until crispy on the outside and tender on the inside.
3. Drizzle with balsamic vinegar and honey (or maple syrup) before serving.

Nutritional Information: 180 calories, 6g protein, 20g carbohydrates, 10g fat, 6g fiber, 0mg cholesterol, 300mg sodium, 670mg potassium.

Ratatouille with Baked Polenta

Yield: 4 servings | **Prep time:** 20 minutes | **Cook time:** 40 minutes

Ingredients:
- For the ratatouille:
  - 2 tablespoons olive oil
  - 1 onion, diced
  - 2 cloves garlic, minced
  - 1 eggplant, cubed
  - 1 zucchini, sliced
  - 1 yellow squash, sliced
  - 1 bell pepper, diced
  - 1 can (14 oz) diced tomatoes
  - 1 teaspoon thyme
  - Salt and pepper to taste
- For the baked polenta:
  - 1 cup polenta
  - 4 cups water
  - 1 teaspoon salt

Directions:
1. For the ratatouille, heat olive oil in a large pan over medium heat. Add onion and garlic; cook until soft. Add eggplant, zucchini, squash, and bell pepper; cook until vegetables are tender. Stir in diced tomatoes and thyme; simmer for 20 minutes. Season with salt and pepper.
2. For the polenta, bring water and salt to a boil. Gradually whisk in polenta. Reduce heat and simmer, stirring frequently, until thickened. Spread polenta in a baking dish and bake at 375°F (190°C) for 20 minutes.
3. Serve ratatouille over baked polenta.

Nutritional Information: 310 calories, 7g protein, 50g carbohydrates, 10g fat, 9g fiber, 0mg cholesterol, 300mg sodium, 750mg potassium.

Baked Garlic Mushroom and Spinach Quesadillas

Yield: 4 servings | **Prep time:** 15 minutes | **Cook time:** 20 minutes

Ingredients:
- 8 whole wheat tortillas
- 2 cups mushrooms, sliced
- 2 cups spinach, chopped
- 4 cloves garlic, minced
- 1 tablespoon olive oil
- 1 cup vegan cheese, shredded
- Salt and pepper to taste

Directions:
1. Preheat oven to 375°F (190°C). In a skillet, heat olive oil over medium heat. Add garlic and mushrooms; cook until mushrooms are soft. Add spinach and cook until wilted. Season with salt and pepper.
2. Place tortillas on a baking sheet. Spread the mushroom and spinach mixture on half of each tortilla, top with vegan cheese, and fold.
3. Bake for 10 minutes, until tortillas are crispy and cheese has melted.
4. Cut into wedges and serve.

Nutritional Information: 320 calories, 12g protein, 42g carbohydrates, 12g fat, 6g fiber, 0mg cholesterol, 580mg sodium, 300mg potassium.

Simple Vegan Pesto Gnocchi

Yield: 4 servings | **Prep time:** 10 minutes | **Cook time:** 15 minutes

Ingredients:
- 1 package (16 oz) gnocchi
- For the pesto:
  - 2 cups fresh basil leaves
  - 1/2 cup pine nuts
  - 2 cloves garlic
  - 1/2 cup olive oil
  - 1/4 cup nutritional yeast
  - Salt and pepper to taste

Directions:
1. Cook gnocchi according to package instructions; drain and set aside.
2. For the pesto, blend basil, pine nuts, garlic, olive oil, and nutritional yeast in a food processor until smooth. Season with salt and pepper.
3. Toss gnocchi with the pesto sauce until well coated.
4. Serve immediately, garnished with additional basil leaves if desired.

Nutritional Information: 520 calories, 12g protein, 58g carbohydrates, 28g fat, 4g fiber, 0mg cholesterol, 580mg sodium, 300mg potassium.

Vegan Paella with Artichokes and Bell Peppers

Yield: 4 servings | **Prep time:** 15 minutes | **Cook time:** 35 minutes

Ingredients:
- 2 tablespoons olive oil
- 1 onion, diced
- 2 cloves garlic, minced
- 1 red bell pepper, sliced
- 1 yellow bell pepper, sliced
- 1 cup Arborio rice
- 1/4 teaspoon saffron threads
- 2 1/2 cups vegetable broth
- 1 can (14 oz) artichoke hearts, drained and quartered
- 1 cup frozen peas
- Salt and pepper to taste
- Lemon wedges, for serving

Directions:
1. Heat olive oil in a large skillet or paella pan over medium heat. Add onion, garlic, and bell peppers; cook until soft.
2. Stir in rice and saffron, cooking for 1 minute. Add vegetable broth and bring to a simmer. Cover and cook for 20 minutes.
3. Add artichoke hearts and peas, cooking for an additional 10 minutes. Season with salt and pepper.
4. Serve with lemon wedges.

Nutritional Information: 380 calories, 9g protein, 68g carbohydrates, 8g fat, 9g fiber, 0mg cholesterol, 700mg sodium, 400mg potassium.

Vegan Fajitas with Portobello Mushrooms and Bell Peppers

Yield: 4 servings | **Prep time:** 20 minutes | **Cook time:** 15 minutes

Ingredients:
- 3 portobello mushrooms, sliced
- 2 bell peppers (1 red, 1 yellow), sliced
- 1 large onion, sliced
- 2 tablespoons olive oil
- 1 teaspoon chili powder
- 1 teaspoon cumin
- 1/2 teaspoon smoked paprika
- Salt and pepper to taste
- 8 small flour tortillas
- Optional toppings: avocado slices, lime wedges, fresh cilantro

Directions:
1. Preheat a large skillet over medium-high heat. Toss mushrooms, bell peppers, and onion with olive oil, chili powder, cumin, smoked paprika, salt, and pepper.
2. Cook the vegetable mixture in the skillet for about 10-12 minutes until vegetables are tender and slightly charred.
3. Warm tortillas in the oven or on a skillet. Serve the vegetable mixture in tortillas with optional toppings as desired.

Nutritional Information: 320 calories, 8g protein, 45g carbohydrates, 12g fat, 6g fiber, 0mg cholesterol, 400mg sodium, 500mg potassium.

Lemon Garlic Orzo with Roasted Vegetables

Yield: 4 servings | **Prep time:** 15 minutes | **Cook time:** 25 minutes

Ingredients:
- 1 cup orzo
- 2 cups vegetable broth
- 2 zucchinis, cubed
- 1 red onion, chopped
- 2 tablespoons olive oil
- 2 cloves garlic, minced
- Juice and zest of 1 lemon
- 1/4 cup fresh parsley, chopped
- Salt and pepper to taste

Directions:
1. Preheat oven to 400°F (200°C). Toss zucchini and red onion with 1 tablespoon olive oil, salt, and pepper. Roast for 20 minutes, until tender.
2. Cook orzo in vegetable broth according to package instructions; drain.
3. In a large bowl, mix roasted vegetables, cooked orzo, garlic, lemon juice, lemon zest, parsley, and remaining olive oil. Season with salt and pepper.
4. Serve warm or at room temperature.

Nutritional Information: 290 calories, 8g protein, 50g carbohydrates, 7g fat, 3g fiber, 0mg cholesterol, 300mg sodium, 450mg potassium.

Vegan Mushroom Risotto with a Side of Steamed Green Beans

Yield: 4 servings | **Prep time:** 10 minutes | **Cook time:** 30 minutes

Ingredients:
- For the Risotto:
- 1 tablespoon olive oil
- 1 small onion, finely chopped
- 2 cloves garlic, minced
- 1 pound mushrooms, sliced
- 1 cup Arborio rice
- 1/2 cup white wine (optional)
- 4 cups vegetable broth, warmed
- 1 tablespoon nutritional yeast (for a cheesy flavor)
- Salt and pepper to taste
- For the Green Beans:
- 1 pound green beans, ends trimmed
- Salt to taste

Directions:
1. In a large pan, heat olive oil over medium heat. Add onion and garlic; cook until softened. Add mushrooms and cook until they release their juices.

2. Stir in Arborio rice and cook for 1-2 minutes. Add white wine (if using) and cook until absorbed. Add warm vegetable broth, 1/2 cup at a time, stirring constantly until each addition is absorbed before adding the next, until rice is creamy and al dente.
3. While risotto cooks, steam green beans in a steamer or in the microwave with a bit of water until tender-crisp, about 3-4 minutes. Season with salt.
4. Serve risotto with a sprinkle of nutritional yeast and a side of steamed green beans.

Nutritional Information: 380 calories, 12g protein, 68g carbohydrates, 7g fat, 8g fiber, 0mg cholesterol, 470mg sodium, 900mg potassium.

Spicy Potato Soup

Yield: 4 servings | **Prep time:** 15 minutes | **Cook time:** 25 minutes
Ingredients:
- 4 large potatoes, peeled and diced
- 1 tablespoon olive oil
- 1 onion, chopped
- 2 cloves garlic, minced
- 1 teaspoon red pepper flakes (adjust to taste)
- 4 cups vegetable broth
- 1 cup coconut milk
- Salt and black pepper to taste
- Chopped green onions and cilantro for garnish

Directions:
1. Heat olive oil in a large pot over medium heat. Add onion and garlic, cooking until soft, about 5 minutes.
2. Add potatoes, red pepper flakes, and vegetable broth. Bring to a boil, then reduce heat and simmer until potatoes are tender, about 15-20 minutes.
3. Use an immersion blender to partially blend the soup for a creamy yet chunky texture. Stir in coconut milk and season with salt and pepper.
4. Heat through for another 5 minutes. Serve hot, garnished with green onions and cilantro.

Nutritional Information: 300 calories, 6g protein, 45g carbohydrates, 12g fat, 6g fiber, 0mg cholesterol, 600mg sodium, 900mg potassium.

Mushroom Soup with Curry

Yield: 4 servings | **Prep time:** 10 minutes | **Cook time:** 30 minutes
Ingredients:
- 1 lb fresh mushrooms, sliced
- 1 medium onion, chopped
- 2 cloves garlic, minced
- 2 tablespoons olive oil
- 1 tablespoon curry powder
- 4 cups vegetable broth
- 1 cup coconut milk
- Salt and pepper to taste
- Fresh cilantro, for garnish

Directions:
1. In a large pot, heat the olive oil over medium heat. Add the onion and garlic, sautéing until soft, about 5 minutes.
2. Stir in the mushrooms and curry powder, cooking until the mushrooms are tender, about 10 minutes.
3. Pour in the vegetable broth and bring to a boil. Reduce heat and simmer for 15 minutes.
4. Stir in the coconut milk and season with salt and pepper. Cook for an additional 5 minutes.
5. Serve hot, garnished with fresh cilantro.

Nutritional Information: 250 calories, 6g protein, 15g carbohydrates, 20g fat, 4g fiber, 0mg cholesterol, 500mg sodium, 600mg potassium.

Broccoli and Fennel Soup

Yield: 4 servings | **Prep time:** 10 minutes | **Cook time:** 20 minutes
Ingredients:
- 1 tablespoon olive oil
- 1 fennel bulb, thinly sliced
- 1 onion, chopped
- 2 cloves garlic, minced
- 4 cups vegetable broth
- 1 head broccoli, cut into florets
- Salt and pepper to taste
- 1/4 cup coconut milk (optional for creaminess)
- Lemon zest, for garnish

Directions:
1. Heat olive oil in a large pot over medium heat. Add fennel and onion, cooking until softened, about 5 minutes. Add garlic and cook for another minute.
2. Pour in the vegetable broth and bring to a boil. Add the broccoli florets, reduce heat, and simmer until broccoli is tender, about 10-15 minutes.
3. Use an immersion blender to puree the soup until smooth. Stir in coconut milk (if using) and season with salt and pepper.
4. Serve hot, garnished with lemon zest.

Nutritional Information: 120 calories, 4g protein, 15g carbohydrates, 5g fat, 5g fiber, 0mg cholesterol, 300mg sodium, 500mg potassium.

Chapter 5:
Chapter 5: Hearty Beans and Grains

Butternut Squash and Cannellini Bean Ragout

Yield: 4 servings | **Prep time:** 15 minutes | **Cook time:** 30 minutes

Ingredients:
- 2 cups butternut squash, cubed
- 1 can (15 oz) cannellini beans, drained and rinsed
- 1 onion, diced
- 2 cloves garlic, minced
- 1 can (14.5 oz) diced tomatoes
- 1 teaspoon rosemary
- 1/2 teaspoon thyme
- 2 tablespoons olive oil
- Salt and pepper to taste
- Fresh parsley, chopped, for garnish

Directions:
1. Heat olive oil in a large skillet over medium heat. Sauté onion and garlic until translucent.
2. Add butternut squash, cooking until slightly softened, about 10 minutes.
3. Stir in cannellini beans, diced tomatoes, rosemary, and thyme. Season with salt and pepper.
4. Simmer for 20 minutes until the squash is tender and flavors have melded.
5. Garnish with fresh parsley before serving.

Nutritional Information: 250 calories, 9g protein, 45g carbohydrates, 5g fat, 12g fiber, 0mg cholesterol, 200mg sodium, 800mg potassium.

Black Bean and Quinoa Chili

Yield: 4 servings | **Prep time:** 10 minutes | **Cook time:** 30 minutes

Ingredients:
- 1 cup quinoa, rinsed
- 2 cups vegetable broth
- 1 can (15 oz) black beans, drained and rinsed
- 1 can (14.5 oz) diced tomatoes
- 1 onion, diced
- 2 cloves garlic, minced
- 1 bell pepper, diced
- 1 tablespoon chili powder
- 1 teaspoon cumin
- Salt and pepper to taste
- 2 tablespoons olive oil

Directions:
1. In a large pot, heat olive oil over medium heat. Add onion, garlic, and bell pepper; sauté until softened.
2. Stir in quinoa, vegetable broth, black beans, diced tomatoes, chili powder, and cumin. Season with salt and pepper.
3. Bring to a boil, then reduce heat and simmer covered for 20 minutes or until quinoa is cooked.
4. Adjust seasoning if necessary and serve.

Nutritional Information: 320 calories, 12g protein, 54g carbohydrates, 7g fat, 10g fiber, 0mg cholesterol, 400mg sodium, 700mg potassium.

Spicy Kidney Bean and Farro Salad

Yield: 4 servings | **Prep time:** 10 minutes | **Cook time:** 30 minutes (for farro)

Ingredients:
- 1 cup farro, cooked
- 1 can (15 oz) kidney beans, drained and rinsed
- 1 bell pepper, diced
- 1/4 cup red onion, finely chopped
- 1/4 cup cilantro, chopped
- For the dressing:
  - 2 tablespoons olive oil
  - Juice of 1 lime
  - 1 teaspoon chili flakes
  - Salt and pepper to taste

Directions:
1. In a large bowl, combine cooked farro, kidney beans, bell pepper, red onion, and cilantro.
2. Whisk together olive oil, lime juice, chili flakes, salt, and pepper for the dressing.
3. Pour the dressing over the salad and toss to combine.

Nutritional Information: 290 calories, 10g protein, 50g carbohydrates, 7g fat, 13g fiber, 0mg cholesterol, 200mg sodium, 600mg potassium.

Lentil and Mushroom Stuffed Peppers

Yield: 4 servings | **Prep time:** 20 minutes | **Cook time:** 40 minutes

Ingredients:
- 4 large bell peppers, halved and seeded
- 1 cup lentils, cooked
- 1 cup mushrooms, chopped
- 1 onion, diced
- 2 cloves garlic, minced
- 1 teaspoon thyme
- 1/2 cup breadcrumbs
- 1/4 cup vegetable broth
- Salt and pepper to taste
- 2 tablespoons olive oil

Directions:
1. Preheat oven to 375°F (190°C). Place bell pepper halves in a baking dish.
2. In a skillet, heat olive oil over medium heat. Sauté onion, garlic, mushrooms, and thyme until softened.
3. Stir in cooked lentils, breadcrumbs, and vegetable broth. Season with salt and pepper.
4. Stuff the bell pepper halves with the lentil mixture. Cover with foil and bake for 30 minutes. Uncover and bake for an additional 10 minutes.
5. Serve warm.

Nutritional Information: 250 calories, 10g protein, 38g carbohydrates, 7g fat, 9g fiber, 0mg cholesterol, 300mg sodium, 600mg potassium.

Sweet Potato and Black Bean Enchiladas

Yield: 4 servings | **Prep time:** 20 minutes | **Cook time:** 25 minutes

Ingredients:
- 2 sweet potatoes, cubed and roasted
- 1 can (15 oz) black beans, drained and rinsed
- 8 small tortillas
- 1 cup enchilada sauce
- 1 onion, diced
- 1 teaspoon cumin
- Salt and pepper to taste
- 1/4 cup cilantro, chopped
- 2 tablespoons olive oil

Directions:
1. Preheat oven to 375°F (190°C). In a skillet, heat olive oil over medium heat. Sauté onion until translucent.
2. Add roasted sweet potatoes, black beans, cumin, salt, and pepper to the skillet. Cook for 5 minutes.
3. Spoon the mixture into tortillas, roll up, and place seam-side down in a baking dish. Cover with enchilada sauce.
4. Bake for 25 minutes. Garnish with cilantro before serving.

Nutritional Information: 350 calories, 11g protein, 60g carbohydrates, 9g fat, 12g fiber, 0mg cholesterol, 700mg sodium, 800mg potassium.

Bulgur Wheat Salad with Lemon and Herbs

Yield: 4 servings | **Prep time:** 10 minutes | **Cook time:** 15 minutes

Ingredients:
- 1 cup bulgur wheat
- 2 cups water
- Juice and zest of 1 lemon
- 1/4 cup chopped parsley
- 1/4 cup chopped mint
- 1/4 cup olive oil
- Salt and pepper to taste
- 1 cucumber, diced
- 1/2 cup cherry tomatoes, halved

Directions:
1. Cook bulgur in water according to package instructions; let cool.
2. Whisk together lemon juice, zest, olive oil, salt, and pepper.
3. Toss bulgur with lemon dressing, parsley, mint, cucumber, and cherry tomatoes.
4. Serve chilled or at room temperature.

Nutritional Information: 280 calories, 6g protein, 40g carbohydrates, 14g fat, 8g fiber, 0mg cholesterol, 10mg sodium, 300mg potassium.

Vegan Jambalaya with Black-Eyed Peas

Yield: 4 servings | **Prep time:** 15 minutes | **Cook time:** 35 minutes

Ingredients:
- 1 cup rice
- 2 cups vegetable broth
- 1 can (15 oz) black-eyed peas, drained and rinsed
- 1 can (14.5 oz) diced tomatoes
- 1 onion, diced
- 1 bell pepper, diced
- 2 stalks celery, diced
- 2 cloves garlic, minced
- 1 teaspoon paprika
- 1/2 teaspoon cayenne pepper
- Salt and pepper to taste
- 2 tablespoons olive oil

Directions:
1. In a large pot, heat olive oil over medium heat. Sauté onion, bell pepper, celery, and garlic until softened.
2. Stir in rice, vegetable broth, black-eyed peas, diced tomatoes, paprika, and cayenne pepper. Season with salt and pepper.
3. Bring to a boil, then reduce heat, cover, and simmer for 25 minutes or until rice is cooked.
4. Adjust seasoning if necessary and serve.

Nutritional Information: 340 calories, 10g protein, 62g carbohydrates, 7g fat, 8g fiber, 0mg cholesterol, 500mg sodium, 700mg potassium.

Spicy Kidney Bean and Farro Salad

Yield: 4 servings | **Prep time:** 10 minutes | **Cook time:** 30 minutes (for farro)

Ingredients:
- 1 cup farro, cooked
- 1 can (15 oz) kidney beans, drained and rinsed
- 1 bell pepper, diced
- 1/4 cup red onion, finely chopped
- 1/4 cup cilantro, chopped
- For the dressing:
  - 2 tablespoons olive oil
  - Juice of 1 lime
  - 1 teaspoon chili flakes
  - Salt and pepper to taste

Directions:
1. In a large bowl, combine cooked farro, kidney beans, bell pepper, red onion, and cilantro.
2. Whisk together olive oil, lime juice, chili flakes, salt, and pepper for the dressing.
3. Pour the dressing over the salad and toss to combine.

Nutritional Information: 290 calories, 10g protein, 50g carbohydrates, 7g fat, 13g fiber, 0mg cholesterol, 200mg sodium, 600mg potassium.

Lentil Loaf with Smoky Tomato Glaze

Yield: 4 servings | **Prep time:** 20 minutes | **Cook time:** 60 minutes

Ingredients:
- 1 cup lentils, cooked
- 1 onion, diced
- 2 cloves garlic, minced
- 1 carrot, grated
- 1/2 cup breadcrumbs
- 1/4 cup ketchup
- 2 tablespoons soy sauce
- 1 teaspoon smoked paprika
- For the glaze:
  - 1/4 cup ketchup
  - 1 tablespoon apple cider vinegar
  - 1 tablespoon maple syrup
  - 1 teaspoon smoked paprika
- Salt and pepper to taste
- 2 tablespoons olive oil

Directions:
1. Preheat oven to 350°F (175°C). Sauté onion, garlic, and carrot in olive oil until softened.
2. In a bowl, mix cooked lentils, sautéed vegetables, breadcrumbs, ketchup, soy sauce, and smoked paprika. Season with salt and pepper.
3. Press mixture into a loaf pan. For the glaze, mix ketchup, apple cider vinegar, maple syrup, and smoked paprika. Spread over the top of the loaf.
4. Bake for 60 minutes. Let cool for 10 minutes before slicing.

Nutritional Information: 320 calories, 12g protein, 54g carbohydrates, 7g fat, 10g fiber, 0mg cholesterol, 600mg sodium, 800mg potassium.

Vegan Risotto with Asparagus and Peas

Yield: 4 servings | **Prep time:** 10 minutes | **Cook time:** 30 minutes

Ingredients:
- 1 cup Arborio rice
- 1 bunch asparagus, trimmed and cut into pieces
- 1/2 cup peas
- 4 cups vegetable broth, warmed
- 1 onion, diced
- 2 cloves garlic, minced
- 1/2 cup white wine (optional)
- 2 tablespoons olive oil
- Salt and pepper to taste
- 1/4 cup nutritional yeast (for a cheesy flavor)

Directions:
1. In a large pan, heat olive oil over medium heat. Sauté onion and garlic until translucent.
2. Add Arborio rice, stirring until the grains are well-coated and slightly translucent.
3. Pour in white wine, stirring until mostly absorbed. Add vegetable broth, one cup at a time, stirring frequently until each addition is absorbed before adding more.

4. About halfway through cooking, add asparagus and peas. Continue adding broth and stirring.
5. Once the risotto is creamy and the rice is tender, stir in nutritional yeast. Season with salt and pepper.

Nutritional Information: 320 calories, 10g protein, 55g carbohydrates, 7g fat, 6g fiber, 0mg cholesterol, 300mg sodium, 400mg potassium.

Mexican Spicy Rice

Yield: 4 servings | **Prep time:** 10 minutes | **Cook time:** 20 minutes

Ingredients:
- 1 cup long-grain white rice
- 2 tablespoons olive oil
- 1 onion, finely chopped
- 2 cloves garlic, minced
- 1 jalapeño, seeded and finely chopped
- 1 teaspoon ground cumin
- 1/2 teaspoon chili powder
- 1/4 teaspoon cayenne pepper (adjust to taste)
- 2 cups vegetable broth
- 1 can (15 oz) diced tomatoes, drained
- Salt to taste
- Fresh cilantro and lime wedges for garnish

Directions:
1. Heat olive oil in a large skillet over medium heat. Add the onion and garlic, cooking until soft, about 5 minutes. Stir in jalapeño, cumin, chili powder, and cayenne pepper, cooking for another minute.
2. Stir in the rice, coating it well with the onion mixture. Cook until lightly toasted, about 2 minutes.
3. Add the vegetable broth and diced tomatoes. Bring to a boil, then reduce heat to low, cover, and simmer until rice is cooked and liquid is absorbed, about 15 minutes.
4. Remove from heat, fluff with a fork, and let sit covered for 5 minutes. Season with salt.
5. Serve garnished with fresh cilantro and lime wedges.

Nutritional Information: 250 calories, 5g protein, 45g carbohydrates, 7g fat, 2g fiber, 0mg cholesterol, 500mg sodium, 300mg potassium.

Baked Rice with Sweet Potatoes and Fennel

Yield: 4 servings | **Prep time:** 15 minutes | **Cook time:** 45 minutes

Ingredients:
- 1 cup basmati rice, rinsed
- 2 cups vegetable broth
- 1 large sweet potato, peeled and diced
- 1 fennel bulb, thinly sliced
- 1 onion, diced
- 2 tablespoons olive oil
- 1 teaspoon dried thyme
- Salt and pepper to taste
- Fresh parsley, chopped for garnish

Directions:
1. Preheat oven to 375°F (190°C). In a baking dish, combine the rinsed basmati rice with vegetable broth, sweet potato, fennel bulb, and onion. Drizzle with olive oil and sprinkle with thyme, salt, and pepper. Stir to mix well.
2. Cover the baking dish tightly with aluminum foil. Bake in the preheated oven for about 45 minutes, or until the rice is fluffy and all the liquid has been absorbed.
3. Remove from oven and let it stand covered for 5 minutes. Then fluff the rice with a fork, mixing the ingredients gently.
4. Serve hot, garnished with fresh parsley.

Nutritional Information: 320 calories, 6g protein, 58g carbohydrates, 7g fat, 5g fiber, 0mg cholesterol, 300mg sodium, 400mg potassium.

Eggplant and Chickpea Rice Pilaf

Yield: 4 servings | **Prep time:** 15 minutes | **Cook time:** 30 minutes

Ingredients:
- 1 cup basmati rice, rinsed
- 2 tablespoons olive oil
- 1 medium eggplant, cubed
- 1 can (15 oz) chickpeas, drained and rinsed
- 1 onion, chopped
- 2 cloves garlic, minced
- 1 teaspoon ground cumin
- 1/2 teaspoon ground coriander
- 2 cups vegetable broth
- Salt and pepper to taste
- Fresh parsley, chopped for garnish

Directions:
1. Heat olive oil in a large skillet over medium heat. Add the eggplant and sauté until beginning to soften, about 5 minutes. Remove eggplant and set aside.
2. In the same skillet, add the onion and garlic, cooking until the onion is translucent, about 5 minutes. Stir in cumin and coriander.
3. Add the rice to the skillet, stirring to coat with the onion mixture. Pour in the vegetable broth and bring to a boil. Reduce heat to low, add the eggplant and chickpeas, cover, and simmer until the rice is cooked and the liquid is absorbed, about 20 minutes.
4. Season with salt and pepper. Fluff the pilaf with a fork before serving.
5. Garnish with fresh parsley.

Nutritional Information: 380 calories, 10g protein, 65g carbohydrates, 10g fat, 8g fiber, 0mg cholesterol, 300mg sodium, 400mg potassium.

Hearty White Bean and Kale Stew

Yield: 4 servings | **Prep time:** 10 minutes | **Cook time:** 30 minutes

Ingredients:
- 2 cans (15 oz each) white beans, drained and rinsed
- 1 onion, diced
- 2 carrots, diced
- 2 stalks celery, diced
- 2 cloves garlic, minced
- 4 cups vegetable broth
- 4 cups kale, chopped
- 1 teaspoon thyme
- Salt and pepper to taste
- 2 tablespoons olive oil

Directions:
1. In a large pot, heat olive oil over medium heat. Sauté onion, carrots, celery, and garlic until softened.
2. Add vegetable broth, white beans, and thyme. Bring to a boil, then reduce heat and simmer for 20 minutes.
3. Stir in kale and cook until wilted. Season with salt and pepper before serving.

Nutritional Information: 260 calories, 14g protein, 45g carbohydrates, 4g fat, 11g fiber, 0mg cholesterol, 700mg sodium, 1000mg potassium.

Quinoa Stuffed Acorn Squash with Pecans and Cranberries

Yield: 4 servings | **Prep time:** 20 minutes | **Cook time:** 40 minutes

Ingredients:
- 2 acorn squash, halved and seeded
- 1 cup quinoa, rinsed
- 2 cups vegetable broth
- 1/2 cup pecans, chopped
- 1/2 cup dried cranberries
- 1 teaspoon cinnamon
- Salt and pepper to taste
- 2 tablespoons olive oil

Directions:
1. Preheat oven to 375°F (190°C). Brush acorn squash halves with olive oil and season with salt and pepper. Place cut side down on a baking sheet and roast for 25 minutes.
2. In a medium saucepan, combine quinoa and vegetable broth. Bring to a boil, reduce heat, cover, and simmer for 15 minutes or until liquid is absorbed.
3. Stir pecans, cranberries, and cinnamon into cooked quinoa. Season with salt and pepper.
4. Fill roasted acorn squash halves with quinoa mixture and bake for an additional 15 minutes.

Nutritional Information: 410 calories, 8g protein, 65g carbohydrates, 14g fat, 9g fiber, 0mg cholesterol, 300mg sodium, 900mg potassium.

Barley and Roasted Vegetable Pilaf

Yield: 4 servings | **Prep time:** 15 minutes | **Cook time:** 45 minutes

Ingredients:
- 1 cup barley, rinsed
- 2 1/2 cups vegetable broth
- 1 zucchini, cubed
- 1 red bell pepper, cubed
- 1 onion, cubed
- 2 cloves garlic, minced
- 2 tablespoons olive oil
- Salt and pepper to taste
- 2 tablespoons fresh parsley, chopped

Directions:
1. Preheat oven to 425°F (220°C). Toss zucchini, bell pepper, onion, and garlic with olive oil, salt, and pepper. Spread on a baking sheet and roast for 25 minutes, stirring halfway through.
2. In a large saucepan, bring vegetable broth to a boil. Add barley, reduce heat, cover, and simmer for 40 minutes or until tender and liquid is absorbed.
3. Mix roasted vegetables into cooked barley. Garnish with fresh parsley before serving.

Nutritional Information: 320 calories, 8g protein, 55g carbohydrates, 7g fat, 10g fiber, 0mg cholesterol, 200mg sodium, 400mg potassium.

Quinoa and Black Bean Stuffed Bell Peppers

Yield: 4 servings | **Prep time:** 20 minutes | **Cook time:** 30 minutes

Ingredients:
- 4 large bell peppers, halved and seeded
- 1 cup quinoa, cooked
- 1 can (15 oz) black beans, drained and rinsed
- 1 cup corn kernels
- 1/2 cup salsa
- 1 teaspoon cumin
- 1/2 teaspoon chili powder
- 1/4 cup cilantro, chopped
- Salt and pepper to taste
- 1 tablespoon olive oil

Directions:
1. Preheat oven to 375°F (190°C).
2. In a bowl, combine cooked quinoa, black beans, corn, salsa, cumin, chili powder, cilantro, salt, and pepper.
3. Arrange bell pepper halves in a baking dish. Stuff each half with the quinoa mixture.
4. Drizzle with olive oil and bake for 30 minutes, until peppers are tender.
5. Serve warm.

Nutritional Information: 320 calories, 12g protein, 55g carbohydrates, 5g fat, 10g fiber, 0mg cholesterol, 200mg sodium, 700mg potassium.

Spicy Ethiopian Lentil Stew

Yield: 4 servings | **Prep time:** 15 minutes | **Cook time:** 45 minutes

Ingredients:

- 1 cup red lentils, rinsed
- 1 onion, diced
- 2 cloves garlic, minced
- 1 tablespoon ginger, minced
- 1 tablespoon berbere spice blend
- 1 can (14.5 oz) diced tomatoes
- 3 cups vegetable broth
- Salt to taste
- 2 tablespoons olive oil

Directions:

1. In a large pot, heat olive oil over medium heat. Sauté onion, garlic, and ginger until softened.
2. Stir in berbere spice blend, cooking for 1 minute. Add lentils, diced tomatoes, and vegetable broth.
3. Bring to a boil, reduce heat, and simmer for 30-35 minutes or until lentils are tender. Season with salt.
4. Serve hot, optionally, with injera or rice.

Nutritional Information: 290 calories, 18g protein, 45g carbohydrates, 5g fat, 15g fiber, 0mg cholesterol, 400mg sodium, 800mg potassium.

Vegan Baked Beans with Smoked Paprika

Yield: 4 servings | **Prep time:** 10 minutes | **Cook time:** 1 hour

Ingredients:

- 2 cans (15 oz each) navy beans, drained and rinsed
- 1 onion, finely chopped
- 2 cloves garlic, minced
- 1/4 cup tomato paste
- 3 tablespoons maple syrup
- 2 tablespoons apple cider vinegar
- 1 tablespoon smoked paprika
- 2 cups vegetable broth
- Salt and pepper to taste
- 1 tablespoon olive oil

Directions:

1. Preheat oven to 350°F (175°C).
2. In a skillet, heat olive oil over medium heat. Sauté onion and garlic until translucent.
3. Stir in tomato paste, maple syrup, apple cider vinegar, and smoked paprika. Add navy beans and vegetable broth. Season with salt and pepper.
4. Transfer to a baking dish and bake, uncovered, for 1 hour or until thick and flavorful.
5. Let cool slightly before serving.

Nutritional Information: 320 calories, 14g protein, 58g carbohydrates, 3g fat, 15g fiber, 0mg cholesterol, 700mg sodium, 1200mg potassium.

Rice and Bean Casserole with Guajillo Sauce

Yield: 4 servings | **Prep time:** 15 minutes | **Cook time:** 45 minutes

Ingredients:

- 1 cup rice
- 2 cups vegetable broth
- 1 can (15 oz) black beans, drained and rinsed
- 1 onion, diced
- 2 cloves garlic, minced
- 3 guajillo chiles, seeded and soaked
- 1 can (14.5 oz) diced tomatoes
- 1 teaspoon cumin
- Salt and pepper to taste
- 2 tablespoons olive oil
- Cilantro for garnish

Directions:

1. Preheat oven to 350°F (175°C). In a saucepan, cook rice in vegetable broth according to package instructions.
2. Sauté onion and garlic in olive oil until soft. Blend guajillo chiles and diced tomatoes to make the sauce.
3. In a casserole dish, combine cooked rice, black beans, guajillo sauce, cumin, salt, and pepper.
4. Bake for 30 minutes. Garnish with cilantro before serving.

Nutritional Information: 340 calories, 10g protein, 60g carbohydrates, 7g fat, 10g fiber, 0mg cholesterol, 400mg sodium, 700mg potassium.

Falafel Bowls with Quinoa and Hummus

Yield: 4 servings | **Prep time:** 20 minutes | **Cook time:** 30 minutes

Ingredients:

- 1 cup quinoa, cooked
- 16 falafel balls (homemade or store-bought)
- 1 cup hummus
- 2 cups mixed greens
- 1 cucumber, diced
- 1 tomato, diced
- For the dressing:
  - Juice of 1 lemon
  - 2 tablespoons olive oil
  - Salt and pepper to taste

Directions:

1. Divide cooked quinoa among four bowls.
2. Top each bowl with falafel balls, hummus, mixed greens, cucumber, and tomato.
3. Whisk together lemon juice, olive oil, salt, and pepper for the dressing. Drizzle over each bowl.

Nutritional Information: 450 calories, 18g protein, 60g carbohydrates, 18g fat, 12g fiber, 0mg cholesterol, 400mg sodium, 800mg potassium.

Vegan Paella with Artichokes and Olives

Yield: 4 servings | **Prep time:** 20 minutes | **Cook time:** 40 minutes

Ingredients:
- 1 cup paella rice
- 2 1/2 cups vegetable broth
- 1 can (14 oz) artichoke hearts, drained and quartered
- 1/2 cup green olives, pitted
- 1 red bell pepper, sliced
- 1 onion, diced
- 2 cloves garlic, minced
- 1 teaspoon smoked paprika
- 1/2 teaspoon saffron threads
- Salt and pepper to taste
- 2 tablespoons olive oil
- Lemon wedges for serving

Directions:
1. Sauté onion, garlic, and bell pepper in olive oil until soft. Stir in smoked paprika and saffron.
2. Add rice and vegetable broth. Bring to a boil, then reduce heat to low. Cover and simmer for 30 minutes.
3. Stir in artichokes and olives. Cook for an additional 10 minutes.
4. Serve with lemon wedges.

Nutritional Information: 360 calories, 8g protein, 60g carbohydrates, 10g fat, 6g fiber, 0mg cholesterol, 400mg sodium, 600mg potassium.

Garlicky White Bean Avocado Toast

Yield: 4 servings | **Prep time:** 10 minutes | **Cook time:** 0 minutes

Ingredients:
- 1 can (15 oz) white beans, drained and rinsed
- 2 cloves garlic, minced
- 2 tablespoons olive oil
- Salt and pepper to taste
- 1 avocado, mashed
- 4 slices whole grain bread, toasted
- Red pepper flakes for garnish

Directions:
1. Mash white beans with garlic, olive oil, salt, and pepper.
2. Spread mashed avocado on toasted bread.
3. Top avocado with white bean mixture. Garnish with red pepper flakes.

Nutritional Information: 310 calories, 10g protein, 35g carbohydrates, 15g fat, 10g fiber, 0mg cholesterol, 200mg sodium, 500mg potassium.

Quinoa and Red Lentil Kitchari

Yield: 4 servings | **Prep time:** 10 minutes | **Cook time:** 30 minutes

Ingredients:
- 1/2 cup quinoa
- 1/2 cup red lentils
- 4 cups water
- 1 teaspoon turmeric
- 1 teaspoon cumin seeds
- 1/2 teaspoon ground ginger
- Salt to taste
- 2 tablespoons olive oil
- 1 onion, diced
- 1 carrot, diced

Directions:
1. Rinse quinoa and lentils. In a pot, combine quinoa, lentils, water, turmeric, cumin, ginger, and salt. Bring to a boil, then simmer for 20 minutes.
2. In a skillet, sauté onion and carrot in olive oil until soft. Stir into the quinoa-lentil mixture.
3. Serve hot.

Nutritional Information: 260 calories, 12g protein, 40g carbohydrates, 7g fat, 8g fiber, 0mg cholesterol, 10mg sodium, 500mg potassium.

Chickpea Pancakes with Avocado and Tomato

Yield: 4 servings | **Prep time:** 10 minutes | **Cook time:** 20 minutes

Ingredients:
- 1 cup chickpea flour
- 1 1/4 cups water
- 1 avocado, sliced
- 1 tomato, sliced
- 1/4 cup cilantro, chopped
- 1/2 teaspoon turmeric
- Salt and pepper to taste
- Olive oil for cooking

Directions:
1. Whisk chickpea flour, water, turmeric, salt, and pepper until smooth. Let the batter sit for a few minutes.
2. Heat olive oil in a skillet. Pour batter to form pancakes. Cook until edges are dry, then flip.
3. Serve pancakes topped with avocado, tomato, and cilantro.

Nutritional Information: 220 calories, 9g protein, 24g carbohydrates, 10g fat, 6g fiber, 0mg cholesterol, 150mg sodium, 600mg potassium.

Smoky Tempeh with Brown Rice and Broccoli

Yield: 4 servings | **Prep time:** 15 minutes |
Cook time: 25 minutes
Ingredients:
- 8 oz tempeh, sliced
- 1 cup brown rice
- 2 cups vegetable broth
- 4 cups broccoli florets
- 2 tablespoons soy sauce
- 1 tablespoon maple syrup
- 1 teaspoon smoked paprika
- 2 tablespoons olive oil
- Salt and pepper to taste

Directions:
1. Cook brown rice in vegetable broth according to package instructions.
2. In a bowl, mix soy sauce, maple syrup, and smoked paprika. Marinate tempeh slices in the mixture for 10 minutes.
3. Heat olive oil in a skillet over medium heat. Add tempeh and cook until browned on both sides.
4. Steam broccoli until tender.
5. Serve smoky tempeh over brown rice with steamed broccoli on the side.

Nutritional Information: 350 calories, 18g protein, 50g carbohydrates, 10g fat, 8g fiber, 0mg cholesterol, 400mg sodium, 800mg potassium.

Red Bean and Quinoa Burgers with Avocado

Yield: 4 servings | **Prep time:** 20 minutes |
Cook time: 10 minutes
Ingredients:
- 1 cup red beans, mashed
- 1/2 cup quinoa, cooked
- 1/4 cup breadcrumbs
- 1 egg (use flax egg for the vegan version)
- 1 teaspoon cumin
- Salt and pepper to taste
- 1 avocado, sliced
- Olive oil for cooking

Directions:
1. In a bowl, mix mashed red beans, cooked quinoa, breadcrumbs, egg, cumin, salt, and pepper.
2. Form into patties. Heat olive oil in a skillet and cook patties until browned on both sides.
3. Serve burgers with sliced avocado on top.

Nutritional Information: 320 calories, 12g protein, 45g carbohydrates, 10g fat, 10g fiber, 53mg cholesterol (0mg if using flax egg), 300mg sodium, 700mg potassium.

Lentil and Sweet Potato Shepherd's Pie

Yield: 4 servings | **Prep time:** 20 minutes |
Cook time: 40 minutes
Ingredients:
- 1 cup lentils, rinsed
- 2 large sweet potatoes, peeled and cubed
- 1 onion, diced
- 2 carrots, diced
- 2 cloves garlic, minced
- 2 cups vegetable broth
- 1 teaspoon thyme
- 1/2 teaspoon rosemary
- 2 tablespoons olive oil
- Salt and pepper to taste

Directions:
1. Boil sweet potatoes until tender, mash, and set aside.
2. Sauté onion, carrots, and garlic in olive oil until softened. Add lentils, vegetable broth, thyme, and rosemary. Simmer until lentils are tender.
3. Transfer the lentil mixture to a baking dish. Top with mashed sweet potatoes.
4. Bake at 375°F (190°C) for 20 minutes. Broil for the last few minutes for a crispy top.

Nutritional Information: 380 calories, 18g protein, 65g carbohydrates, 7g fat, 15g fiber, 0mg cholesterol, 300mg sodium, 1000mg potassium.

Millet Tabbouleh with Tomatoes and Cucumbers

Yield: 4 servings | **Prep time:** 15 minutes |
Cook time: 20 minutes
Ingredients:
- 1 cup millet, cooked
- 1 cup tomatoes, diced
- 1 cup cucumbers, diced
- 1/4 cup fresh parsley, chopped
- 1/4 cup fresh mint, chopped
- Juice of 1 lemon
- 2 tablespoons olive oil
- Salt and pepper to taste

Directions:
1. In a large bowl, combine cooked millet with tomatoes, cucumbers, parsley, and mint.
2. Whisk together lemon juice, olive oil, salt, and pepper. Pour over the millet mixture and toss to combine.
3. Chill before serving.

Nutritional Information: 210 calories, 6g protein, 35g carbohydrates, 7g fat, 5g fiber, 0mg cholesterol, 10mg sodium, 300mg potassium.

Cuban Black Beans and Rice

Yield: 4 servings | **Prep time:** 10 minutes |
Cook time: 1 hour 20 minutes (includes bean soaking time)

Ingredients:
- 1 cup dry black beans, soaked overnight
- 1 cup white rice
- 4 cups water
- 1 onion, diced
- 1 bell pepper, diced
- 2 cloves garlic, minced
- 1 teaspoon cumin
- 2 tablespoons olive oil
- Salt and pepper to taste
- Fresh cilantro for garnish

Directions:
1. Drain soaked black beans. In a large pot, cover beans with water. Bring to a boil, then simmer for 1 hour until tender.
2. In another pot, cook rice according to package instructions.
3. In a skillet, heat olive oil. Sauté onion, bell pepper, and garlic until soft. Add cumin and cooked beans. Season with salt and pepper.
4. Serve black beans over rice, garnished with fresh cilantro.

Nutritional Information: 380 calories, 14g protein, 70g carbohydrates, 7g fat, 14g fiber, 0mg cholesterol, 200mg sodium, 1000mg potassium.

Chickpea and Spinach Stuffed Portobello Mushrooms

Yield: 4 servings | **Prep time:** 20 minutes |
Cook time: 20 minutes

Ingredients:
- 4 large Portobello mushrooms, stems removed
- 1 can (15 oz) chickpeas, drained and rinsed
- 2 cups spinach, chopped
- 1 onion, diced
- 2 cloves garlic, minced
- 1/2 cup breadcrumbs
- 2 tablespoons olive oil
- Salt and pepper to taste
- 1 teaspoon thyme

Directions:
1. Preheat oven to 375°F (190°C). Brush mushrooms with olive oil, season with salt and pepper, and place on a baking sheet.
2. In a skillet, heat olive oil. Sauté onion and garlic until translucent. Add chickpeas, spinach, and thyme, and cook until spinach is wilted.
3. Stir in breadcrumbs. Adjust seasoning.
4. Fill each mushroom cap with the chickpea mixture. Bake for 20 minutes.
5. Serve warm.

Nutritional Information: 260 calories, 10g protein, 35g carbohydrates, 10g fat, 8g fiber, 0mg cholesterol, 300mg sodium, 600mg potassium.

Baked Falafel with Quinoa Tabbouleh

Yield: 4 servings | **Prep time:** 20 minutes |
Cook time: 30 minutes

Ingredients:
- For the falafel:
  - 1 can (15 oz) chickpeas, drained and rinsed
  - 1 onion, chopped
  - 2 cloves garlic, minced
  - 1/4 cup parsley, chopped
  - 2 tablespoons flour
  - 1 teaspoon cumin
  - Salt and pepper to taste
  - Olive oil for brushing
- For the tabbouleh:
  - 1 cup quinoa, cooked
  - 1/2 cup parsley, chopped
  - 1/4 cup mint, chopped
  - 1 tomato, diced
  - Juice of 1 lemon
  - 2 tablespoons olive oil
  - Salt and pepper to taste

Directions:
1. Preheat oven to 375°F (190°C). In a food processor, blend chickpeas, onion, garlic, parsley, flour, cumin, salt, and pepper until combined. Form into balls and place on a baking sheet. Brush with olive oil and bake for 25-30 minutes.
2. Mix cooked quinoa, parsley, mint, tomato, lemon juice, olive oil, salt, and pepper to make the tabbouleh.
3. Serve falafel with quinoa tabbouleh on the side.

Nutritional Information: 370 calories, 15g protein, 55g carbohydrates, 12g fat, 10g fiber, 0mg cholesterol, 300mg sodium, 700mg potassium.

Vegan Stuffed Bell Peppers with Lentils and Quinoa

Yield: 4 servings | **Prep time:** 20 minutes |
Cook time: 30 minutes

Ingredients:
- 4 large bell peppers, tops cut off and seeds removed
- 1/2 cup quinoa, rinsed
- 1 cup green lentils, cooked
- 1 onion, diced
- 2 cloves garlic, minced
- 1 can (14.5 oz) diced tomatoes
- 1 teaspoon oregano
- 1 teaspoon basil
- Salt and pepper to taste
- 2 tablespoons olive oil
- 1/2 cup vegetable broth
- 1/4 cup fresh parsley, chopped

Directions:
1. Preheat oven to 375°F (190°C). In a saucepan, cook quinoa according to package instructions.
2. Heat olive oil in a skillet over medium heat. Sauté onion and garlic until softened. Stir in cooked lentils, cooked quinoa, diced tomatoes, oregano, basil, salt, and pepper.
3. Fill each bell pepper with the lentil-quinoa mixture. Place in a baking dish and pour vegetable broth around the peppers.
4. Bake covered for 25 minutes, then uncover and bake for an additional 5 minutes.
5. Garnish with fresh parsley before serving.

Nutritional Information: 320 calories, 14g protein, 55g carbohydrates, 7g fat, 15g fiber, 0mg cholesterol, 200mg sodium, 800mg potassium.

Pinto Bean Pozole with Hominy and Lime

Yield: 4 servings | **Prep time:** 10 minutes | **Cook time:** 25 minutes

Ingredients:
- 1 can (15 oz) pinto beans, drained and rinsed
- 1 can (15 oz) hominy, drained
- 4 cups vegetable broth
- 1 onion, chopped
- 2 cloves garlic, minced
- 1 teaspoon chili powder
- 1/2 teaspoon smoked paprika
- Juice of 1 lime
- Salt and pepper to taste
- 2 tablespoons olive oil
- Fresh cilantro, chopped, for garnish

Directions:
1. Heat olive oil in a pot over medium heat. Add onion and garlic; sauté until translucent.
2. Stir in chili powder and smoked paprika; cook for 1 minute.
3. Add pinto beans, hominy, and vegetable broth. Bring to a boil, then simmer for 20 minutes.
4. Stir in lime juice and season with salt and pepper.
5. Garnish with fresh cilantro before serving.

Nutritional Information: 250 calories, 8g protein, 45g carbohydrates, 5g fat, 10g fiber, 0mg cholesterol, 700mg sodium, 500mg potassium.

Gumbo with Okra and Red Beans

Yield: 4 servings | **Prep time:** 15 minutes | **Cook time:** 1 hour

Ingredients:
- 1 cup red beans, soaked overnight and drained
- 2 cups okra, sliced
- 1 onion, diced
- 1 bell pepper, diced
- 3 cloves garlic, minced
- 1 can (14.5 oz) diced tomatoes
- 4 cups vegetable broth
- 1 teaspoon smoked paprika
- 1/2 teaspoon cayenne pepper
- 2 tablespoons vegetable oil
- Salt to taste

Directions:
1. In a large pot, heat oil over medium heat. Sauté onion, bell pepper, and garlic until softened.
2. Add okra, red beans, diced tomatoes, vegetable broth, smoked paprika, and cayenne pepper. Bring to a boil, then reduce heat and simmer for 45 minutes.
3. Season with salt. Serve with rice if desired.

Nutritional Information: 250 calories, 12g protein, 40g carbohydrates, 5g fat, 10g fiber, 0mg cholesterol, 700mg sodium, 800mg potassium.

Quinoa Pilaf with Almonds and Cranberries

Yield: 4 servings | **Prep time:** 5 minutes | **Cook time:** 20 minutes

Ingredients:
- 1 cup quinoa, rinsed
- 2 cups vegetable broth
- 1/2 cup dried cranberries
- 1/2 cup almonds, sliced and toasted
- 1/2 teaspoon cinnamon
- Salt to taste
- 2 tablespoons olive oil

Directions:
1. In a saucepan, bring vegetable broth to a boil. Add quinoa, reduce heat, cover, and simmer for 15 minutes or until liquid is absorbed.
2. Stir in dried cranberries, toasted almonds, and cinnamon. Season with salt.
3. Drizzle with olive oil before serving.

Nutritional Information: 320 calories, 8g protein, 48g carbohydrates, 12g fat, 6g fiber, 0mg cholesterol, 200mg sodium, 400mg potassium.

Barbecue Lentil Stuffed Sweet Potatoes

Yield: 4 servings | **Prep time:** 10 minutes | **Cook time:** 1 hour

Ingredients:
- 4 large sweet potatoes, washed
- 1 cup lentils, cooked
- 1/2 cup barbecue sauce
- 1/4 cup red onion, finely chopped
- 2 tablespoons olive oil
- Salt and pepper to taste
- Green onions, sliced, for garnish

Directions:
1. Preheat oven to 400°F (200°C). Prick sweet potatoes with a fork, rub with olive oil, and season with salt and pepper. Bake for 45-50 minutes, until tender.
2. Mix cooked lentils with barbecue sauce and red onion.
3. Split baked sweet potatoes open and stuff with barbecue lentil mixture.
4. Garnish with sliced green onions before serving.

Nutritional Information: 380 calories, 12g protein, 70g carbohydrates, 6g fat, 15g fiber, 0mg cholesterol, 400mg sodium, 1000mg potassium.

Spiced Chickpea Wrap with Tahini Dressing

Yield: 4 servings | **Prep time:** 15 minutes | **Cook time:** 10 minutes

Ingredients:
- 1 can (15 oz) chickpeas, drained and rinsed
- 4 whole wheat wraps
- 1 tablespoon olive oil
- 1 teaspoon cumin
- 1/2 teaspoon smoked paprika
- Salt and pepper to taste
- 2 cups mixed greens
- 1 carrot, shredded
- 1/2 cucumber, sliced
  For the tahini dressing:
    - 1/4 cup tahini
    - 2 tablespoons lemon juice
    - 1 clove garlic, minced
    - Water, as needed, to thin
    - Salt to taste

Directions:
1. Heat olive oil in a skillet over medium heat. Add chickpeas, cumin, smoked paprika, salt, and pepper. Cook for 5-7 minutes until fragrant.
2. Whisk together tahini, lemon juice, minced garlic, and salt. Add water as needed to achieve a drizzle-able consistency.
3. Lay out wraps and divide mixed greens, shredded carrot, cucumber slices, and spiced chickpeas among them.

4. Drizzle tahini dressing over the fillings, roll up the wraps, and serve.

Nutritional Information: 350 calories, 12g protein, 45g carbohydrates, 15g fat, 9g fiber, 0mg cholesterol, 300mg sodium, 600mg potassium.

Lentil Bolognese over Spaghetti Squash

Yield: 4 servings | **Prep time:** 15 minutes | **Cook time:** 45 minutes

Ingredients:
- 1 large spaghetti squash, halved and seeded
- 1 cup lentils, cooked
- 1 onion, diced
- 2 cloves garlic, minced
- 1 can (14.5 oz) diced tomatoes
- 1 teaspoon oregano
- 1 teaspoon basil
- 2 tablespoons olive oil
- Salt and pepper to taste

Directions:
1. Roast spaghetti squash at 400°F (200°C) for 40 minutes or until tender.
2. Sauté onion and garlic in olive oil until softened. Add lentils, diced tomatoes, oregano, and basil. Simmer for 20 minutes.
3. Use a fork to shred the inside of the spaghetti squash into "noodles." Top with lentil Bolognese.

Nutritional Information: 280 calories, 12g protein, 45g carbohydrates, 7g fat, 10g fiber, 0mg cholesterol, 300mg sodium, 800mg potassium.

Lentil Walnut Tacos with Avocado Cream

Yield: 4 servings | **Prep time:** 20 minutes | **Cook time:** 30 minutes

Ingredients:
- 1 cup lentils, cooked
- 1/2 cup walnuts, chopped
- 1 tablespoon taco seasoning
- 8 corn tortillas

For the avocado cream:
- 1 ripe avocado
- 1/4 cup cilantro
- Juice of 1 lime
- Salt to taste

For topping:
- diced tomatoes
- shredded lettuce.

Directions:
1. Pulse lentils and walnuts in a food processor with taco seasoning until well mixed.
2. Heat mixture in a skillet for 5-7 minutes.
3. Blend avocado, cilantro, lime juice, and salt for the avocado cream.
4. Assemble tacos with lentil-walnut mixture, avocado cream, tomatoes, and lettuce.

Nutritional Information: 320 calories, 12g protein, 40g carbohydrates, 15g fat, 10g fiber, 0mg cholesterol, 150mg sodium, 700mg potassium.

Basmati Rice Pilaf

Yield: 4 servings | **Prep time:** 5 minutes |
Cook time: 25 minutes
Ingredients:

- 1 cup basmati rice
- 2 tablespoons olive oil
- 1 small onion, finely chopped
- 1/4 cup carrot, finely diced
- 1/4 cup peas (fresh or frozen)
- 2 cups vegetable broth
- 1 bay leaf
- 1/2 teaspoon salt
- 1/4 teaspoon black pepper
- 1/4 teaspoon turmeric (optional for color)

Directions:

1. Rinse basmati rice under cold water until the water runs clear. Drain.
2. In a saucepan, heat olive oil over medium heat. Add the onion and carrot, sauté until softened, for about 5 minutes.
3. Stir in the rice, peas, vegetable broth, bay leaf, salt, pepper, and turmeric if using. Bring to a boil.
4. Reduce heat to low, cover, and simmer for 20 minutes or until all liquid is absorbed. Remove from heat and let sit, covered, for 5 minutes. Fluff with a fork before serving.

Nutritional Information: 280 calories, 5g protein, 49g carbohydrates, 7g fat, 2g fiber, 0mg cholesterol, 300mg sodium, 150mg potassium.

Spiced Lentil and Carrot Burgers

Yield: 4 servings | **Prep time:** 20 minutes |
Cook time: 40 minutes
Ingredients:

- 1 cup lentils, cooked
- 2 large carrots, grated
- 1 onion, diced
- 2 cloves garlic, minced
- 1/2 cup breadcrumbs
- 2 teaspoons cumin
- 1 teaspoon smoked paprika
- Salt and pepper to taste
- 2 tablespoons olive oil

Directions:

1. Preheat oven to 375°F (190°C).
2. In a bowl, mash half of the lentils. Mix in the remaining lentils, grated carrots, diced onion, garlic, breadcrumbs, cumin, smoked paprika, salt, and pepper.
3. Form the mixture into patties and place on a baking sheet.
4. Brush each patty with olive oil. Bake for 30-40 minutes, flipping halfway through, until crispy and golden.
5. Serve on buns with your favorite toppings.

Nutritional Information: 280 calories, 12g protein, 45g carbohydrates, 7g fat, 12g fiber, 0mg cholesterol, 300mg sodium, 600mg potassium.

Creamy Chickpea and Vegetable Curry

Yield: 4 servings | **Prep time:** 15 minutes |
Cook time: 30 minutes
Ingredients:

- 1 can (15 oz) chickpeas, drained and rinsed
- 1 can (14 oz) coconut milk
- 2 cups mixed vegetables (carrots, peas, bell peppers), chopped
- 1 onion, diced
- 2 cloves garlic, minced
- 1 tablespoon curry powder
- 1 teaspoon turmeric
- 1 teaspoon cumin
- Salt and pepper to taste
- 2 tablespoons olive oil
- Cooked rice for serving

Directions:

1. In a large skillet, heat olive oil over medium heat. Sauté onion and garlic until softened.
2. Add curry powder, turmeric, and cumin; cook for 1 minute until fragrant.
3. Stir in chickpeas, mixed vegetables, and coconut milk. Season with salt and pepper.
4. Simmer for 20 minutes, until vegetables are tender and curry is thickened.
5. Serve over cooked rice.

Nutritional Information: 360 calories, 10g protein, 40g carbohydrates, 18g fat, 8g fiber, 0mg cholesterol, 300mg sodium, 600mg potassium.

Saffron Rice with Garbanzo Beans and Vegetables

Yield: 4 servings | **Prep time:** 10 minutes |
Cook time: 20 minutes
Ingredients:

- 1 cup basmati rice
- 2 cups vegetable broth
- 1 pinch saffron threads
- 1 can (15 oz) garbanzo beans, drained and rinsed
- 1 bell pepper, diced
- 1/2 cup peas
- 1 onion, diced
- 2 cloves garlic, minced
- 2 tablespoons olive oil
- Salt to taste.

Directions:

1. Soak saffron in 1/4 cup warm vegetable broth for 5 minutes.
2. In a saucepan, heat olive oil over medium heat. Sauté onion and garlic until translucent. Add rice, saffron mixture, and remaining broth. Bring to a boil, then cover and simmer for 15 minutes.
3. Stir in garbanzo beans, bell pepper, and peas. Cook for an additional 5 minutes. Season with salt.

Vegan Chana Masala with Basmati Rice

Yield: 4 servings | **Prep time:** 10 minutes |
Cook time: 30 minutes
Ingredients:
- 1 cup basmati rice
- 2 cans (15 oz each) chickpeas
- drained and rinsed
- 1 onion, diced
- 2 tomatoes, diced
- 2 cloves garlic, minced
- 1 tablespoon ginger, minced
- 2 teaspoons garam masala
- 1 teaspoon cumin
- 1 teaspoon turmeric
- 1/2 teaspoon chili powder
- 3 cups vegetable broth
- 2 tablespoons olive oil
- Salt to taste
- Fresh cilantro for garnish.

Directions:
1. Cook basmati rice according to package instructions.
2. Heat olive oil in a large skillet over medium heat. Sauté onion, garlic, and ginger until onion is translucent.
3. Add spices, stirring for 1 minute. Add tomatoes and cook until softened.
4. Stir in chickpeas and vegetable broth. Simmer for 20 minutes. Season with salt.
5. Serve chana masala over rice, garnished with cilantro.
Nutritional Information: 420 calories, 15g protein, 75g carbohydrates, 9g fat, 12g fiber, 0mg cholesterol, 300mg sodium, 800mg potassium.

Moroccan-Spiced Lentil and Vegetable Stew

Yield: 4 servings | **Prep time:** 20 minutes |
Cook time: 40 minutes
Ingredients:
- 1 cup lentils, rinsed
- 1 sweet potato, cubed
- 1 carrot, diced
- 1 onion, diced
- 2 cloves garlic, minced
- 1 teaspoon cumin
- 1/2 teaspoon cinnamon
- 1/2 teaspoon turmeric
- 1/4 teaspoon ginger
- 4 cups vegetable broth
- 2 tablespoons olive oil
- Salt and pepper to taste
- Fresh parsley for garnish.

Directions:
1. Heat olive oil in a large pot over medium heat. Sauté onion, garlic, sweet potato, and carrot until slightly softened.
2. Add spices, stirring until fragrant. Add lentils and vegetable broth. Bring to a boil, then simmer for 30 minutes.

3. Season with salt and pepper. Serve garnished with parsley.
Nutritional Information: 280 calories, 14g protein, 45g carbohydrates, 5g fat, 15g fiber, 0mg cholesterol, 200mg sodium, 700mg potassium.

Vegan Mushroom and Spinach Risotto

Yield: 4 servings | **Prep time:** 10 minutes |
Cook time: 30 minutes
Ingredients:
- 1 cup Arborio rice
- 4 cups vegetable broth, warmed
- 2 cups mushrooms, sliced
- 2 cups spinach, roughly chopped
- 1 onion, diced
- 2 cloves garlic, minced
- 1/2 cup white wine (optional)
- 2 tablespoons olive oil
- Salt and pepper to taste
- Nutritional yeast for serving (optional)

Directions:
1. In a large pan, heat olive oil over medium heat. Sauté onion and garlic until translucent.
2. Add mushrooms and cook until they begin to release their juices.
3. Stir in Arborio rice until coated in the oil and lightly toasted.
4. Pour in wine (if using) and stir until mostly absorbed. Then, add the vegetable broth, 1/2 cup at a time, stirring constantly, until the liquid is absorbed before adding more.
5. When the rice is al dente and creamy, stir in the spinach until wilted. Season with salt and pepper.
6. Serve hot, sprinkled with nutritional yeast if desired.
Nutritional Information: 350 calories, 8g protein, 60g carbohydrates, 7g fat, 4g fiber, 0mg cholesterol, 300mg sodium, 400mg potassium.

Chickpea Flour Frittata with Vegetables

Yield: 4 servings | **Prep time:** 10 minutes |
Cook time: 25 minutes
Ingredients:
- 1 cup chickpea flour
- 1 1/2 cups water
- 2 cups mixed vegetables (bell peppers, spinach, tomatoes), chopped
- 1 onion, diced
- 2 cloves garlic, minced
- 1/4 cup nutritional yeast
- 2 tablespoons olive oil
- 1 teaspoon turmeric
- Salt and pepper to taste
Directions:
1. Preheat oven to 375°F (190°C).

2. Whisk together chickpea flour, water, nutritional yeast, turmeric, salt, and pepper until smooth. Let sit for 5 minutes.
3. Heat olive oil in an oven-proof skillet over medium heat. Sauté onion, garlic, and vegetables until soft.
4. Pour the chickpea flour mixture over the vegetables. Cook for 5 minutes without stirring.
5. Transfer the skillet to the oven and bake for 20 minutes or until the frittata is firm and golden.
6. Serve warm, cut into wedges.

Nutritional Information: 250 calories, 13g protein, 30g carbohydrates, 10g fat, 7g fiber, 0mg cholesterol, 300mg sodium, 500mg potassium.

Stuffed Acorn Squash with Wild Rice and Cranberries

Yield: 4 servings | **Prep time:** 15 minutes | **Cook time:** 60 minutes
Ingredients:
- 2 acorn squash, halved and seeded
- 1 cup wild rice blend, cooked
- 1/2 cup dried cranberries
- 1/2 cup pecans, chopped
- 1 onion, diced
- 2 cloves garlic, minced
- 1/4 cup parsley, chopped
- 2 tablespoons olive oil
- Salt and pepper to taste

Directions:
1. Preheat oven to 375°F (190°C). Brush acorn squash halves with 1 tablespoon olive oil and season with salt and pepper. Place cut side down on a baking sheet and bake for 40 minutes.
2. In a skillet, heat the remaining olive oil over medium heat. Sauté onion and garlic until soft.
3. Mix sautéed onion and garlic with cooked wild rice, cranberries, pecans, and parsley.
4. Fill the roasted acorn squash halves with the rice mixture and return to the oven. Bake for an additional 20 minutes.
5. Serve warm.

Nutritional Information: 400 calories, 8g protein, 65g carbohydrates, 14g fat, 8g fiber, 0mg cholesterol, 200mg sodium, 800mg potassium.

Butternut Squash and Black Bean Chili

Yield: 4 servings | **Prep time:** 15 minutes | **Cook time:** 45 minutes
Ingredients:
- 1 butternut squash, peeled and cubed
- 1 can (15 oz) black beans, drained and rinsed
- 1 onion, diced, 2 cloves garlic, minced
- 1 can (14.5 oz) diced tomatoes
- 1 tablespoon chili powder
- 1 teaspoon cumin
- 4 cups vegetable broth
- 2 tablespoons olive oil
- Salt and pepper to taste
- Avocado and cilantro for garnish.

Directions:
1. Heat olive oil in a large pot over medium heat. Sauté onion and garlic until soft.
2. Add butternut squash, black beans, diced tomatoes, chili powder, and cumin. Stir to combine.
3. Pour in vegetable broth, bring to a boil, then simmer for 30 minutes until squash is tender. Season with salt and pepper.
4. Serve garnished with avocado and cilantro.

Nutritional Information: 300 calories, 9g protein, 45g carbohydrates, 10g fat, 12g fiber, 0mg cholesterol, 300mg sodium, 800mg potassium.

Fried Pinto Beans with Tomatoes

Yield: 4 servings | **Prep time:** 10 minutes | **Cook time:** 20 minutes
Ingredients:
- 2 tablespoons olive oil
- 1 onion, diced
- 2 cloves garlic, minced
- 1 can (15 oz) pinto beans, drained and rinsed
- 1 can (14.5 oz) diced tomatoes, undrained
- 1 teaspoon ground cumin
- 1/2 teaspoon chili powder
- Salt and pepper to taste
- Fresh cilantro, chopped for garnish

Directions:
1. Heat olive oil in a large skillet over medium heat. Add the onion and garlic, and sauté until soft, about 5 minutes.
2. Add the pinto beans, diced tomatoes with their juice, cumin, and chili powder to the skillet. Stir to combine.
3. Cook, stirring occasionally, until the mixture thickens and the flavors meld, about 15 minutes. Mash the beans slightly with a fork if desired.
4. Season with salt and pepper to taste. Serve garnished with fresh cilantro.

Nutritional Informaion: 200 calories, 8g protein, 30g carbohydrates, 5g fat, 8g fiber, 0mg cholesterol, 400mg sodium, 600mg potassium.

Chapter 6: Yummy Smoothie

Avocado and Spinach Smoothie

Yield: 2 servings | **Prep time:** 5 minutes
Ingredients:
- 1 ripe avocado
- 2 cups fresh spinach
- 1 banana
- 1 cup unsweetened almond milk
- Ice cubes (optional)

Directions:
1. Combine all ingredients in a blender.
2. Blend until smooth.
3. Serve immediately.

Nutritional Information: 230 calories, 4g protein, 27g carbohydrates, 13g fat, 7g fiber, 0mg cholesterol, 100mg sodium, 700mg potassium.

Green Smoothie (Spinach, Pineapple, Banana)

Yield: 2 servings | **Prep time:** 5 minutes
Ingredients:
- 2 cups spinach
- 1 cup pineapple chunks
- 1 banana
- 1 cup coconut water

Directions:
1. Place all ingredients in a blender.
2. Blend until smooth.
3. Enjoy immediately.

Nutritional Information: 180 calories, 3g protein, 44g carbohydrates, 0.5g fat, 5g fiber, 0mg cholesterol, 30mg sodium, 600mg potassium.

Zucchini Bread Batter Smoothie

Yield: 2 servings | **Prep time:** 5 minutes
Ingredients:
- 1 cup almond milk
- 1/2 cup rolled oats
- 1 small zucchini, chopped
- 1 banana
- 1/2 teaspoon cinnamon
- 1 tablespoon almond butter
- 1 teaspoon vanilla extract
- Ice cubes

Directions:
1. Combine all ingredients in a blender.
2. Blend until smooth and creamy.
3. Serve immediately, topped with a sprinkle of cinnamon.

Nutritional Information: 180 calories, 5g protein, 32g carbohydrates, 5g fat, 5g fiber, 0mg cholesterol, 100mg sodium, 350mg potassium.

Carrot Ginger Zing Smoothie

Yield: 2 servings | **Prep time:** 5 minutes
Ingredients:
- 2 carrots, chopped
- 1 inch ginger, peeled
- 1 apple, cored and sliced
- 1 orange, peeled and sectioned
- 1 cup water or orange juice

Directions:
1. Add all ingredients to a blender.
2. Blend until smooth.
3. Serve chilled.

Nutritional Information: 150 calories, 2g protein, 36g carbohydrates, 0.5g fat, 6g fiber, 0mg cholesterol, 40mg sodium, 500mg potassium.

Celery Apple Cleanse Smoothie

Yield: 2 servings | **Prep time:** 5 minutes
Ingredients:
- 4 stalks celery
- 2 apples, cored and sliced
- 1 tablespoon lemon juice
- 1 cup water

Directions:
1. Combine celery, apples, lemon juice, and water in a blender.
2. Blend until smooth.
3. Enjoy immediately.

Nutritional Information: 95 calories, 1g protein, 24g carbohydrates, 0.3g fat, 5g fiber, 0mg cholesterol, 80mg sodium, 400mg potassium.

Pomegranate Beetroot Boost Smoothie

Yield: 2 servings | **Prep time:** 10 minutes
Ingredients:
- 1 medium beetroot, cooked and peeled
- 1/2 cup pomegranate seeds
- 1 apple, cored and sliced
- 1/2 cup water or coconut water
- Ice cubes (optional)

Directions:
1. Combine beetroot, pomegranate seeds, apple, and water in a blender.
2. Blend until smooth, adding ice if desired.
3. Serve immediately.

Nutritional Information: 120 calories, 2g protein, 28g carbohydrates, 0.3g fat, 6g fiber, 0mg cholesterol, 65mg sodium, 400mg potassium.

Golden Milk Spice Smoothie

Yield: 2 servings | **Prep time:** 5 minutes
Ingredients:
- 1 cup almond milk
- 1/2 teaspoon turmeric
- 1/4 teaspoon cinnamon
- 1/4 teaspoon ginger
- 1 tablespoon honey
- 1 banana
- Ice cubes

Directions:
1. Combine all ingredients in a blender.
2. Blend until smooth.
3. Serve immediately.

Nutritional Information: 120 calories, 2g protein, 26g carbohydrates, 2g fat, 3g fiber, 0mg cholesterol, 80mg sodium, 300mg potassium.

Cucumber Melon Hydrator Smoothie

Yield: 2 servings | **Prep time:** 5 minutes
Ingredients:
- 1 cup cucumber, sliced
- 2 cups honeydew melon, cubed
- 1/2 cup Greek yogurt (use plant-based for vegan option)
- Mint leaves for garnish

Directions:
1. Blend cucumber, honeydew melon, and yogurt until smooth.
2. Garnish with mint leaves.
3. Serve chilled.

Nutritional Information: 100 calories, 4g protein, 22g carbohydrates, 0.2g fat, 1.5g fiber, 0mg cholesterol, 45mg sodium, 400mg potassium.

Sweet Potato Cinnamon Spice Smoothie

Yield: 2 servings | **Prep time:** 5 minutes
Ingredients:
- 1/2 cup cooked sweet potato, cooled
- 1 cup almond milk
- 1 banana
- 1/2 teaspoon cinnamon
- Pinch of nutmeg
- 1 tablespoon maple syrup
- Ice cubes

Directions:
1. Blend sweet potato, almond milk, banana, cinnamon, nutmeg, maple syrup, and ice until smooth.
2. Taste and adjust sweetness if necessary.
3. Serve chilled.

Nutritional Information: 150 calories, 2g protein, 35g carbohydrates, 1g fat, 4g fiber, 0mg cholesterol, 100mg sodium, 400mg potassium.

Roasted Butternut Squash Smoothie

Yield: 2 servings | **Prep time:** 10 minutes (plus roasting time)
Ingredients:
- 1 cup roasted butternut squash, cooled
- 1 cup almond milk
- 1 banana
- 1/2 teaspoon cinnamon
- Pinch of nutmeg
- 1 tablespoon maple syrup
- Ice cubes

Directions:
1. Blend roasted butternut squash, almond milk, banana, cinnamon, nutmeg, maple syrup, and ice until smooth.
2. Adjust sweetness to taste.
3. Serve chilled, sprinkled with extra cinnamon.

Nutritional Information: 160 calories, 3g protein, 37g carbohydrates, 1g fat, 5g fiber, 0mg cholesterol, 80mg sodium, 500mg potassium.

Acai Antioxidant Supreme Smoothie

Yield: 2 servings | **Prep time:** 5 minutes
Ingredients:
- 1 packet of frozen acai berry puree
- 1 banana
- 1/2 cup mixed berries
- 1 cup spinach leaves
- 1 tablespoon flaxseeds
- 1 cup almond milk
- Ice cubes

Directions:
1. Blend acai puree, banana, mixed berries, spinach, flaxseeds, and almond milk until smooth.
2. Add ice to reach the desired consistency and blend again.
3. Serve immediately.

Nutritional Information: 200 calories, 3g protein, 35g carbohydrates, 5g fat, 7g fiber, 0mg cholesterol, 70mg sodium, 400mg potassium.

Beetroot and Berry Fusion Smoothie

Yield: 2 servings | **Prep time:** 5 minutes
Ingredients:
- 1 small beetroot, cooked and peeled
- 1 cup mixed berries (fresh or frozen)
- 1 banana
- 1 cup almond milk
- 1 tablespoon flaxseed meal
- Ice cubes

Directions:
1. Combine beetroot, mixed berries, banana, almond milk, and flaxseed meal in a blender.

2. Blend until smooth, adding ice to reach desired consistency.
3. Serve immediately, garnished with a few berries.

Nutritional Information: 140 calories, 3g protein, 30g carbohydrates, 2g fat, 6g fiber, 0mg cholesterol, 90mg sodium, 400mg potassium.

Matcha Green Tea Energy Smoothie

Yield: 2 servings | **Prep time:** 5 minutes
Ingredients:
- 1 teaspoon matcha green tea powder
- 1 banana
- 1 cup spinach leaves
- 1/2 avocado
- 1 cup almond milk
- 1 tablespoon honey (or to taste)
- Ice cubes

Directions:
1. Blend matcha powder, banana, spinach, avocado, almond milk, and honey until smooth.
2. Add ice cubes and blend again until desired consistency is reached.
3. Serve immediately.

Nutritional Information: 180 calories, 3g protein, 31g carbohydrates, 7g fat, 5g fiber, 0mg cholesterol, 60mg sodium, 450mg potassium.

Raspberry and Almond Butter Smoothie

Yield: 2 servings | **Prep time:** 5 minutes
Ingredients:
- 1 cup raspberries
- 1 banana
- 2 tablespoons almond butter
- 1 cup almond milk
- Ice cubes

Directions:
1. Blend raspberries, banana, almond butter, and almond milk until smooth.
2. Add ice and blend to desired thickness.
3. Serve immediately.

Nutritional Information: 220 calories, 4g protein, 30g carbohydrates, 11g fat, 7g fiber, 0mg cholesterol, 100mg sodium, 400mg potassium.

Mango Coconut Bliss Smoothie

Yield: 2 servings | **Prep time:** 5 minutes
Ingredients:
- 1 cup mango chunks
- 1/2 cup coconut milk
- 1 banana
- 1/2 cup orange juice
- Ice cubes

Directions:

1. Place mango, coconut milk, banana, and orange juice in a blender.
2. Blend until smooth, adding ice as needed for consistency.
3. Serve chilled.

Nutritional Information: 200 calories, 2g protein, 35g carbohydrates, 7g fat, 3g fiber, 0mg cholesterol, 15mg sodium, 500mg potassium.

Blueberry Flaxseed Power Smoothie

Yield: 2 servings | **Prep time:** 5 minutes
Ingredients:

- 1 cup blueberries (fresh or frozen)
- 1 banana
- 1 tablespoon ground flaxseed
- 1 cup almond milk
- 1/2 cup Greek yogurt (use plant-based for vegan option)
- Ice cubes (optional)

Directions:

1. Place all ingredients in a blender.
2. Blend until smooth.
3. Serve immediately.

Nutritional Information: 180 calories, 5g protein, 35g carbohydrates, 3g fat, 6g fiber, 0mg cholesterol, 80mg sodium, 400mg potassium.

Chocolate Peanut Butter Protein Smoothie

Yield: 2 servings | **Prep time:** 5 minutes
Ingredients:

- 2 tablespoons peanut butter
- 1 banana
- 2 tablespoons cocoa powder
- 1 scoop plant-based protein powder
- 1 cup almond milk
- Ice cubes

Directions:

1. Combine all ingredients in a blender.
2. Blend until smooth and creamy.
3. Serve immediately.

Nutritional Information: 250 calories, 15g protein, 30g carbohydrates, 10g fat, 5g fiber, 0mg cholesterol, 150mg sodium, 500mg potassium.

Peachy Green Detox Smoothie

Yield: 2 servings | **Prep time:** 5 minutes
Ingredients:

- 2 peaches, sliced
- 1 cup spinach leaves
- 1/2 cucumber, sliced
- 1 tablespoon chia seeds
- 1 cup coconut water

Directions:

1. Blend peaches, spinach, cucumber, chia seeds, and coconut water until smooth.
2. If it is too thick, add more coconut water to achieve the desired consistency.
3. Serve chilled.

Nutritional Information: 120 calories, 3g protein, 25g carbohydrates, 2g fat, 5g fiber, 0mg cholesterol, 60mg sodium, 450mg potassium.

Cherry Vanilla Recovery Smoothie

Yield: 2 servings | **Prep time:** 5 minutes
Ingredients:

- 1 cup cherries (fresh or frozen)
- 1 banana
- 1/2 teaspoon vanilla extract
- 1 cup almond milk
- 1/2 cup Greek yogurt (use plant-based for vegan option)
- Ice cubes

Directions:

1. Place all ingredients in a blender.
2. Blend until smooth.
3. Serve immediately for a refreshing recovery drink.

Nutritional Information: 160 calories, 5g protein, 33g carbohydrates, 2g fat, 4g fiber, 0mg cholesterol, 80mg sodium, 400mg potassium.

Red Velvet Beet Smoothie

Yield: 2 servings | **Prep time:** 10 minutes
Ingredients:

- 1 small beet, cooked and peeled
- 1 cup frozen raspberries
- 1 banana
- 1 tablespoon cocoa powder
- 1 cup almond milk
- Ice cubes

Directions:

1. Place cooked beet, raspberries, banana, cocoa powder, and almond milk in a blender.
2. Blend until smooth, adding ice as needed.
3. Serve immediately, optionally topped with a sprinkle of cocoa powder.

Nutritional Information: 150 calories, 4g protein, 30g carbohydrates, 2g fat, 6g fiber, 0mg cholesterol, 100mg sodium, 450mg potassium.

Chapter 7: Lively Salads

Roasted Beet and Quinoa Salad with Orange Tahini Dressing

Yield: 4 servings | **Prep time:** 15 minutes | **Cook time:** 30 minutes

Ingredients:
- 2 cups cooked quinoa
- 4 medium beets, roasted and cubed
- 1/2 cup chopped walnuts
- 2 cups spinach leaves
- For the dressing:
    - 1/4 cup tahini
    - Juice of 1 orange
    - 2 tablespoons maple syrup
    - Salt and pepper to taste

Directions:
1. In a large bowl, mix quinoa, roasted beets, walnuts, and spinach.
2. Whisk together tahini, orange juice, maple syrup, salt, and pepper for the dressing.
3. Toss the salad with the dressing before serving.

Nutritional Information: 350 calories, 9g protein, 40g carbohydrates, 18g fat, 6g fiber, 0mg cholesterol, 200mg sodium, 600mg potassium.

Wild Rice and Arugula Salad with Zesty Lemon Dressing

Yield: 4 servings | **Prep time:** 15 minutes | **Cook time:** 45 minutes (for wild rice)

Ingredients:
- 1 cup wild rice, cooked
- 4 cups arugula
- 1/2 cup dried cranberries
- 1/2 cup walnuts, toasted and chopped
- For the dressing:
    - 1/4 cup olive oil
    - Juice of 1 lemon
    - 1 teaspoon honey
    - Salt and pepper to taste

Directions:
1. Prepare wild rice according to package instructions; let cool.
2. In a large salad bowl, mix cooled wild rice, arugula, dried cranberries, and toasted walnuts.
3. Whisk together olive oil, lemon juice, honey, salt, and pepper for the dressing.
4. Drizzle dressing over salad, toss to combine, and serve.

Nutritional Information: 310 calories, 7g protein, 40g carbohydrates, 16g fat, 5g fiber, 10mg sodium, 390mg potassium.

Vegan Cobb Salad with Coconut Bacon

Yield: 4 servings | **Prep time:** 20 minutes |
Cook time: 20 minutes
Ingredients:
- 6 cups mixed salad greens
- 1 cup cherry tomatoes, halved
- 1 avocado, diced
- 1/2 cup corn kernels
- 1/2 cup shredded carrots
- 1/2 cup coconut bacon
- 1/4 cup red onion, thinly sliced
- For the dressing:
    - 1/4 cup olive oil
    - 2 tablespoons apple cider vinegar
    - 1 tablespoon Dijon mustard
    - 1 tablespoon maple syrup
    - Salt and pepper to taste

Directions:
1. Arrange salad greens on a large platter. Top with cherry tomatoes, avocado, corn, carrots, coconut bacon, and red onion.
2. Whisk together olive oil, apple cider vinegar, Dijon mustard, maple syrup, salt, and pepper for the dressing.
3. Drizzle the dressing over the salad before serving.

Nutritional Information: 290 calories, 4g protein, 20g carbohydrates, 22g fat, 7g fiber, 0mg cholesterol, 250mg sodium, 700mg potassium.

Pineapple Cucumber Salad

Yield: 4 servings | **Prep time:** 10 minutes
Ingredients:
- 2 cups pineapple, cubed
- 2 cups cucumber, cubed
- 1/4 cup red onion, thinly sliced
- 1/4 cup cilantro, chopped
- Juice of 1 lime
- Salt and chili powder to taste

Directions:
1. In a large bowl, combine pineapple, cucumber, red onion, and cilantro.
2. Squeeze lime juice over the salad and season with salt and chili powder.
3. Toss well before serving chilled.

Nutritional Information: 70 calories, 1g protein, 17g carbohydrates, 0g fat, 2g fiber, 0mg cholesterol, 5mg sodium, 200mg potassium.

Beetroot, Walnut, and Baby Spinach Salad

Yield: 4 servings | **Prep time:** 10 minutes
Ingredients:
- 4 medium beetroots, cooked and sliced
- 1/2 cup walnuts, toasted
- 4 cups baby spinach
- 2 tablespoons balsamic vinegar
- 2 tablespoons olive oil
- Salt and pepper to taste

Directions:
1. Arrange baby spinach on a serving platter. Top with sliced beetroots and toasted walnuts.
2. Whisk together balsamic vinegar, olive oil, salt, and pepper. Drizzle over the salad before serving.

Nutritional Information: 220 calories, 5g protein, 18g carbohydrates, 16g fat, 5g fiber, 0mg cholesterol, 200mg sodium, 500mg potassium.

Roasted Sweet Potato, Kale, and Avocado Salad

Yield: 4 servings | **Prep time:** 15 minutes | **Cook time:** 25 minutes
Ingredients:
- 2 sweet potatoes, cubed
- 2 tablespoons olive oil
- Salt and pepper to taste
- 4 cups kale, stems removed & leaves torn
- 1 avocado, diced
- 1/4 cup pumpkin seeds
- For the dressing:
    - 3 tablespoons olive oil
    - 1 tablespoon apple cider vinegar
    - 1 teaspoon Dijon mustard
    - 1 teaspoon honey

Directions:
1. Preheat oven to 425°F (220°C). Toss sweet potatoes with olive oil, salt, and pepper. Roast for 25 minutes until tender.
2. Massage kale with a little olive oil until the leaves begin to soften.
3. Combine roasted sweet potato, kale, avocado, and pumpkin seeds in a salad bowl.
4. Whisk together dressing ingredients and drizzle over salad before serving.

Nutritional Information: 350 calories, 7g protein, 37g carbohydrates, 21g fat, 9g fiber, 0mg cholesterol, 300mg sodium, 890mg potassium.

Roasted Pumpkin and Chickpea Salad with Maple-Dijon Dressing

Yield: 4 servings | **Prep time:** 20 minutes |
Cook time: 30 minutes
Ingredients:
- 2 cups pumpkin, cubed and roasted
- 1 can (15 oz) chickpeas, drained, rinsed, and roasted
- 4 cups mixed salad greens
- 1/4 cup pumpkin seeds
- For the dressing:
  - 3 tablespoons olive oil
  - 2 tablespoons Dijon mustard
  - 1 tablespoon maple syrup
  - Salt and pepper to taste

Directions:
1. Toss roasted pumpkin and chickpeas with mixed salad greens and pumpkin seeds in a large bowl.
2. Whisk together olive oil, Dijon mustard, maple syrup, salt, and pepper for the dressing.
3. Drizzle the dressing over the salad before serving.

Nutritional Information: 320 calories, 9g protein, 34g carbohydrates, 16g fat, 8g fiber, 0mg cholesterol, 300mg sodium, 700mg potassium.

Avocado, Tomato, and Spinach Quinoa Salad

Yield: 4 servings | **Prep time:** 15 minutes |
Cook time: 20 minutes
Ingredients:
- 1 cup quinoa
- 2 cups water
- 1 avocado, diced
- 1 cup cherry tomatoes, halved
- 2 cups baby spinach
- 2 tablespoons olive oil
- Juice of 1 lemon
- Salt and pepper to taste

Directions:
1. Rinse quinoa under cold water. In a medium saucepan, bring quinoa and water to a boil. Reduce heat, cover, and simmer for 15 minutes. Let it cool.
2. In a large bowl, combine cooked quinoa, avocado, cherry tomatoes, and baby spinach.
3. Whisk together olive oil, lemon juice, salt, and pepper. Drizzle over salad and gently toss to combine.

Nutritional Information: 320 calories, 8g protein, 40g carbohydrates, 16g fat, 8g fiber, 0mg cholesterol, 200mg sodium, 700mg potassium.

Mediterranean Chickpea and Cucumber Salad

Yield: 4 servings | **Prep time:** 15 minutes
Ingredients:
- 1 can (15 oz) chickpeas, drained and rinsed
- 1 cucumber, diced
- 1 bell pepper, diced
- 1/4 cup red onion, finely chopped
- 1/4 cup Kalamata olives, halved
- 1/4 cup feta cheese, crumbled (use vegan feta for a vegan version)
- For the dressing:
  - 3 tablespoons olive oil
  - 2 tablespoons lemon juice
  - 1 teaspoon dried oregano
  - Salt and pepper to taste

Directions:
1. In a large bowl, combine chickpeas, cucumber, bell pepper, red onion, olives, and feta cheese.
2. Whisk together the dressing ingredients in a small bowl.
3. Pour dressing over salad and toss to combine. Serve immediately or chill before serving.

Nutritional Information: 280 calories, 8g protein, 30g carbohydrates, 15g fat, 7g fiber, 15mg cholesterol, 400mg sodium, 450mg potassium.

Moroccan Carrot and Lentil Salad

Yield: 4 servings | **Prep time:** 15 minutes |
Cook time: 25 minutes (for lentils)
Ingredients:
- 1 cup green lentils, cooked
- 4 carrots, grated
- 1/4 cup cilantro, chopped
- 1/4 cup raisins
- For the dressing:
  - 3 tablespoons olive oil
  - 2 tablespoons lemon juice
  - 1 teaspoon cumin
  - 1/2 teaspoon cinnamon
  - Salt to taste

Directions:
1. Cook lentils according to package instructions; let cool.
2. In a large bowl, mix cooled lentils, grated carrots, cilantro, and raisins.
3. Whisk together olive oil, lemon juice, cumin, cinnamon, and salt for the dressing.
4. Toss salad with dressing before serving.

Nutritional Information: 290 calories, 10g protein, 45g carbohydrates, 9g fat, 15g fiber, 0mg cholesterol, 300mg sodium, 700mg potassium.

Rainbow Chopped Salad with Orange-Ginger Dressing

Yield: 4 servings | **Prep time:** 20 minutes
Ingredients:
- 2 cups romaine lettuce, chopped
- 1/2 cup red cabbage, shredded
- 1 carrot, julienned
- 1 yellow bell pepper, diced
- 1/2 cup cherry tomatoes, halved
- 1/4 cup red onion, finely diced
- For the dressing:
    - 1/4 cup orange juice
    - 2 tablespoons olive oil
    - 1 tablespoon ginger, minced
    - 1 tablespoon soy sauce
    - 1 teaspoon honey

Directions:
1. In a large salad bowl, combine lettuce, red cabbage, carrot, bell pepper, cherry tomatoes, and red onion.
2. Whisk together orange juice, olive oil, ginger, soy sauce, and honey for the dressing.
3. Pour dressing over salad, toss to coat, and serve.

Nutritional Information: 150 calories, 2g protein, 18g carbohydrates, 9g fat, 3g fiber, 0mg cholesterol, 150mg sodium, 400mg potassium.

Green Goddess Broccoli Salad

Yield: 4 servings | **Prep time:** 20 minutes
Ingredients:
- 4 cups broccoli florets
- 1/2 cup plain yogurt
- 1/4 cup mayonnaise
- 2 tablespoons chives, chopped
- 2 tablespoons parsley, chopped
- Juice of 1/2 lemon
- Salt and pepper to taste

Directions:
1. Blanch broccoli florets in boiling water for 2 minutes, then plunge into ice water. Drain well.
2. In a bowl, mix yogurt, mayonnaise, chives, parsley, and lemon juice. Season with salt and pepper.
3. Toss broccoli in the dressing until well coated. Refrigerate until ready to serve.

Nutritional Information: 180 calories, 4g protein, 12g carbohydrates, 14g fat, 3g fiber, 10mg cholesterol, 250mg sodium, 450mg potassium.

Spicy Southwest Sweet Potato Salad

Yield: 4 servings | **Prep time:** 15 minutes |
Cook time: 25 minutes
Ingredients:
- 2 large sweet potatoes, cubed
- 1 tablespoon olive oil
- 1 teaspoon chili powder
- 1 can (15 oz) black beans, rinsed and drained
- 1 red bell pepper, diced
- 1/2 red onion, diced
- 2 tablespoons cilantro, chopped
- For the dressing:
    - Juice of 1 lime
    - 2 tablespoons olive oil
    - 1 teaspoon cumin
    - Salt and pepper to taste

Directions:
1. Preheat oven to 425°F (220°C). Toss sweet potatoes with olive oil and chili powder. Roast for 25 minutes, until tender.
2. In a large bowl, mix roasted sweet potatoes, black beans, red bell pepper, red onion, and cilantro.
3. Whisk together dressing ingredients and pour over the salad. Toss to combine.

Nutritional Information: 280 calories, 8g protein, 45g carbohydrates, 10g fat, 10g fiber, 0mg cholesterol, 300mg sodium, 800mg potassium.

Pomegranate and Pear Salad with Balsamic Reduction

Yield: 4 servings | **Prep time:** 15 minutes |
Cook time: 10 minutes (for balsamic reduction)
Ingredients:
- 1/2 cup balsamic vinegar
- 4 cups mixed greens
- 1 pear, sliced
- 1/2 cup pomegranate seeds
- 1/4 cup walnuts, toasted
- Salt and pepper to taste

Directions:
1. In a small saucepan, simmer balsamic vinegar over low heat until reduced by half. Let cool.
2. Arrange mixed greens on a platter. Top with pear slices, pomegranate seeds, and toasted walnuts.
3. Drizzle with balsamic reduction and season with salt and pepper before serving.

Nutritional Information: 150 calories, 2g protein, 20g carbohydrates, 7g fat, 3g fiber, 0mg cholesterol, 150mg sodium, 300mg potassium.

Crunchy Thai Peanut & Quinoa Salad

Yield: 4 servings | **Prep time:** 20 minutes | **Cook time:** 15 minutes

Ingredients:
- 1 cup quinoa, rinsed
- 2 cups water
- 1 red bell pepper, thinly sliced
- 1 carrot, julienned
- 1 cucumber, julienned
- 1/4 cup cilantro, chopped
- 1/4 cup peanuts, chopped
- For the dressing:
  - 1/4 cup peanut butter
  - 2 tablespoons soy sauce
  - 1 tablespoon lime juice
  - 1 tablespoon maple syrup
  - 1 teaspoon ginger, grated
  - 1 clove garlic, minced

Directions:
1. Cook quinoa in water according to package instructions; let cool.
2. In a large bowl, combine cooled quinoa, red bell pepper, carrot, cucumber, and cilantro.
3. Whisk together dressing ingredients until smooth. Pour over salad and toss to combine.
4. Garnish with chopped peanuts before serving.

Nutritional Information: 320 calories, 10g protein, 45g carbohydrates, 12g fat, 6g fiber, 0mg cholesterol, 430mg sodium, 600mg potassium.

Summer Watermelon and Mint Salad

Yield: 4 servings | **Prep time:** 10 minutes

Ingredients:
- 4 cups watermelon, cubed
- 1/4 cup mint leaves, chopped
- Juice of 1 lime
- 1 tablespoon honey (optional for sweetness)
- Pinch of salt

Directions:
1. In a large bowl, combine watermelon and mint leaves.
2. Whisk together lime juice, honey (if using), and a pinch of salt.
3. Drizzle the lime dressing over the watermelon and mint, gently toss to combine.

Nutritional Information: 90 calories, 2g protein, 23g carbohydrates, 0.5g fat, 1g fiber, 0mg cholesterol, 50mg sodium, 300mg potassium.

Roasted Butternut Squash and Pecan Salad

Yield: 4 servings | **Prep time:** 15 minutes | **Cook time:** 25 minutes

Ingredients:
- 4 cups butternut squash, cubed
- 1/2 cup pecans, toasted
- 6 cups mixed greens
- 1/4 cup dried cranberries
- For the dressing:
  - 3 tablespoons olive oil
  - 2 tablespoons balsamic vinegar
  - 1 teaspoon maple syrup
  - Salt and pepper to taste

Directions:
1. Preheat oven to 400°F (200°C). Toss butternut squash with 1 tablespoon olive oil, salt, and pepper. Roast for 25 minutes until tender.
2. In a bowl, mix mixed greens, roasted butternut squash, toasted pecans, and dried cranberries.
3. Whisk together 2 tablespoons of olive oil, balsamic vinegar, maple syrup, salt, and pepper for the dressing. Drizzle over the salad before serving.

Nutritional Information: 290 calories, 4g protein, 30g carbohydrates, 18g fat, 5g fiber, 0mg cholesterol, 150mg sodium, 600mg potassium.

Asian Sesame Noodle Salad

Yield: 4 servings | **Prep time:** 15 minutes | **Cook time:** 10 minutes

Ingredients:
- 8 oz noodles (e.g., soba, rice)
- 1/4 cup soy sauce
- 2 tablespoons sesame oil
- 1 tablespoon rice vinegar
- 1 tablespoon maple syrup
- 1 teaspoon ginger, grated
- 1 cup shredded carrot
- 1 red bell pepper, thinly sliced
- 1/4 cup green onions, chopped
- 1/4 cup cilantro, chopped
- 2 tablespoons sesame seeds

Directions:
1. Cook noodles according to package instructions; rinse under cold water and drain.
2. Whisk together soy sauce, sesame oil, rice vinegar, maple syrup, and ginger for the dressing.
3. Toss noodles with carrot, bell pepper, green onions, cilantro, and dressing.
4. Sprinkle with sesame seeds before serving.

Nutritional Information: 320 calories, 8g protein, 48g carbohydrates, 12g fat, 3g fiber, 0mg cholesterol, 800mg sodium, 400mg potassium.

Grilled Peach and Corn Salad with Basil Vinaigrette

Yield: 4 servings | **Prep time:** 15 minutes |
Cook time: 10 minutes
Ingredients:
- 4 peaches, halved and pitted
- 2 ears of corn, husked
- 6 cups mixed greens
- 1/4 cup basil leaves for the vinaigrette
- 2 tablespoons olive oil, plus more for grilling
- 1 tablespoon white balsamic vinegar
- Salt and pepper to taste

Directions:
1. Preheat the grill to medium-high heat. Brush peaches and corn with olive oil and season with salt and pepper.
2. Grill peaches and corn, turning occasionally, until charred and tender, about 10 minutes for corn and 5 minutes for peaches.
3. Let corn cool slightly, then cut kernels off the cob. Slice grilled peaches.
4. For the vinaigrette, blend basil leaves, 2 tablespoons olive oil, balsamic vinegar, salt, and pepper until smooth.
5. Toss mixed greens with corn, peach slices, and basil vinaigrette.

Nutritional Information: 180 calories, 3g protein, 27g carbohydrates, 7g fat, 4g fiber, 0mg cholesterol, 150mg sodium, 500mg potassium.

Kale and Brussels Sprout Salad with Almonds and Lemon Dressing

Yield: 4 servings | **Prep time:** 20 minutes
Ingredients:
- 4 cups kale, thinly sliced
- 2 cups Brussels sprouts, thinly sliced
- 1/2 cup almonds, chopped and toasted
- For the dressing:
  - Juice of 1 lemon
  - 1/4 cup olive oil
  - 1 tablespoon Dijon mustard
  - 1 teaspoon honey
  - Salt and pepper to taste

Directions:
1. In a large bowl, combine kale, Brussels sprouts, and toasted almonds.
2. Whisk together lemon juice, olive oil, Dijon mustard, honey, salt, and pepper to make the dressing.
3. Toss the salad with the dressing before serving.

Nutritional Information: 250 calories, 6g protein, 14g carbohydrates, 20g fat, 4g fiber, 0mg cholesterol, 200mg sodium, 450mg potassium.

Creamy Avocado and Spirulina Salad

Yield: 4 servings | **Prep time:** 10 minutes
Ingredients:
- 2 avocados, diced
- 1/2 cup cherry tomatoes, halved
- 1/4 cup red onion, thinly sliced
- 1 tablespoon spirulina powder
- 2 tablespoons lime juice
- Salt and pepper to taste

Directions:
1. In a bowl, combine avocados, cherry tomatoes, and red onion.
2. Sprinkle spirulina powder over the salad.
3. Drizzle lime juice and season with salt and pepper. Gently toss to combine.

Nutritional Information: 170 calories, 3g protein, 12g carbohydrates, 14g fat, 7g fiber, 0mg cholesterol, 100mg sodium, 500mg potassium.

Vegan Taco Salad with Creamy Cilantro Dressing

Yield: 4 servings | **Prep time:** 20 minutes |
Cook time: 10 minutes
Ingredients:
- 2 cups cooked black beans
- 1 cup corn kernels
- 1 avocado, diced
- 6 cups romaine lettuce, chopped
- 1 cup cherry tomatoes, halved
- 1/2 cup red onion, diced
- For the dressing:
  - 1/2 cup cashews, soaked and drained
  - 1/4 cup water
  - 1/4 cup cilantro leaves
  - Juice of 1 lime
  - 1 clove garlic
  - Salt to taste

Directions:
1. In a large salad bowl, combine black beans, corn, avocado, romaine lettuce, cherry tomatoes, and red onion.
2. For the dressing, blend cashews, water, cilantro, lime juice, garlic, and salt until smooth.
3. Drizzle the creamy cilantro dressing over the salad and toss well before serving.

Nutritional Information: 320 calories, 12g protein, 40g carbohydrates, 15g fat, 12g fiber, 0mg cholesterol, 300mg sodium, 800mg potassium.

Cucumber Noodle, Edamame, and Mango Salad

Yield: 4 servings | **Prep time:** 20 minutes
Ingredients:
- 2 large cucumbers, spiralized
- 1 cup edamame, shelled and cooked
- 1 mango, peeled and diced
- 1/4 cup red bell pepper, thinly sliced
- 1/4 cup cilantro, chopped
- For the dressing:
  - 2 tablespoons lime juice
  - 1 tablespoon soy sauce
  - 1 tablespoon sesame oil
  - 1 teaspoon honey
  - Salt to taste

Directions:
1. In a large bowl, combine cucumber noodles, edamame, mango, red bell pepper, and cilantro.
2. Whisk together lime juice, soy sauce, sesame oil, honey, and salt for the dressing.
3. Pour dressing over the salad and toss to combine.

Nutritional Information: 160 calories, 6g protein, 22g carbohydrates, 7g fat, 5g fiber, 0mg cholesterol, 200mg sodium, 600mg potassium.

Lemon Herb Mediterranean Pasta Salad

Yield: 4 servings | **Prep time:** 15 minutes |
Cook time: 10 minutes
Ingredients:
- 8 oz whole wheat pasta
- 1 cup cherry tomatoes, halved
- 1 cup cucumber, diced
- 1/2 cup Kalamata olives, pitted
- 1/4 cup red onion, thinly sliced
- 1/4 cup feta cheese, crumbled (use vegan feta for vegan version)
- For the dressing:
  - Juice of 1 lemon
  - 1/4 cup olive oil
  - 2 garlic cloves, minced
  - 1 teaspoon dried oregano
  - Salt and pepper to taste

Directions:
1. Cook pasta according to package instructions. Drain and rinse under cold water.
2. In a large bowl, mix pasta with cherry tomatoes, cucumber, olives, red onion, and feta cheese.
3. Whisk together lemon juice, olive oil, garlic, oregano, salt, and pepper for the dressing.
4. Pour dressing over pasta salad and toss to combine.

Nutricional Information: 310 calories, 8g protein, 45g carbohydrates, 14g fat, 8g fiber, 15mg cholesterol, 300mg sodium, 350mg potassium.

Smoky BBQ Chickpea and Crispy Polenta Salad

Yield: 4 servings | **Prep time:** 20 minutes |
Cook time: 25 minutes
Ingredients:
- 1 can (15 oz) chickpeas, drained, rinsed, and dried
- 2 tablespoons BBQ sauce
- 1 cup polenta, cooked and cooled
- 4 cups mixed greens
- ½ cup cherry tomatoes, halved
- For the dressing:
  - 2 tablespoons olive oil
  - 1 tablespoon balsamic vinegar
  - 1 teaspoon smoked paprika
  - Salt and pepper to taste

Directions:
1. Toss chickpeas with BBQ sauce. Spread on a baking sheet and bake at 400°F (200°C) for 20 minutes.
2. Cut polenta into cubes and pan-fry in a little oil until crispy on all sides.
3. On a serving platter, arrange mixed greens, cherry tomatoes, roasted chickpeas, and crispy polenta.
4. Whisk together olive oil, balsamic vinegar, smoked paprika, salt, and pepper for the dressing. Drizzle over the salad before serving.

Nutritional Information: 320 calories, 10g protein, 45g carbohydrates, 12g fat, 8g fiber, 0mg cholesterol, 580mg sodium, 400mg potassium.

Vegan Potato Salad with Dijon Mustard Dressing

Yield: 4 servings | **Prep time:** 15 minutes |
Cook time: 20 minutes
Ingredients:
- 2 lbs potatoes, cubed and boiled
- 1/2 cup red onion, finely chopped
- 1/2 cup celery, chopped
- For the dressing:
  - 1/4 cup vegan mayonnaise
  - 2 tablespoons Dijon mustard
  - 1 tablespoon apple cider vinegar
  - Salt and pepper to taste

Directions:
1. In a large bowl, combine boiled potatoes, red onion, and celery.
2. Whisk together vegan mayonnaise, Dijon mustard, apple cider vinegar, salt, and pepper for the dressing.
3. Pour dressing over the potato mixture and toss to coat.

Nutritional Information: 250 calories, 5g protein, 38g carbohydrates, 8g fat, 4g fiber, 0mg cholesterol, 250mg sodium, 900mg potassium.

Rainbow Detox Salad with Ginger Lime Dressing

Yield: 4 servings | **Prep time:** 20 minutes
Ingredients:
- 2 cups kale, chopped
- 1 cup red cabbage, shredded
- 1/2 cup carrots, julienned
- 1/2 cup bell peppers, thinly sliced
- 1/4 cup almonds, sliced
- 1/4 cup cranberries
- For the dressing:
  - Juice of 1 lime
  - 1 tablespoon ginger, grated
  - 2 tablespoons olive oil
  - 1 teaspoon honey
  - Salt to taste

Directions:
1. Combine kale, red cabbage, carrots, bell peppers, almonds, and cranberries in a large salad bowl.
2. Whisk together lime juice, ginger, olive oil, honey, and salt for the dressing.
3. Drizzle the dressing over the salad and toss well before serving.

Nutritional Information: 190 calories, 4g protein, 20g carbohydrates, 11g fat, 4g fiber, 0mg cholesterol, 150mg sodium, 400mg potassium.

Spicy Kale and Quinoa Black Bean Salad

Yield: 4 servings | **Prep time:** 15 minutes |
Cook time: 15 minutes
Ingredients:
- 1 cup quinoa, cooked
- 4 cups kale, chopped
- 1 can (15 oz) black beans, drained and rinsed
- 1 avocado, diced
- 1/2 cup cherry tomatoes, halved
- 1 jalapeno, minced (optional)
- For the dressing:
  - Juice of 1 lime
  - 2 tablespoons olive oil
  - 1 teaspoon chili powder
  - Salt and pepper to taste

Directions:
1. In a large bowl, mix cooked quinoa, kale, black beans, avocado, cherry tomatoes, and jalapeno.
2. Whisk together lime juice, olive oil, chili powder, salt, and pepper for the dressing.
3. Pour the dressing over the salad and toss to combine thoroughly.

Nutritional Information: 330 calories, 12g protein, 45g carbohydrates, 13g fat, 12g fiber, 0mg cholesterol, 300mg sodium, 800mg potassium.

Roasted Beet, Citrus, and Fennel Salad

Yield: 4 servings | **Prep time:** 15 minutes |
Cook time: 45 minutes
Ingredients:
- 4 medium beets, peeled and cubed
- 2 oranges, peeled and segments
- 1 fennel bulb, thinly sliced
- 1/4 cup walnuts, toasted
- 2 tablespoons olive oil
- 2 tablespoons balsamic vinegar
- Salt and pepper to taste

Directions:
1. Preheat oven to 400°F (200°C). Toss beets with 1 tablespoon olive oil, salt, and pepper. Roast for 45 minutes or until tender.
2. Arrange roasted beets, orange segments, and fennel slices on a platter.
3. Drizzle with remaining olive oil and balsamic vinegar. Garnish with toasted walnuts.

Nutritional Information: 220 calories, 4g protein, 24g carbohydrates, 12g fat, 6g fiber, 0mg cholesterol, 200mg sodium, 500mg potassium.

Charred Corn and Avocado Salad with Chili Lime Dressing

Yield: 4 servings | **Prep time:** 10 minutes |
Cook time: 10 minutes
Ingredients:
- 4 ears of corn, husked
- 1 avocado, diced
- 1/2 cup cherry tomatoes, halved
- 1/4 cup cilantro, chopped
- For the dressing:
  - Juice of 2 limes
  - 1 tablespoon olive oil
  - 1 teaspoon chili powder
  - Salt to taste

Directions:
1. Grill corn over medium heat until charred on all sides. Let cool, then cut kernels off the cob.
2. In a bowl, combine corn kernels, avocado, cherry tomatoes, and cilantro.
3. Whisk together lime juice, olive oil, chili powder, and salt. Drizzle over salad and toss to combine.

Nutritional Information: 250 calories, 5g protein, 35g carbohydrates, 12g fat, 7g fiber, 0mg cholesterol, 150mg sodium, 600mg potassium.

Refreshing Cucumber, Dill, and Red Onion Salad

Yield: 4 servings | **Prep time:** 10 minutes
Ingredients:
- 2 large cucumbers, thinly sliced
- 1/4 red onion, thinly sliced
- 1/4 cup fresh dill, chopped
- For the dressing:
    - 3 tablespoons apple cider vinegar
    - 1 tablespoon olive oil
    - 1 teaspoon sugar (optional)
    - Salt and pepper to taste

Directions:
1. In a salad bowl, combine cucumbers, red onion, and dill.
2. Whisk together apple cider vinegar, olive oil, sugar (if using), salt, and pepper for the dressing.
3. Pour dressing over the cucumber mixture and toss to combine. Chill before serving.

Nutritional Information: 80 calories, 1g protein, 10g carbohydrates, 4g fat, 2g fiber, 0mg cholesterol, 10mg sodium, 250mg potassium.

Heirloom Tomato and Peach Salad with Basil Vinaigrette

Yield: 4 servings | **Prep time:** 15 minutes
Ingredients:
- 3 heirloom tomatoes, sliced
- 2 peaches, sliced
- 1/4 cup basil leaves
- For the vinaigrette:
    - 1/4 cup olive oil
    - 2 tablespoons white balsamic vinegar
    - 1/4 cup fresh basil, finely chopped
    - Salt and pepper to taste

Directions:
1. Arrange tomato and peach slices on a platter, alternating and overlapping them.
2. For the vinaigrette, whisk together olive oil, white balsamic vinegar, chopped basil, salt, and pepper in a small bowl.
3. Drizzle the basil vinaigrette over the tomatoes and peaches. Garnish with whole basil leaves.

Nutritional Information: 180 calories, 2g protein, 14g carbohydrates, 14g fat, 3g fiber, 0mg cholesterol, 10mg sodium, 400mg potassium.

Zucchini Ribbon Salad with Lemon and Almond Pesto

Yield: 4 servings | **Prep time:** 20 minutes
Ingredients:
- 2 zucchinis, sliced into ribbons
- 1/2 cup almonds, toasted
- 1/4 cup olive oil
- Juice and zest of 1 lemon
- 1 garlic clove
- Salt and pepper to taste

Directions:
1. Use a vegetable peeler or mandoline to slice the zucchini into thin ribbons.
2. In a food processor, blend almonds, olive oil, lemon juice and zest, garlic, salt, and pepper until smooth to make the pesto.
3. Toss zucchini ribbons with the almond pesto. Adjust seasoning if necessary.

Nutritional Information: 230 calories, 6g protein, 8g carbohydrates, 20g fat, 3g fiber, 0mg cholesterol, 150mg sodium, 400mg potassium.

Grilled Vegetable Salad with Salsa Verde

Yield: 4 servings | **Prep time:** 20 minutes | **Cook time:** 10 minutes
Ingredients:
- 2 zucchinis, sliced lengthwise
- 2 bell peppers, quartered
- 1 red onion, sliced into rings
- 2 tablespoons olive oil
- Salt and pepper to taste
- For the salsa verde:
    - 1 cup fresh parsley
    - 1/2 cup olive oil
    - 2 tablespoons capers
    - 1 garlic clove
    - Juice of 1 lemon
    - Salt to taste

Directions:
1. Preheat grill to medium-high. Brush vegetables with olive oil and season with salt and pepper. Grill until charred and tender, about 5 minutes per side.
2. For the salsa verde, blend parsley, olive oil, capers, garlic, lemon juice, and salt until smooth.
3. Arrange grilled vegetables on a platter and drizzle with salsa verde before serving.

Nutritional Information: 250 calories, 3g protein, 15g carbohydrates, 21g fat, 4g fiber, 0mg cholesterol, 200mg sodium, 500mg potassium.

Shaved Asparagus and Arugula Salad

Yield: 4 servings | **Prep time:** 15 minutes
Ingredients:
- 1 bunch asparagus, tough ends trimmed
- 4 cups arugula
- 1/4 cup shaved Parmesan (use vegan Parmesan for a vegan version)
- 1/4 cup pine nuts, toasted
- For the dressing:
    - 3 tablespoons olive oil
    - 1 tablespoon lemon juice
    - 1 teaspoon Dijon mustard
    - Salt and pepper to taste

Directions:
1. Use a vegetable peeler to shave the asparagus into thin ribbons.
2. In a large bowl, combine asparagus ribbons, arugula, shaved Parmesan, and toasted pine nuts.
3. Whisk together olive oil, lemon juice, Dijon mustard, salt, and pepper for the dressing.
4. Toss the salad with the dressing before serving.

Nutritional Information: 210 calories, 7g protein, 8g carbohydrates, 18g fat, 3g fiber, 4mg cholesterol, 250mg sodium, 350mg potassium.

Carrot, Apple, and Cabbage Coleslaw

Yield: 4 servings | **Prep time:** 15 minutes
Ingredients:
- 2 cups cabbage, shredded
- 1 carrot, grated
- 1 apple, julienned
- For the dressing:
  - 1/4 cup mayonnaise (use vegan mayonnaise for a vegan version)
  - 2 tablespoons apple cider vinegar
  - 1 tablespoon maple syrup
  - Salt and pepper to taste

Directions:
1. In a large bowl, combine cabbage, carrot, and apple.
2. In a small bowl, whisk together mayonnaise, apple cider vinegar, maple syrup, salt, and pepper.
3. Toss the coleslaw with the dressing until well coated. Chill before serving.

Nutritional Information: 150 calories, 1g protein, 18g carbohydrates, 9g fat, 3g fiber, 5mg cholesterol, 180mg sodium, 250mg potassium.

Spinach, Avocado, and Strawberry Salad with Poppy Seed Dressing

Yield: 4 servings | **Prep time:** 15 minutes
Ingredients:
- 4 cups baby spinach
- 1 avocado, sliced
- 1 cup strawberries, sliced
- 1/4 cup almonds, sliced
- For the dressing:
  - 1/4 cup olive oil
  - 2 tablespoons white wine vinegar
  - 1 tablespoon honey
  - 1 teaspoon poppy seeds
  - Salt and pepper to taste

Directions:
1. In a large salad bowl, combine baby spinach, avocado slices, strawberry slices, and sliced almonds.
2. In a small bowl, whisk together olive oil, white wine vinegar, honey, poppy seeds, salt, and pepper to create the dressing.
3. Drizzle the dressing over the salad and gently toss to combine before serving.

Nutritional Information: 270 calories, 4g protein, 19g carbohydrates, 21g fat, 7g fiber, 0mg cholesterol, 100mg sodium, 600mg potassium.

Roasted Cauliflower and Chickpea Salad with Tahini Dressing

Yield: 4 servings | **Prep time:** 15 minutes |
Cook time: 25 minutes
Ingredients:
- 1 head cauliflower, cut into florets
- 1 can (15 oz) chickpeas, drained, rinsed, and dried
- 4 cups spinach leaves
- 1/4 cup red onion, thinly sliced
- For the dressing:
  - 1/4 cup tahini
  - 2 tablespoons lemon juice
  - 1 garlic clove, minced
  - 2-4 tablespoons water
  - Salt to taste

Directions:
1. Toss cauliflower and chickpeas with a little olive oil, salt, and pepper. Roast at 425°F (220°C) for 25 minutes.
2. Arrange spinach and red onion on a serving platter. Top with roasted cauliflower and chickpeas.
3. Whisk together tahini, lemon juice, minced garlic, water (as needed for consistency), and salt for the dressing. Drizzle over the salad before serving.

Nutritional Information: 280 calories, 12g protein, 33g carbohydrates, 13g fat, 10g fiber, 0mg cholesterol, 300mg sodium, 600mg potassium.

Warm Lentil Salad with Roasted Vegetables and Apple Cider Vinaigrette

Yield: 4 servings | **Prep time:** 20 minutes |
Cook time: 30 minutes
Ingredients:
- 1 cup lentils, cooked
- 2 cups mixed vegetables (e.g., carrots, zucchini, bell peppers), roasted
- For the vinaigrette:
  - 1/4 cup apple cider vinegar
  - 1/4 cup olive oil
  - 1 tablespoon Dijon mustard
  - 1 teaspoon honey
  - Salt and pepper to taste

Directions:
1. Preheat oven to 425°F (220°C). Toss vegetables with olive oil, salt, and pepper. Roast for 30 minutes or until tender.
2. Mix cooked lentils with roasted vegetables.
3. Whisk together the vinaigrette ingredients and pour over the salad. Serve warm.

Chapter 8: Supportive Snacks & Appetizers

Pita Pockets with Cucumber and Vegan Tzatziki

Yield: 4 servings | **Prep time:** 15 minutes |
Cook time: 0 minutes
Ingredients:
- 4 whole wheat pita pockets
- 1 cucumber, sliced
- For the vegan tzatziki:
    - 1 cup vegan yogurt
    - 1/2 cucumber, grated and drained
    - 2 cloves garlic, minced
    - 2 tablespoons lemon juice
    - 1 tablespoon dill, chopped
    - Salt to taste

Directions:
1. Mix all ingredients for the vegan tzatziki in a bowl. Chill for at least 10 minutes.
2. Fill each pita pocket with sliced cucumber and a generous dollop of vegan tzatziki.

Nutritional Information: 250 calories, 9g protein, 50g carbohydrates, 2g fat, 6g fiber, 0mg cholesterol, 200mg sodium, 300mg potassium.

Roasted Chickpeas

Yield: 4 servings | **Prep time:** 5 minutes |
Cook time: 30 minutes
Ingredients:
- 2 cans (15 oz each) chickpeas, drained, rinsed, and dried
- 2 tablespoons olive oil
- 1/2 teaspoon salt
- 1 teaspoon smoked paprika
- 1 teaspoon chili powder

Directions:
1. Preheat oven to 400°F (200°C). Toss chickpeas with olive oil, salt, smoked paprika, and chili powder.
2. Spread on a baking sheet in a single layer. Bake for 30 minutes, stirring halfway through, until crispy.
3. Let cool before serving.

Nutritional Information: 210 calories, 10g protein, 30g carbohydrates, 7g fat, 8g fiber, 0mg cholesterol, 300mg sodium, 290mg potassium.

Bell Pepper Strips with Salsa

Yield: 4 servings | **Prep time:** 10 minutes |
Cook time: 0 minutes
Ingredients:

- 2 large bell peppers cut into strips
- 1 cup salsa

Directions:

1. Wash and slice bell peppers into thin strips.
2. Serve bell pepper strips with a bowl of salsa for dipping.

Nutritional Information: 60 calories, 2g protein, 14g carbohydrates, 0g fat, 4g fiber, 0mg cholesterol, 400mg sodium, 400mg potassium.

Rice Cakes with Avocado

Yield: 2 servings | **Prep time:** 5 minutes |
Cook time: 0 minutes
Ingredients:

- 4 rice cakes
- 1 ripe avocado
- Salt and pepper to taste
- Lemon juice (optional)

Directions:

1. Mash the avocado in a small bowl. Season with salt, pepper, and a squeeze of lemon juice.
2. Spread the mashed avocado evenly over the rice cakes.

Nutritional Information: 200 calories, 3g protein, 27g carbohydrates, 10g fat, 7g fiber, 0mg cholesterol, 150mg sodium, 500mg potassium.

Stuffed Bell Peppers

Yield: 4 servings | **Prep time:** 20 minutes |
Cook time: 40 minutes
Ingredients:

- 4 large bell peppers, tops removed, seeded
- 1 tablespoon olive oil
- 1 onion, diced
- 2 cloves garlic, minced
- 1 cup quinoa, cooked
- 1 can (14 oz) black beans, drained and rinsed
- 1 cup corn kernels (fresh or frozen)
- 1 teaspoon chili powder
- 1 teaspoon cumin
- 1/2 cup tomato sauce
- Salt and pepper to taste
- 1/2 cup shredded vegan cheese
- Fresh cilantro for garnish

Directions:

1. Preheat oven to 375°F (190°C). Place bell peppers in a baking dish; set aside.
2. In a skillet, heat olive oil over medium heat. Add onion and garlic; sauté until softened, about 5 minutes. Stir in cooked quinoa, black beans, corn, chili powder, cumin, and tomato sauce. Season with salt and pepper.
3. Spoon the mixture into each bell pepper. Top with shredded vegan cheese.
4. Cover with foil and bake for 35 minutes. Uncover and bake for an additional 5 minutes or until the cheese is melted and the peppers are tender.
5. Garnish with fresh cilantro before serving.

Nutritional Information: 350 calories, 15g protein, 55g carbohydrates, 9g fat, 11g fiber, 0mg cholesterol, 500mg sodium, 800mg potassium.

Chilled Creamy Tofu Cheese

Yield: 4 servings | **Prep time:** 10 minutes |
Cook time: 0 minutes (plus chilling time)
Ingredients:

- 1 block (14 oz) firm tofu, drained
- 2 tablespoons nutritional yeast
- 1 tablespoon lemon juice
- 1 garlic clove, minced
- 1/2 teaspoon salt
- 2 tablespoons fresh herbs (e.g., chives or dill), chopped

Directions:

1. Blend tofu, nutritional yeast, lemon juice, garlic, and salt in a food processor until smooth.
2. Stir in fresh herbs. Transfer to a bowl and chill for at least 1 hour before serving.
3. Serve with crackers or vegetable sticks.

Nutritional Information: 120 calories, 12g protein, 4g carbohydrates, 6g fat, 2g fiber, 0mg cholesterol, 300mg sodium, 200mg potassium.

Homemade Granola Bars

Yield: 6 servings | **Prep time:** 15 minutes |
Cook time: 20 minutes
Ingredients:

- 2 cups rolled oats
- 1/2 cup almonds, chopped
- 1/4 cup honey (use maple syrup for a vegan option)
- 1/4 cup almond butter
- 1/2 cup dried cranberries
- 1/2 teaspoon vanilla extract

Directions:

1. Preheat oven to 350°F (175°C). Mix all ingredients in a bowl until well combined.
2. Press the mixture firmly into a lined 8-inch square baking pan.
3. Bake for 20 minutes. Let cool before cutting into bars.

Nutritional Information: 300 calories, 8g protein, 45g carbohydrates, 12g fat, 6g fiber, 0mg cholesterol, 50mg sodium, 250mg potassium.

Rice Cakes with Tahini and Honey

Yield: 2 servings | **Prep time:** 5 minutes |
Cook time: 0 minutes
Ingredients:
- 4 rice cakes
- 4 tablespoons tahini
- 2 tablespoons honey

Directions:
1. Spread 1 tablespoon of tahini on each rice cake.
2. Drizzle honey over the tahini.

Nutritional Information: 210 calories, 5g protein, 28g carbohydrates, 10g fat, 2g fiber, 0mg cholesterol, 70mg sodium, 120mg potassium.

Avocado and Tomato Sandwich on Whole Grain Bread

Yield: 2 servings | **Prep time:** 5 minutes |
Cook time: 0 minutes
Ingredients:
- 4 slices whole grain bread
- 1 ripe avocado, sliced
- 1 tomato, sliced
- Salt and pepper to taste

Directions:
1. Layer avocado and tomato slices on two slices of bread. Season with salt and pepper.
2. Top with the remaining slices of bread to make two sandwiches.

Nutritional Information: 300 calories, 9g protein, 45g carbohydrates, 12g fat, 10g fiber, 0mg cholesterol, 300mg sodium, 600mg potassium.

Almond Protein Bars

Yield: 6 servings | **Prep time:** 15 minutes |
Cook time: 0 minutes (plus refrigeration)
Ingredients:
- 1 cup almonds
- 1 cup dates, pitted
- 1/4 cup protein powder (vegan)
- 2 tablespoons almond butter
- 1 tablespoon chia seeds
- 2 tablespoons water

Directions:
1. Process almonds and dates in a food processor until crumbly. Add protein powder, almond butter, chia seeds, and water; process until the mixture sticks together.
2. Press the mixture into a lined loaf pan. Refrigerate for at least 2 hours before cutting into bars.

Nutritional Information: 260 calories, 10g protein, 30g carbohydrates, 14g fat, 6g fiber, 0mg cholesterol, 20mg sodium, 360mg potassium.

Roasted Cauliflower Bites with Curry Dip

Yield: 4 servings | **Prep time:** 15 minutes |
Cook time: 25 minutes
Ingredients:
- For the cauliflower:
  - 1 head cauliflower, cut into bite-sized pieces
  - 2 tablespoons olive oil
  - Salt and pepper to taste
- For the curry dip:
  - 1/2 cup vegan mayonnaise
  - 1 tablespoon curry powder
  - 1 teaspoon lime juice
  - Salt to taste

Directions:
1. Preheat oven to 425°F (220°C). Toss cauliflower pieces with olive oil, salt, and pepper. Spread on a baking sheet and roast for 25 minutes, until tender and golden.
2. Mix vegan mayonnaise, curry powder, lime juice, and salt to make the dip.
3. Serve cauliflower bites with curry dip on the side.

Nutritional Information: 220 calories, 3g protein, 14g carbohydrates, 17g fat, 4g fiber, 0mg cholesterol, 350mg sodium, 400mg potassium.

Kale Chips

Yield: 4 servings | **Prep time:** 10 minutes |
Cook time: 15 minutes
Ingredients:
- 1 bunch kale, stems removed, leaves torn
- 1 tablespoon olive oil
- 1/2 teaspoon salt

Directions:
1. Preheat oven to 350°F (175°C). Toss kale leaves with olive oil and salt.
2. Spread on a baking sheet in a single layer. Bake for 15 minutes, until crispy.
3. Let cool before serving.

Nutritional Information: 58 calories, 2g protein, 7g carbohydrates, 3g fat, 1g fiber, 0mg cholesterol, 300mg sodium, 299mg potassium.

Air-Popped Popcorn with Nutritional Yeast

Yield: 4 servings | **Prep time:** 2 minutes |
Cook time: 5 minutes
Ingredients:
- 1/2 cup popcorn kernels, air-popped
- 2 tablespoons nutritional yeast
- 1/4 teaspoon salt
- 1 teaspoon olive oil (optional)

Directions:
1. Pop the popcorn kernels using an air popper.

2. While still hot, sprinkle popcorn with nutritional yeast, salt, and drizzle with olive oil if using. Toss to coat evenly.
3. Serve immediately.

Nutritional Information: 110 calories, 5g protein, 18g carbohydrates, 2g fat, 4g fiber, 0mg cholesterol, 150mg sodium, 180mg potassium.

Veggie Spring Rolls with Peanut Dipping Sauce

Yield: 4 servings | **Prep time:** 30 minutes | **Cook time:** 0 minutes

Ingredients:
- 8 rice paper wrappers
- 1 cup shredded carrots
- 1 cup sliced cucumber
- 1 cup sliced bell pepper
- 1 cup cooked vermicelli noodles
- 1/4 cup chopped cilantro
- For the sauce:
  - 1/4 cup peanut butter
  - 2 tablespoons soy sauce
  - 1 tablespoon lime juice
  - 1 tablespoon maple syrup
  - 2 tablespoons water

Directions:
1. Dip rice paper wrappers in warm water for a few seconds to soften. Place on a clean surface.
2. On each wrapper, place a small number of carrots, cucumber, bell pepper, vermicelli noodles, and cilantro.
3. Roll the wrappers tightly.
4. Mix peanut butter, soy sauce, lime juice, maple syrup, and water to make the dipping sauce.
5. Serve spring rolls with peanut dipping sauce.

Nutritional Information: 210 calories, 6g protein, 38g carbohydrates, 5g fat, 3g fiber, 0mg cholesterol, 430mg sodium, 220mg potassium.

Vegan Cheese and Whole Grain Crackers

Yield: 4 servings | **Prep time:** 5 minutes | **Cook time:** 0 minutes

Ingredients:
- 1 cup vegan cheese, sliced or spreadable
- 1 box (8 oz) whole grain crackers

Directions:
1. Arrange vegan cheese and whole grain crackers on a serving plate.
2. Serve immediately, allowing guests to assemble their own crackers and cheese.

Nutritional Information: 250 calories, 7g protein, 30g carbohydrates, 12g fat, 4g fiber, 0mg cholesterol, 450mg sodium, 100mg potassium.

Cucumber and Jicama with Lime Juice

Yield: 4 servings | **Prep time:** 15 minutes | **Cook time:** 0 minutes

Ingredients:
- 1 large cucumber, julienned
- 1 large jicama, julienned
- Juice of 2 limes
- Salt and chili powder to taste

Directions:
1. Mix cucumber and jicama in a bowl.
2. Add lime juice, salt, and chili powder. Toss to combine.
3. Serve chilled.

Nutritional Information: 50 calories, 1g protein, 12g carbohydrates, 0g fat, 6g fiber, 0mg cholesterol, 5mg sodium, 290mg potassium.

Guacamole with Whole Grain Crackers

Yield: 4 servings | **Prep time:** 10 minutes | **Cook time:** 0 minutes

Ingredients:
- 2 ripe avocados, mashed
- 1 lime, juiced
- 1/4 cup red onion, finely chopped
- 1/4 cup cilantro, chopped
- Salt and pepper to taste
- Whole grain crackers for serving

Directions:
1. In a bowl, mix mashed avocados with lime juice, red onion, cilantro, salt, and pepper until well combined.
2. Serve immediately with whole grain crackers.

Nutritional Information: 220 calories, 3g protein, 15g carbohydrates, 17g fat, 7g fiber, 0mg cholesterol, 200mg sodium, 500mg potassium.

Zucchini Chips

Yield: 4 servings | **Prep time:** 15 minutes | **Cook time:** 2 hours

Ingredients:
- 2 large zucchinis, thinly sliced
- 1 tablespoon olive oil
- 1/2 teaspoon salt

Directions:
1. Preheat oven to 225°F (105°C). Toss zucchini slices with olive oil and salt.
2. Arrange slices in a single layer on a baking sheet lined with parchment paper.
3. Bake for 2 hours, flipping halfway through, until crispy.
4. Let cool before serving.

Nutritional Information: 60 calories, 2g protein, 4g carbohydrates, 4g fat, 1g fiber, 0mg cholesterol, 300mg sodium, 400mg potassium.

Spiced Pear Chips

Yield: 4 servings | **Prep time:** 10 minutes |
Cook time: 2 hours
Ingredients:
- 3 pears, thinly sliced
- 1/2 teaspoon ground cinnamon
- 1/4 teaspoon ground nutmeg

Directions:
1. Preheat oven to 225°F (105°C). Arrange pear slices in a single layer on a baking sheet lined with parchment paper.
2. Sprinkle with cinnamon and nutmeg.
3. Bake for 2 hours, flipping halfway through, until dried and crispy.
4. Let cool before serving.

Nutritional Information: 95 calories, 1g protein, 25g carbohydrates, 0g fat, 5g fiber, 0mg cholesterol, 0mg sodium, 200mg potassium.

Baked Apple Chips

Yield: 4 servings | **Prep time:** 10 minutes |
Cook time: 2 hours
Ingredients:
- 4 apples, thinly sliced
- 1 teaspoon ground cinnamon

Directions:
1. Preheat oven to 200°F (90°C). Arrange apple slices in a single layer on baking sheets lined with parchment paper.
2. Sprinkle apple slices with cinnamon.
3. Bake for 2 hours, flipping halfway through, until dried and crisp.
4. Let cool before serving.

Nutritional Information: 95 calories, 0g protein, 25g carbohydrates, 0g fat, 5g fiber, 0mg cholesterol, 0mg sodium, 200mg potassium.

Roasted Seaweed Snacks

Yield: 4 servings | **Prep time:** 5 minutes |
Cook time: 10 minutes
Ingredients:
- 4 sheets nori (seaweed)
- 1 teaspoon sesame oil
- Salt to taste

Directions:
1. Preheat oven to 300°F (150°C). Brush nori sheets lightly with sesame oil and sprinkle with salt.
2. Cut into small squares and place on a baking sheet. Bake for 10 minutes or until crispy.
3. Let cool before serving.

Nutritional Information: 35 calories, 2g protein, 1g carbohydrates, 2g fat, 1g fiber, 0mg cholesterol, 100mg sodium, 50mg potassium.

Smoked Paprika Almonds

Yield: 4 servings | **Prep time:** 5 minutes |
Cook time: 10 minutes
Ingredients:
- 2 cups raw almonds
- 1 tablespoon olive oil
- 1 teaspoon smoked paprika
- 1/2 teaspoon salt
- 1/4 teaspoon garlic powder

Directions:
1. Preheat oven to 350°F (175°C). In a bowl, toss almonds with olive oil, smoked paprika, salt, and garlic powder.
2. Spread almonds on a baking sheet in a single layer. Bake for 10 minutes, stirring once.
3. Let cool before serving.

Nutritional Information: 250 calories, 9g protein, 9g carbohydrates, 21g fat, 5g fiber, 0mg cholesterol, 300mg sodium, 350mg potassium.

Chili Lime Edamame

Yield: 4 servings | **Prep time:** 5 minutes |
Cook time: 10 minutes
Ingredients:
- 2 cups edamame, shelled
- 1 tablespoon olive oil
- Juice of 1 lime
- 1 teaspoon chili powder
- Salt to taste

Directions:
1. Cook edamame according to package instructions; drain.
2. Toss edamame with olive oil, lime juice, chili powder, and salt.
3. Serve warm or at room temperature.

Nutritional Information: 150 calories, 12g protein, 9g carbohydrates, 8g fat, 4g fiber, 0mg cholesterol, 200mg sodium, 400mg potassium.

Vegan Yogurt with Mixed Berries

Yield: 4 servings | **Prep time:** 5 minutes |
Cook time: 0 minutes
Ingredients:
- 2 cups vegan yogurt
- 1 cup mixed berries (strawberries, blueberries, raspberries)
- 1 tablespoon maple syrup (optional)

Directions:
1. Divide the yogurt into four bowls.
2. Top each bowl with mixed berries.
3. Drizzle with maple syrup if desired.

Nutritional Information: 120 calories, 3g protein, 25g carbohydrates, 2g fat, 3g fiber, 0mg cholesterol, 60mg sodium, 200mg potassium.

Vegan Pesto Stuffed Mushrooms

Yield: 4 servings | **Prep time:** 15 minutes | **Cook time:** 20 minutes

Ingredients:
- 16 large mushrooms, stems removed
- 1 cup basil leaves
- 1/2 cup walnuts
- 2 cloves garlic
- 1/4 cup olive oil
- Salt and pepper to taste

Directions:
1. Preheat oven to 375°F (190°C).
2. In a food processor, blend basil, walnuts, garlic, and olive oil until smooth. Season with salt and pepper.
3. Stuff each mushroom cap with the pesto mixture. Place on a baking sheet.
4. Bake for 20 minutes, until mushrooms are tender.

Nutritional Information: 200 calories, 5g protein, 6g carbohydrates, 19g fat, 2g fiber, 0mg cholesterol, 150mg sodium, 300mg potassium.

Steamed Edamame sprinkled with Sea Salt

Yield: 4 servings | **Prep time:** 2 minutes | **Cook time:** 5 minutes

Ingredients:
- 2 cups edamame in pods
- Sea salt to taste

Directions:
1. Steam edamame in pods for about 5 minutes until tender.
2. Sprinkle with sea salt.
3. Serve warm.

Nutritional Information: 100 calories, 8g protein, 9g carbohydrates, 4g fat, 4g fiber, 0mg cholesterol, 120mg sodium, 363mg potassium.

Carrot Sticks with Almond Butter Dip

Yield: 4 servings | **Prep time:** 10 minutes | **Cook time:** 0 minutes

Ingredients:
- 4 large carrots, peeled and cut into sticks
- 1/2 cup almond butter
- 2 tablespoons maple syrup
- 1 tablespoon lemon juice
- Pinch of salt

Directions:
1. In a small bowl, mix almond butter, maple syrup, lemon juice, and a pinch of salt until smooth.
2. Serve carrot sticks with almond butter dip.

Nutritional Information: 230 calories, 6g protein, 24g carbohydrates, 14g fat, 5g fiber, 0mg cholesterol, 150mg sodium, 400mg potassium.

Crispy Tofu Bites

Yield: 4 servings | **Prep time:** 15 minutes | **Cook time:** 25 minutes

Ingredients:
- 1 block (14 oz) extra-firm tofu, pressed and cubed
- 1/4 cup soy sauce
- 2 tablespoons olive oil
- 2 tablespoons cornstarch

Directions:
1. Preheat oven to 400°F (200°C). Toss tofu cubes with soy sauce, then coat with cornstarch.
2. Arrange tofu on a baking sheet lined with parchment paper. Drizzle with olive oil.
3. Bake for 25 minutes, flipping halfway through, until crispy.
4. Serve warm.

Nutritional Information: 200 calories, 12g protein, 10g carbohydrates, 14g fat, 1g fiber, 0mg cholesterol, 800mg sodium, 300mg potassium.

Cherry Tomato Bites

Yield: 4 servings | **Prep time:** 10 minutes | **Cook time:** 0 minutes

Ingredients:
- 1 cup cherry tomatoes, halved
- 1/2 cup vegan feta cheese, crumbled
- 1/4 cup chopped basil
- 1 tablespoon olive oil
- Salt and pepper to taste

Directions:
1. Toss cherry tomatoes with vegan feta, basil, olive oil, salt, and pepper.
2. Serve as a bite-sized appetizer.

Nutritional Information: 90 calories, 2g protein, 4g carbohydrates, 7g fat, 1g fiber, 0mg cholesterol, 200mg sodium, 150mg potassium.

Baked Sweet Potato Fries

Yield: 4 servings | **Prep time:** 10 minutes | **Cook time:** 25 minutes

Ingredients:
- 2 large sweet potatoes, cut into fries
- 2 tablespoons olive oil
- 1 teaspoon paprika
- Salt to taste

Directions:
1. Preheat oven to 425°F (220°C). Toss sweet potato fries with olive oil, paprika, and salt.
2. Spread in a single layer on a baking sheet. Bake for 25 minutes, flipping halfway through, until crispy.
3. Serve immediately.

Nutritional Information: 190 calories, 2g protein, 27g carbohydrates, 7g fat, 4g fiber, 0mg cholesterol, 300mg sodium, 450mg potassium.

Falafel Balls

Yield: 4 servings | **Prep time:** 20 minutes (plus soaking time) | **Cook time:** 10 minutes
Ingredients:
- 1 cup dried chickpeas, soaked overnight
- 1 onion, chopped
- 2 cloves garlic, minced
- 1/4 cup fresh parsley, chopped
- 1 teaspoon ground cumin
- Salt and oil for frying

Directions:
1. Drain chickpeas and blend with onion, garlic, parsley, and cumin until smooth. Season with salt.
2. Form mixture into small balls and fry in hot oil until golden and crispy.
3. Drain on paper towels and serve.

Nutritional Information: 220 calories, 9g protein, 33g carbohydrates, 7g fat, 6g fiber, 0mg cholesterol, 300mg sodium, 400mg potassium.

Sweet Potato Hummus

Yield: 4 servings | **Prep time:** 15 minutes | **Cook time:** 30 minutes
Ingredients:
- 1 large sweet potato, roasted and peeled
- 1 can (15 oz) chickpeas, drained and rinsed
- 2 tablespoons tahini
- 2 tablespoons olive oil
- 1 lemon, juiced
- Salt to taste

Directions:
1. Blend roasted sweet potato, chickpeas, tahini, olive oil, and lemon juice until smooth. Season with salt.
2. Serve with vegetable sticks or crackers.

Nutritional Information: 280 calories, 8g protein, 38g carbohydrates, 12g fat, 8g fiber, 0mg cholesterol, 200mg sodium, 600mg potassium.

Crispy Brussels Sprout Leaves

Yield: 4 servings | **Prep time:** 10 minutes | **Cook time:** 15 minutes
Ingredients:
- 2 cups Brussels sprouts, leaves separated
- 2 tablespoons olive oil
- Salt and pepper to taste

Directions:
1. Preheat oven to 400°F (200°C).
2. Toss Brussels sprouts leaves with olive oil, salt, and pepper. Spread on a baking sheet.
3. Bake for 15 minutes, until crispy.

Nutritional Information: 80 calories, 3g protein, 7g carbohydrates, 5g fat, 3g fiber, 0mg cholesterol, 150mg sodium, 250mg potassium.

Vegan Caprese Skewers

Yield: 4 servings | **Prep time:** 10 minutes | **Cook time:** 0 minutes
Ingredients:
- 16 cherry tomatoes
- 16 small balls vegan of mozzarella cheese
- 16 fresh basil leaves
- Balsamic reduction for drizzling

Directions:
1. Thread a cherry tomato, a basil leaf, and a vegan mozzarella ball onto skewers.
2. Drizzle with balsamic reduction before serving.

Nutritional Information: 100 calories, 2g protein, 5g carbohydrates, 7g fat, 1g fiber, 0mg cholesterol, 150mg sodium, 150mg potassium.

Vegan Caesar Salad Cups

Yield: 4 servings | **Prep time:** 15 minutes
Ingredients:
- 8 large romaine lettuce leaves
- 1/2 cup cashews, soaked and drained
- 1/4 cup water
- 2 tablespoons lemon juice
- 1 tablespoon capers
- 1 garlic clove
- Salt and pepper to taste

Directions:
1. Blend cashews, water, lemon juice, capers, and garlic until smooth for the dressing. Season with salt and pepper.
2. Spoon dressing into the center of each romaine leaf.
3. Serve as individual cups.

Nutritional Information: 120 calories, 4g protein, 8g carbohydrates, 9g fat, 2g fiber, 0mg cholesterol, 150mg sodium, 200mg potassium.

Matcha Energy Balls

Yield: 4 servings (about 12 balls) | **Prep time:** 15 minutes | **Cook time:** 0 minutes
Ingredients:
- 1 cup dates, pitted
- 1/2 cup almonds
- 1/2 cup cashews
- 2 tablespoons matcha powder
- 1 tablespoon coconut oil

Directions:
1. Blend dates, almonds, cashews, matcha powder, and coconut oil in a food processor until sticky.
2. Roll mixture into small balls.
3. Refrigerate for 1 hour before serving.

Nutritional Information: 220 calories, 5g protein, 24g carbohydrates, 13g fat, 4g fiber, 0mg cholesterol, 5mg sodium, 300mg potassium.

Avocado Lime Popsicles

Yield: 4 servings | **Prep time:** 10 minutes |
Cook time: 0 minutes (Freeze time: 4 hours)
Ingredients:
- 2 ripe avocados
- 1/2 cup coconut milk
- 1/4 cup lime juice
- 1/3 cup maple syrup
- Pinch of salt

Directions:
1. Blend avocados, coconut milk, lime juice, maple syrup, and a pinch of salt until smooth.
2. Pour the mixture into popsicle molds and freeze for at least 4 hours or until set.
3. To serve, run warm water over the molds to release the popsicles.

Nutritional Information: 250 calories, 2g protein, 24g carbohydrates, 17g fat, 6g fiber, 0mg cholesterol, 50mg sodium, 400mg potassium.

Vegan Garlic Knots

Yield: 4 servings (12 knots) | **Prep time:** 20 minutes | **Cook time:** 15 minutes
Ingredients:
- 1 pound pizza dough
- 1/4 cup olive oil
- 3 cloves garlic, minced
- 1 tablespoon dried parsley
- Salt to taste

Directions:
1. Preheat oven to 400°F (200°C). Roll out pizza dough and cut into strips. Tie each strip into a knot and place it on a baking sheet.
2. Mix olive oil, garlic, parsley, and salt. Brush over knots.
3. Bake for 15 minutes, until golden brown.
4. Serve warm.

Nutritional Information: 300 calories, 8g protein, 38g carbohydrates, 14g fat, 2g fiber, 0mg cholesterol, 580mg sodium, 100mg potassium.

Vegan Buffalo Cauliflower Wings

Yield: 4 servings | **Prep time:** 15 minutes | **Cook time:** 20 minutes
Ingredients:
- 1 head cauliflower, cut into florets
- 1 cup flour
- 1 cup water
- 1/2 teaspoon garlic powder
- 1 cup vegan buffalo sauce
- 2 tablespoons olive oil

Directions:
1. Preheat oven to 450°F (230°C). Mix flour, water, and garlic powder in a bowl to create a batter.
2. Dip cauliflower florets into the batter, then place on a greased baking sheet.
3. Bake for 20 minutes, flipping halfway through. Toss baked florets with buffalo sauce and olive oil.
4. Serve hot.

Nutritional Information: 260 calories, 5g protein, 35g carbohydrates, 12g fat, 4g fiber, 0mg cholesterol, 1500mg sodium, 300mg potassium.

Marinated Artichoke Hearts Skewers

Yield: 4 servings | **Prep time:** 15 minutes (plus marinating time) | **Cook time:** 0 minutes
Ingredients:
- 1 jar (12 oz) marinated artichoke hearts, drained
- 1/2 cup cherry tomatoes
- 1/4 cup olives
- 1/4 cup basil leaves
- Wooden skewers

Directions:
1. Thread artichoke hearts, cherry tomatoes, olives, and basil leaves onto skewers.
2. Let marinate in the fridge for at least 1 hour before serving.
3. Serve cold or at room temperature.

Nutritional Information: 100 calories, 2g protein, 10g carbohydrates, 5g fat, 5g fiber, 0mg cholesterol, 700mg sodium, 200mg potassium.

Crispy Baked Avocado Fries

Yield: 4 servings | **Prep time:** 15 minutes | **Cook time:** 20 minutes
Ingredients:
- 2 ripe avocados sliced into wedges
- 1/2 cup flour
- 2 flax eggs (2 tablespoons ground flaxseed mixed with 6 tablespoons water; let sit for 5 minutes)
- 1 cup breadcrumbs
- Salt and pepper to taste

Directions:
1. Preheat oven to 425°F (220°C). Line a baking sheet with parchment paper.
2. Dredge avocado slices in flour, dip in flax eggs, then coat with breadcrumbs. Season with salt and pepper.
3. Arrange on the baking sheet and bake for 20 minutes, flipping halfway through, until golden and crispy.
4. Serve immediately.

Nutritional Information: 330 calories, 7g protein, 37g carbohydrates, 18g fat, 9g fiber, 0mg cholesterol, 200mg sodium, 650mg potassium.

Chapter 9: Flavorful Desserts

Vegan Blueberry Muffins

Yield: 6 servings | **Prep time:** 10 minutes | **Cook time:** 25 minutes

Ingredients:
- 1 1/2 cups all-purpose flour
- 3/4 cup sugar
- 1/2 teaspoon salt
- 2 teaspoons baking powder
- 1/3 cup vegetable oil
- 1 cup plant-based milk
- 1 teaspoon vanilla extract
- 1 cup fresh blueberries

Directions:
1. Preheat oven to 400°F (200°C) and line a muffin tin with paper liners.
2. In a large bowl, mix together flour, sugar, salt, and baking powder. In another bowl, whisk together oil, milk, and vanilla. Combine wet and dry ingredients, then gently fold in blueberries.
3. Fill muffin cups and bake for 25 minutes or until a toothpick comes out clean.

Nutritional Information: 280 calories, 4g protein, 45g carbohydrates, 10g fat, 2g fiber, 0mg cholesterol, 300mg sodium, 100mg potassium.

Almond Flour Chocolate Chip Cookies

Yield: 6 servings | **Prep time:** 10 minutes | **Cook time:** 12 minutes

Ingredients:
- 2 cups almond flour
- 1/4 cup coconut oil, melted
- 1/4 cup maple syrup
- 1 teaspoon vanilla extract
- 1/2 teaspoon baking soda
- 1/4 teaspoon salt
- 1/2 cup dark chocolate chips

Directions:
1. Preheat oven to 350°F (175°C) and line a baking sheet with parchment paper.
2. In a bowl, combine almond flour, baking soda, and salt. Add melted coconut oil, maple syrup, and vanilla extract. Mix until well combined. Fold in chocolate chips.
3. Drop spoonful of dough onto the prepared baking sheet and flatten slightly.
4. Bake for 10-12 minutes, until edges are golden. Let cool on the sheet before transferring to a wire rack.

Nutritional Information: 320 calories, 8g protein, 24g carbohydrates, 24g fat, 4g fiber, 0mg cholesterol, 150mg sodium, 300mg potassium.

Creamy Coconut Millet Porridge

Yield: 4 servings | **Prep time:** 5 minutes |
Cook time: 25 minutes
Ingredients:

- 1 cup millet
- 1 can (14 oz) coconut milk
- 2 cups water
- 2 tablespoons maple syrup
- 1/2 teaspoon vanilla extract
- Pinch of salt
- Fresh fruit and nuts for topping

Directions:

1. Rinse millet thoroughly. In a pot, combine millet, coconut milk, water, and a pinch of salt. Bring to a boil, then reduce heat and simmer covered for 20-25 minutes, until millet is tender and liquid is absorbed.
2. Stir in maple syrup and vanilla extract. Serve warm, topped with fresh fruit and nuts of your choice.

Nutritional Information: 300 calories, 6g protein, 45g carbohydrates, 12g fat, 4g fiber, 0mg cholesterol, 50mg sodium, 200mg potassium.

Vegan Chocolate Avocado Mousse

Yield: 4 servings | **Prep time:** 10 minutes |
Cook time: 0 minutes
Ingredients:

- 2 ripe avocados
- 1/4 cup cocoa powder
- 1/4 cup maple syrup
- 1/2 teaspoon vanilla extract
- Pinch of salt
- Plant-based milk (as needed)

Directions:

1. In a food processor, blend avocados, cocoa powder, maple syrup, vanilla extract, and salt until smooth, adding milk as needed to achieve the desired consistency.
2. Chill before serving, garnished with fruit or nuts if desired.

Nutritional Information: 250 calories, 3g protein, 30g carbohydrates, 15g fat, 7g fiber, 0mg cholesterol, 10mg sodium, 500mg potassium.

Banana Ice Cream

Yield: 2 servings | **Prep time:** 5 minutes (plus freezing time) | **Cook time:** 0 minutes
Ingredients:

- 2 bananas, sliced and frozen

Directions:

1. In a food processor, blend the frozen banana slices until smooth.
2. Serve immediately for a soft-serve texture or freeze for a firmer consistency.

Nutritional Information: 100 calories, 1g protein, 27g carbohydrates, 0g fat, 3g fiber, 0mg cholesterol, 0mg sodium, 400mg potassium.

Peanut Butter Stuffed Dates

Yield: 6 servings | **Prep time:** 10 minutes |
Cook time: 0 minutes
Ingredients:

- 12 Medjool dates, pitted
- 1/2 cup natural peanut butter
- Optional toppings: melted dark chocolate, sea salt

Directions:

1. Slice dates halfway open and fill each with peanut butter.
2. If desired, drizzle with melted dark chocolate and sprinkle with sea salt. Chill before serving.

Nutritional Information: 150 calories, 4g protein, 25g carbohydrates, 5g fat, 3g fiber, 0mg cholesterol, 50mg sodium, 300mg potassium.

Frozen Chocolate Banana Bites

Yield: 4 servings | **Prep time:** 15 minutes |
Cook time: 0 minutes (plus freezing time)
Ingredients:

- 2 bananas
- 1/2 cup melted dark chocolate
- 1/4 cup crushed nuts or desiccated coconut

Directions:

1. Slice bananas and dip each slice into melted chocolate.
2. Roll in crushed nuts or coconut, place on a parchment-lined tray, and freeze.

Nutritional Information: 180 calories, 3g protein, 27g carbohydrates, 8g fat, 4g fiber, 0mg cholesterol, 0mg sodium, 300mg potassium.

Baked Apple with Cinnamon and Nutmeg

Yield: 2 servings | **Prep time:** 5 minutes |
Cook time: 30 minutes
Ingredients:

- 2 apples, cored
- 2 tablespoons raisins
- 1 teaspoon cinnamon
- 1/4 teaspoon nutmeg
- 1/4 cup water

Directions:

1. Preheat oven to 350°F (175°C). Place apples in a baking dish.
2. Mix raisins, cinnamon, and nutmeg, and fill apples with this mixture. Add water to the dish.
3. Bake for 30 minutes or until apples are tender.

Nutritional Information: 120 calories, 0g protein, 31g carbohydrates, 0g fat, 5g fiber, 0mg cholesterol, 0mg sodium, 200mg potassium.

Coconut Chia Pudding

Yield: 4 servings | **Prep time:** 5 minutes (plus chilling time) | **Cook time:** 0 minutes

Ingredients:
- 1 can (14 oz) coconut milk
- 1/4 cup chia seeds
- 2 tablespoons maple syrup
- 1/2 teaspoon vanilla extract
- Fresh berries for topping

Directions:
1. Whisk together coconut milk, chia seeds, maple syrup, and vanilla in a bowl.
2. Cover and refrigerate for at least 4 hours, or overnight, until thickened.
3. Stir well before serving. Top with fresh berries.

Nutritional Information: 250 calories, 4g protein, 18g carbohydrates, 18g fat, 6g fiber, 0mg cholesterol, 15mg sodium, 200mg potassium.

Vegan Raspberry Cheesecake

Yield: 6 servings | **Prep time:** 20 minutes | **Cook time:** 0 minutes (plus chilling time)

Ingredients:
- 1 1/2 cups raw cashews, soaked overnight
- 1 cup dates, pitted
- 1/2 cup almonds
- 1 can (14 oz) coconut cream
- 1/2 cup raspberries
- 1/4 cup maple syrup
- 1 teaspoon vanilla extract
- Pinch of salt

Directions:
1. Process dates and almonds until the mixture sticks together. Press into the bottom of a springform pan to form the crust.
2. Blend cashews, coconut cream, raspberries, maple syrup, vanilla, and salt until smooth. Pour over the crust.
3. Freeze for at least 4 hours. Thaw for 30 minutes before serving. Garnish with fresh raspberries.

Nutritional Information: 450 calories, 10g protein, 40g carbohydrates, 30g fat, 5g fiber, 0mg cholesterol, 20mg sodium, 400mg potassium.

Carrot Cake with Cashew Frosting

Yield: 6 servings | **Prep time:** 20 minutes | **Cook time:** 30 minutes

Ingredients:
- 2 cups grated carrots
- 1 1/2 cups all-purpose flour
- 1 cup sugar
- 1/2 cup vegetable oil
- 2 teaspoons baking powder
- 1 teaspoon cinnamon
- 1/2 teaspoon nutmeg

- **For the frosting:**
  - 1 cup raw cashews, soaked overnight
  - 1/4 cup maple syrup
  - 1/4 cup coconut oil, melted
  - 1 teaspoon vanilla extract
  - Pinch of salt

Directions:
1. Preheat oven to 350°F (175°C). Grease and flour a cake pan.
2. Mix flour, sugar, baking powder, cinnamon, and nutmeg. Stir in grated carrots and oil until well combined.
3. Pour batter into the pan. Bake for 30 minutes until a toothpick comes out clean.
4. For the frosting, blend cashews, maple syrup, coconut oil, vanilla, and salt until smooth. Spread over the cooled cake.

Nutritional Information: 580 calories, 8g protein, 70g carbohydrates, 32g fat, 3g fiber, 0mg cholesterol, 150mg sodium, 400mg potassium.

Chocolate-Dipped Strawberry Pops

Yield: 4 servings | **Prep time:** 15 minutes | **Cook time:** 0 minutes (plus chilling time)

Ingredients:
- 16 large strawberries
- 8 oz dark chocolate, chopped
- 1 tablespoon coconut oil
- Popsicle sticks

Directions:
1. Insert popsicle sticks into the strawberries.
2. Melt dark chocolate and coconut oil together until smooth.
3. Dip strawberries in chocolate, let excess drip off, and place on a parchment-lined tray.
4. Chill until the chocolate sets.

Nutritional Information: 300 calories, 4g protein, 35g carbohydrates, 18g fat, 5g fiber, 0mg cholesterol, 20mg sodium, 400mg potassium.

Lemon Poppy Seed Cake

Yield: 6 servings | **Prep time:** 15 minutes | **Cook time:** 30 minutes

Ingredients:
- 1 3/4 cups all-purpose flour
- 1 cup sugar
- 1/4 cup poppy seeds
- 1 teaspoon baking powder
- 1/2 teaspoon baking soda
- 1/2 cup vegetable oil
- 1 cup plant-based yogurt
- 1/4 cup lemon juice
- Zest of 1 lemon
- 1 teaspoon vanilla extract

Directions:
1. Preheat oven to 350°F (175°C). Grease and flour a loaf pan.
2. In a large bowl, combine flour, sugar, poppy seeds, baking powder, and baking soda.

3. In another bowl, whisk together oil, yogurt, lemon juice, lemon zest, and vanilla. Add to dry ingredients, stirring just until moistened.
4. Pour batter into the prepared pan. Bake for 30 minutes or until a toothpick comes out clean. Let cool before slicing.

Nutritional Information: 380 calories, 6g protein, 52g carbohydrates, 18g fat, 2g fiber, 0mg cholesterol, 200mg sodium, 100mg potassium.

Maple Pecan Bars

Yield: 6 servings | **Prep time:** 15 minutes | **Cook time:** 25 minutes

Ingredients:
- 1 cup almond flour
- 1/4 cup coconut oil, melted
- 2 tablespoons maple syrup (for crust)
- 1/2 cup maple syrup (for filling)
- 1 cup pecans, chopped
- 2 tablespoons almond milk
- 1 teaspoon vanilla extract
- Pinch of salt

Directions:
1. Preheat oven to 350°F (175°C). Mix almond flour, coconut oil, and 2 tablespoons maple syrup; press into a lined baking dish. Bake for 10 minutes.
2. Combine 1/2 cup maple syrup, almond milk, vanilla, and salt; bring to a simmer. Add pecans.
3. Pour filling over the crust. Bake for 15 minutes. Cool before slicing.

Nutritional Information: 350 calories, 6g protein, 24g carbohydrates, 28g fat, 4g fiber, 0mg cholesterol, 10mg sodium, 200mg potassium.

Vegan Pumpkin Pie

Yield: 6 servings | **Prep time:** 20 minutes | **Cook time:** 1 hour

Ingredients:
- 1 (15 oz) can of pumpkin puree
- 3/4 cup coconut milk
- 1/2 cup brown sugar
- 1/4 cup cornstarch
- 1 teaspoon vanilla extract
- 2 teaspoons pumpkin pie spice
- 1 vegan pie crust

Directions:
1. Preheat oven to 350°F (175°C).
2. Whisk together pumpkin puree, coconut milk, brown sugar, cornstarch, vanilla, and pumpkin pie spice until smooth.
3. Pour into pie crust and bake for 1 hour. Chill before serving.

Nutritional Information: 280 calories, 3g protein, 40g carbohydrates, 12g fat, 2g fiber, 0mg cholesterol, 150mg sodium, 250mg potassium.

Vegan Key Lime Pie

Yield: 6 servings | **Prep time:** 20 minutes | **Cook time:** 0 minutes (plus chilling time)

Ingredients:
- 1 1/2 cups raw cashews, soaked
- 1/2 cup key lime juice
- 1/4 cup coconut oil, melted
- 1/3 cup maple syrup
- 1 teaspoon vanilla extract
- 1 vegan graham cracker crust

Directions:
1. Blend cashews, lime juice, coconut oil, maple syrup, and vanilla until smooth.
2. Pour into crust. Chill for at least 4 hours.
3. Garnish with lime slices before serving.

Nutritional Information: 450 calories, 8g protein, 40g carbohydrates, 30g fat, 2g fiber, 0mg cholesterol, 200mg sodium, 300mg potassium.

Vegan Lemon Tart

Yield: 6 servings | **Prep time:** 20 minutes | **Cook time:** 0 minutes (plus chilling time)

Ingredients:
- 1 1/2 cups almond flour
- 1/4 cup coconut oil, melted (for crust)
- 2 tablespoons maple syrup (for crust)
- 1 cup cashews, soaked
- 1/2 cup lemon juice
- 1/4 cup maple syrup (for filling)
- 1/4 cup coconut cream
- Zest of 1 lemon

Directions:
1. Mix almond flour, coconut oil, and 2 tablespoons maple syrup; press into tart pan. Chill.
2. Blend cashews, lemon juice, 1/4 cup maple syrup, coconut cream, and zest until creamy.
3. Fill the crust with lemon mixture. Chill for 4 hours.

Nutritional Information: 420 calories, 10g protein, 36g carbohydrates, 28g fat, 4g fiber, 0mg cholesterol, 10mg sodium, 300mg potassium.

Spiced Pear Crumble

Yield: 6 servings | **Prep time:** 15 minutes | **Cook time:** 30 minutes

Ingredients:
- 4 pears, sliced
- 1/2 cup rolled oats
- 1/2 cup almond flour
- 1/4 cup coconut oil, melted
- 1/4 cup maple syrup
- 1 teaspoon cinnamon
- 1/2 teaspoon nutmeg

Directions:
1. Preheat oven to 375°F (190°C). Toss pears with cinnamon and nutmeg; place in a baking dish.
2. Mix oats, almond flour, coconut oil, and maple syrup; crumble over pears.
3. Bake for 30 minutes. Serve warm.

Nutritional Information: 300 calories, 4g protein, 45g carbohydrates, 14g fat, 6g fiber, 0mg cholesterol, 5mg sodium, 200mg potassium.

Coconut Rice Pudding with Mango

Yield: 4 servings | **Prep time:** 5 minutes | **Cook time:** 25 minutes

Ingredients:
- 1 cup jasmine rice
- 1 can (14 oz) coconut milk
- 1/4 cup sugar
- 1 ripe mango, diced
- Pinch of salt

Directions:
1. Combine rice, coconut milk, sugar, and salt in a pot. Simmer on low heat until rice is tender, about 25 minutes, stirring occasionally.
2. Serve warm or cold, topped with fresh mango.

Nutritional Information: 300 calories, 4g protein, 45g carbohydrates, 12g fat, 2g fiber, 0mg cholesterol, 50mg sodium, 200mg potassium.

Matcha Green Tea Cupcakes

Yield: 6 servings | **Prep time:** 15 minutes | **Cook time:** 20 minutes

Ingredients:
- 1 cup all-purpose flour
- 1/2 cup sugar
- 1 tablespoon matcha green tea powder
- 1 teaspoon baking powder
- 1/2 cup plant-based milk
- 1/4 cup vegetable oil
- 1 teaspoon vanilla extract

Directions:
1. Preheat oven to 350°F (175°C) and line a muffin tin with cupcake liners.
2. In a bowl, whisk together flour, sugar, matcha powder, and baking powder.
3. Stir in milk, oil, and vanilla until just combined. Fill cupcake liners.
4. Bake for 20 minutes. Cool before frosting.

Nutritional Information: 220 calories, 3g protein, 34g carbohydrates, 8g fat, 1g fiber, 0mg cholesterol, 150mg sodium, 50mg potassium.

Gingerbread Cookies with Royal Icing

Yield: 6 servings | **Prep time:** 20 minutes | **Cook time:** 10 minutes

Ingredients:
- 2 cups all-purpose flour
- 1 teaspoon ground ginger
- 1 teaspoon cinnamon
- 1/2 teaspoon baking soda
- 1/4 teaspoon nutmeg
- 1/2 cup vegan butter, softened
- 3/4 cup brown sugar
- 1/4 cup molasses
- 2 tablespoons plant-based milk
- **For icing:**
  - 1 cup powdered sugar
  - 2 tablespoons plant-based milk
  - 1/2 teaspoon vanilla extract

Directions:
1. Mix flour, ginger, cinnamon, baking soda, and nutmeg.
2. Cream butter and sugar, then add molasses and milk. Combine with dry ingredients.
3. Chill dough, roll out, cut into shapes, and bake at 350°F (175°C) for 8-10 minutes.
4. Mix icing ingredients, decorate cookies after cooling.

Nutritional Information: 350 calories, 3g protein, 70g carbohydrates, 8g fat, 1g fiber, 0mg cholesterol, 150mg sodium, 100mg potassium.

Salted Caramel Brownies

Yield: 6 servings | **Prep time:** 15 minutes | **Cook time:** 25 minutes

Ingredients:
- 3/4 cup all-purpose flour
- 1/2 cup cocoa powder
- 1 cup sugar
- 1/2 cup vegan butter, melted
- 2 flax eggs (2 tablespoons flaxseed meal + 5 tablespoons water)
- 1 teaspoon vanilla extract
- 1/4 teaspoon sea salt
- Vegan caramel sauce for drizzling

Directions:
1. Preheat oven to 350°F (175°C). Line an 8x8 inch baking dish with parchment.
2. Mix flour, cocoa, and salt. Add sugar, butter, flax eggs, and vanilla. Combine until smooth.
3. Pour into prepared dish. Bake for 25 minutes. Cool, drizzle with caramel and a pinch of sea salt.

Nutritional Information: 350 calories, 4g protein, 52g carbohydrates, 16g fat, 3g fiber, 0mg cholesterol, 200mg sodium, 150mg potassium.

Vegan Chocolate Lava Cake

Yield: 4 servings | **Prep time:** 10 minutes |
Cook time: 15 minutes
Ingredients:
- 1/2 cup all-purpose flour
- 1/3 cup cocoa powder
- 1/4 cup sugar
- 3/4 cup almond milk
- 1/4 cup coconut oil, melted
- 1 teaspoon vanilla extract
- 1/4 teaspoon salt
- 4 squares of dark chocolate

Directions:
1. Preheat oven to 375°F (190°C). Grease 4 ramekins.
2. Mix flour, cocoa, sugar, and salt. Stir in almond milk, coconut oil, and vanilla until smooth.
3. Pour batter into ramekins. Press a chocolate square into the center of each.
4. Bake for 12-15 minutes. Edges should be firm, but the center should be slightly soft.
5. Let cool for 1 minute before serving.

Nutritional Information: 320 calories, 4g protein, 40g carbohydrates, 18g fat, 4g fiber, 0mg cholesterol, 150mg sodium, 250mg potassium.

Cherry Almond Galette

Yield: 6 servings | **Prep time:** 20 minutes |
Cook time: 25 minutes
Ingredients:
- 1 vegan pie crust
- 2 cups cherries, pitted
- 1/4 cup sugar
- 1 tablespoon cornstarch
- 1/2 teaspoon almond extract
- Sliced almonds for garnish

Directions:
1. Preheat oven to 375°F (190°C). Roll out the pie crust on a baking sheet.
2. Toss cherries with sugar, cornstarch, and almond extract. Arrange on the crust, leaving a border. Fold edges over-filling.
3. Bake until golden, about 25 minutes. Garnish with almonds.

Nutritional Information: 270 calories, 3g protein, 40g carbohydrates, 12g fat, 3g fiber, 0mg cholesterol, 150mg sodium, 150mg potassium.

Vegan Tiramisu

Yield: 6 servings | **Prep time:** 30 minutes |
Cook time: 0 minutes (plus chilling time)
Ingredients:
- 1 1/2 cups cashews, soaked
- 1 cup brewed coffee, cooled
- 1/2 cup maple syrup
- 1 teaspoon vanilla extract
- Vegan ladyfingers or sponge cake
- Cocoa powder for dusting

Directions:
1. Blend cashews, half the coffee, maple syrup, and vanilla until creamy.
2. Dip ladyfingers in the remaining coffee. Layer in a dish with cashew cream.
3. Chill for 4 hours. Dust with cocoa before serving.

Nutritional Information: 400 calories, 10g protein, 50g carbohydrates, 20g fat, 3g fiber, 0mg cholesterol, 70mg sodium, 300mg potassium.

Cinnamon Sugar Pumpkin Donuts

Yield: 6 servings | **Prep time:** 15 minutes |
Cook time: 15 minutes
Ingredients:
- 1 1/2 cups all-purpose flour
- 1/2 cup sugar
- 1/4 cup brown sugar
- 1 teaspoon baking powder
- 1/2 teaspoon salt
- 1 teaspoon cinnamon
- 1/2 teaspoon nutmeg
- 1/2 cup pumpkin puree
- 1/4 cup plant-based milk
- 1/4 cup vegetable oil
- 1 teaspoon vanilla extract
- **For topping:**
  - 1/4 cup sugar
  - 1 tablespoon cinnamon

Directions:
1. Mix dry ingredients, then add pumpkin, milk, oil, and vanilla. Stir until just combined.
2. Pipe into a donut pan and bake at 350°F (175°C) for 15 minutes.
3. Mix topping sugar and cinnamon. Roll warm donuts in the mixture.

Nutritional Information: 320 calories, 4g protein, 60g carbohydrates, 9g fat, 2g fiber, 0mg cholesterol, 200mg sodium, 100mg potassium.

Chocolate Mint Avocado Pudding

Yield: 4 servings | **Prep time:** 10 minutes | **Cook time:** 0 minutes

Ingredients:
- 2 ripe avocados
- 1/4 cup cocoa powder
- 1/4 cup maple syrup
- 1/2 teaspoon mint extract
- Pinch of salt

Directions:
1. Blend all ingredients until smooth.
2. Chill for at least 1 hour before serving.

Nutritional Information: 250 calories, 3g protein, 30g carbohydrates, 15g fat, 7g fiber, 0mg cholesterol, 10mg sodium, 500mg potassium.

Blackberry Sorbet

Yield: 4 servings | **Prep time:** 10 minutes | **Cook time:** 0 minutes (plus freezing time)

Ingredients:
- 4 cups blackberries, fresh or frozen
- 1/2 cup sugar
- 1/2 cup water
- 1 tablespoon lemon juice

Directions:
1. In a saucepan, dissolve sugar in water over medium heat. Cool the syrup.
2. Blend blackberries, lemon juice, and cooled syrup until smooth.
3. Strain to remove seeds, then freeze in an ice cream maker or a shallow pan, stirring occasionally.
4. Serve frozen.

Nutritional Information: 180 calories, 1g protein, 46g carbohydrates, 1g fat, 7g fiber, 0mg cholesterol, 5mg sodium, 200mg potassium.

Vegan S'mores Bars

Yield: 6 servings | **Prep time:** 15 minutes | **Cook time:** 10 minutes

Ingredients:
- 1 1/2 cups graham cracker crumbs
- 1/2 cup vegan butter, melted
- 1 cup dark chocolate chips
- 1 cup marshmallows (vegan)
- 1/2 cup almond milk

Directions:
1. Mix graham cracker crumbs with melted butter and press into the bottom of a baking dish.
2. Melt chocolate with almond milk and pour over the crust. Top with marshmallows.
3. Broil for a few minutes until the marshmallows are golden. Cool before cutting.

Nutritional Information: 400 calories, 5g protein, 52g carbohydrates, 20g fat, 2g fiber, 0mg cholesterol, 250mg sodium, 150mg potassium.

Raspberry Coconut Macaroons

Yield: 6 servings | **Prep time:** 15 minutes | **Cook time:** 20 minutes

Ingredients:
- 2 cups shredded coconut
- 1/2 cup almond flour
- 3/4 cup raspberries
- 1/4 cup maple syrup
- 1 teaspoon vanilla extract
- Pinch of salt

Directions:
1. Preheat oven to 350°F (175°C). Line a baking sheet with parchment.
2. Mash raspberries. Mix with coconut, almond flour, maple syrup, vanilla, and salt.
3. Scoop mixture onto baking sheet. Bake for 18-20 minutes.
4. Cool before serving.

Nutritional Information: 280 calories, 3g protein, 24g carbohydrates, 20g fat, 5g fiber, 0mg cholesterol, 50mg sodium, 200mg potassium.

Apple Pie Smoothie Bowl

Yield: 2 servings | **Prep time:** 10 minutes | **Cook time:** 0 minutes

Ingredients:
- 2 apples, cored and chopped
- 1 banana, frozen
- 1/2 cup rolled oats
- 1 teaspoon cinnamon
- 1/4 teaspoon nutmeg
- 1 cup almond milk
- Toppings: sliced almonds, fresh apple slices, a drizzle of maple syrup

Directions:
1. Blend apples, banana, oats, cinnamon, nutmeg, and almond milk until smooth.
2. Pour into bowls. Top with almonds, apple slices, and maple syrup.

Nutritional Information: 250 calories, 5g protein, 53g carbohydrates, 3g fat, 8g fiber, 0mg cholesterol, 80mg sodium, 400mg potassium.

Chocolate Hazelnut Spread

Yield: 4 servings | **Prep time:** 15 minutes | **Cook time:** 0 minutes

Ingredients:
- 1 cup hazelnuts, roasted and skinned
- 1/4 cup cocoa powder
- 1/2 cup powdered sugar
- 2 tablespoons coconut oil, melted
- 1 teaspoon vanilla extract
- Pinch of salt

Directions:
1. Blend hazelnuts in a food processor until butter forms.
2. Add cocoa powder, powdered sugar, coconut oil, vanilla, and salt. Blend until smooth.
3. Store in an airtight container.

Nutritional Information: 350 calories, 6g protein, 34g carbohydrates, 24g fat, 4g fiber, 0mg cholesterol, 10mg sodium, 200mg potassium.

Raw Cashew Dreamcake

Yield: 6 servings | **Prep time:** 20 minutes | **Cook time:** 0 minutes (plus soaking and freezing time)

Ingredients:
- 2 cups raw cashews, soaked overnight
- 1/2 cup coconut oil, melted
- 1/2 cup maple syrup
- Juice of 1 lemon
- 1 teaspoon vanilla extract
- 1 cup mixed berries for topping
- **For crust:**
  - 1 cup almonds
  - 1 cup dates, pitted

Directions:
1. For the crust, process almonds and dates until mixture sticks together. Press into bottom of a springform pan.
2. Blend cashews, coconut oil, maple syrup, lemon juice, and vanilla until smooth. Pour over the crust.
3. Freeze for at least 4 hours. Top with berries before serving.

Nutritional Information: 600 calories, 15g protein, 50g carbohydrates, 42g fat, 6g fiber, 0mg cholesterol, 10mg sodium, 400mg potassium.

Peach Cobbler with Biscuit Topping

Yield: 6 servings | **Prep time:** 15 minutes | **Cook time:** 35 minutes

Ingredients:
- 4 cups peaches, sliced
- 1/2 cup sugar
- 1 cup all-purpose flour
- 1 1/2 teaspoons baking powder
- 1/2 cup plant-based milk
- 1/4 cup vegan butter, melted
- Pinch of salt

Directions:
1. Preheat oven to 375°F (190°C). Toss peaches with half the sugar. Place in a baking dish.
2. Mix flour, remaining sugar, baking powder, and salt. Stir in milk and butter to form a dough.
3. Drop dough over peaches. Bake until golden, about 35 minutes.

Nutritional Information: 280 calories, 4g protein, 52g carbohydrates, 8g fat, 2g fiber, 0mg cholesterol, 150mg sodium, 200mg potassium.

Pear and Fig Tart

Yield: 6 servings | **Prep time:** 20 minutes | **Cook time:** 30 minutes

Ingredients:
- 1 vegan pie crust
- 4 pears, thinly sliced
- 8 figs, halved
- 1/4 cup sugar
- 1/2 teaspoon cinnamon
- 2 tablespoons almond milk

Directions:
1. Preheat oven to 375°F (190°C). Roll out pie crust into a tart pan.
2. Arrange pear slices and fig halves on the crust. Sprinkle with sugar and cinnamon.
3. Brush edges with almond milk. Bake for 30 minutes.
4. Cool before serving.

Nutritional Information: 300 calories, 4g protein, 50g carbohydrates, 10g fat, 5g fiber, 0mg cholesterol, 100mg sodium, 300mg potassium.

Vegan Chocolate Pecan Pie

Yield: 6 servings | **Prep time:** 20 minutes | **Cook time:** 40 minutes

Ingredients:
- 1 vegan pie crust
- 1 cup pecans, halved
- 3/4 cup dark chocolate chips
- 3/4 cup maple syrup
- 1/2 cup almond milk
- 1/4 cup cornstarch
- 1 teaspoon vanilla extract
- Pinch of salt

Directions:
1. Preheat oven to 350°F (175°C). Arrange pecans and chocolate chips in pie crust.
2. Whisk together maple syrup, almond milk, cornstarch, vanilla, and salt. Pour over pecans.
3. Bake for 40 minutes. Cool before serving.

Nutritional Information: 450 calories, 6g protein, 58g carbohydrates, 24g fat, 5g fiber, 0mg cholesterol, 150mg sodium, 300mg potassium.

Vegan Snickerdoodles

Yield: 6 servings | **Prep time:** 10 minutes |
Cook time: 10 minutes
Ingredients:
- 1 3/4 cups all-purpose flour
- 1 teaspoon baking powder
- 1/2 cup vegan butter, softened
- 3/4 cup sugar
- 1/4 cup almond milk
- 1 teaspoon vanilla extract
- 2 tablespoons sugar (for coating)
- 2 teaspoons ground cinnamon (for coating)

Directions:
1. Preheat oven to 350°F (175°C). Line a baking sheet with parchment paper.
2. In a bowl, mix flour and baking powder. In another bowl, cream together vegan butter and 3/4 cup sugar until smooth. Stir in almond milk and vanilla. Blend in the flour mixture until dough forms.
3. Mix 2 tablespoons sugar and ground cinnamon in a small bowl. Shape dough into 1 inch balls and roll in the cinnamon-sugar mixture. Place on the prepared baking sheet.
4. Bake for 10 to 12 minutes. Let cool on baking sheet for a few minutes before transferring to a wire rack to cool completely.

Nutritional Information: 320 calories, 3g protein, 49g carbohydrates, 12g fat, 1g fiber, 0mg cholesterol, 160mg sodium, 50mg potassium.

Dark Chocolate Orange Truffles

Yield: 4 servings | **Prep time:** 15 minutes |
Cook time: 0 minutes (plus chilling)
Ingredients:
- 8 oz dark chocolate, finely chopped
- 1/2 cup coconut cream
- 1 teaspoon orange zest
- 1 tablespoon orange liqueur (optional)
- Cocoa powder for dusting

Directions:
1. Heat coconut cream until hot but not boiling. Pour over the chocolate in a bowl. Let sit for a minute, then stir until smooth.
2. Mix in orange zest and liqueur if using. Chill until firm.
3. Scoop and roll into balls, dust with cocoa powder.

Nutritional Information: 320 calories, 4g protein, 25g carbohydrates, 24g fat, 5g fiber, 0mg cholesterol, 10mg sodium, 300mg potassium.

Sweet Potato Brownies

Yield: 6 servings | **Prep time:** 15 minutes |
Cook time: 25 minutes
Ingredients:
- 1 cup mashed sweet potato
- 1/2 cup almond butter

- 1/4 cup cocoa powder
- 1/4 cup maple syrup
- 1/2 teaspoon vanilla extract
- 1/2 teaspoon baking powder
- Pinch of salt

Directions:
1. Preheat oven to 350°F (175°C). Line an 8x8-inch baking dish with parchment paper.
2. Mix all ingredients until well combined. Spread in prepared dish.
3. Bake for 25 minutes. Cool before slicing.

Nutritional Information: 220 calories, 5g protein, 24g carbohydrates, 12g fat, 4g fiber, 0mg cholesterol, 100mg sodium, 300mg potassium.

Vegan Oatmeal Raisin Cookies

Yield: 6 servings | **Prep time:** 10 minutes |
Cook time: 12 minutes
Ingredients:
- 1 cup rolled oats
- 1/2 cup almond flour
- 1/2 cup raisins
- 1/4 cup coconut oil, melted
- 1/4 cup maple syrup
- 1 teaspoon cinnamon
- 1/2 teaspoon baking soda
- Pinch of salt

Directions:
1. Preheat oven to 350°F (175°C). Line a baking sheet with parchment.
2. Mix all ingredients. Drop spoonfuls onto a baking sheet.
3. Bake for 12 minutes. Cool on a wire rack.

Nutritional Information: 250 calories, 4g protein, 35g carbohydrates, 12g fat, 3g fiber, 0mg cholesterol, 150mg sodium, 200mg potassium.

Lemon Coconut Energy Bites

Yield: 4 servings | **Prep time:** 10 minutes |
Cook time: 0 minutes
Ingredients:
- 1 cup dates, pitted
- 1/2 cup almonds
- 1/2 cup shredded coconut
- 1 tablespoon lemon zest
- 1 tablespoon lemon juice

Directions:
1. Process dates and almonds in a food processor until finely chopped.
2. Add coconut, lemon zest, and juice; process until the mixture sticks together.
3. Roll into balls and chill.

Nutritional Information: 180 calories, 3g protein, 27g carbohydrates, 9g fat, 4g fiber, 0mg cholesterol, 5mg sodium, 200mg potassium.

Chapter 10: Delectable Souses, Dips and Dressings

Black Bean Dip

Yield: 4 servings | **Prep time:** 5 minutes |
Cook time: 0 minutes
Ingredients:

- 1 can (15 oz) black beans, drained and rinsed
- 2 tablespoons lime juice
- 1/4 cup fresh cilantro
- 1 garlic clove
- 1/2 teaspoon cumin
- Salt to taste
- Water as needed for consistency

Directions:

1. Blend all ingredients until smooth, adding water as needed.
2. Season with salt.
3. Serve with tortilla chips or sliced veggies.

Nutritional Information: 120 calories, 7g protein, 20g carbohydrates, 1g fat, 7g fiber, 0mg cholesterol, 200mg sodium, 400mg potassium.

Spicy Peanut Sauce

Yield: 4 servings | **Prep time:** 5 minutes
Ingredients:

- 1/2 cup peanut butter
- 2 tablespoons soy sauce
- 1 tablespoon maple syrup
- 1 tablespoon lime juice
- 1 clove garlic, minced
- 1 teaspoon grated ginger
- 1/2 teaspoon crushed red pepper flakes
- 1/4 cup warm water

Directions:

1. Whisk together all ingredients in a bowl, gradually adding warm water until the desired consistency is reached.
2. Adjust seasoning to taste.
3. Serve with spring rolls, salads, or grilled vegetables.

Nutritional Information: 200 calories, 8g protein, 12g carbohydrates, 16g fat, 2g fiber, 0mg cholesterol, 400mg sodium, 200mg potassium.

Chimichurri Sauce

Yield: 4 servings | **Prep time:** 10 minutes
Ingredients:
- 1 cup fresh parsley
- 1/4 cup fresh oregano
- 3 cloves garlic
- 1/2 cup olive oil
- 2 tablespoons red wine vinegar
- 1 teaspoon chili flakes
- Salt and pepper to taste

Directions:
1. Pulse parsley, oregano, and garlic in a food processor until finely chopped.
2. Stir in olive oil, vinegar, chili flakes, salt, and pepper.
3. Let sit for 10 minutes before serving. Serve over grilled vegetables or tofu.

Nutritional Information: 250 calories, 1g protein, 2g carbohydrates, 27g fat, 1g fiber, 0mg cholesterol, 10mg sodium, 100mg potassium.

Vegan Tzatziki Sauce

Yield: 4 servings | **Prep time:** 10 minutes
Ingredients:
- 1 cup unsweetened coconut yogurt
- 1 cucumber, grated and drained
- 2 cloves garlic, minced
- 1 tablespoon lemon juice
- 2 tablespoons chopped dill
- Salt and pepper to taste

Directions:
1. Combine all ingredients in a bowl.
2. Chill for at least 30 minutes before serving.
3. Serve with pita bread, falafel, or fresh vegetables.

Nutritional Information: 70 calories, 2g protein, 8g carbohydrates, 3g fat, 1g fiber, 0mg cholesterol, 150mg sodium, 150mg potassium.

Creamy Avocado Cilantro Sauce

Yield: 4 servings | **Prep time:** 5 minutes
Ingredients:
- 1 ripe avocado
- 1/4 cup cilantro leaves
- 1 clove garlic
- 2 tablespoons lime juice
- 1/4 cup water
- Salt and pepper to taste

Directions:
1. Blend all ingredients until smooth, adding more water if needed for desired consistency.
2. Season with salt and pepper to taste.
3. Serve as a dressing or dip for tacos, salads, or vegetables.

Nutritional Information: 100 calories, 2g protein, 8g carbohydrates, 9g fat, 5g fiber, 0mg cholesterol, 10mg sodium, 300mg potassium.

Roasted Red Pepper Hummus

Yield: 4 servings | **Prep time:** 10 minutes
Ingredients:
- 1 can (15 oz) chickpeas, drained and rinsed
- 1/2 cup roasted red peppers
- 1/4 cup tahini
- 2 tablespoons olive oil
- 2 tablespoons lemon juice
- 1 clove garlic
- Salt and smoked paprika to taste

Directions:
1. Combine chickpeas, roasted red peppers, tahini, olive oil, lemon juice, and garlic in a food processor. Blend until smooth.
2. Season with salt and smoked paprika.
3. Serve as a dip or spread, garnished with additional paprika.

Nutritional Information: 220 calories, 7g protein, 21g carbohydrates, 14g fat, 5g fiber, 0mg cholesterol, 320mg sodium, 260mg potassium.

Sun-Dried Tomato Pesto

Yield: 4 servings | **Prep time:** 5 minutes
Ingredients:
- 1/2 cup sun-dried tomatoes
- 1/4 cup almonds
- 1 clove garlic
- 1/4 cup olive oil
- 1/4 cup fresh basil leaves
- Salt and pepper to taste

Directions:
1. Blend sun-dried tomatoes, almonds, garlic, olive oil, and basil until smooth.
2. Season with salt and pepper.
3. Serve with pasta, spread on sandwiches, or as a dip.

Nutritional Information: 220 calories, 4g protein, 6g carbohydrates, 20g fat, 2g fiber, 0mg cholesterol, 150mg sodium, 300mg potassium.

Tahini Lemon Drizzle

Yield: 4 servings | **Prep time:** 5 minutes
Ingredients:
- 1/4 cup tahini
- 2 tablespoons lemon juice
- 1 clove garlic, minced
- 2-4 tablespoons water
- Salt to taste

Directions:
1. Whisk together tahini, lemon juice, and garlic, adding water until the desired consistency is reached.
2. Season with salt.
3. Drizzle over roasted vegetables, salads, or falafel.

Nutritional Information: 110 calories, 3g protein, 4g carbohydrates, 9g fat, 2g fiber, 0mg cholesterol, 20mg sodium, 120mg potassium.

Beet Hummus

Yield: 4 servings | **Prep time:** 10 minutes
Ingredients:
- 1 can (15 oz) chickpeas, drained and rinsed
- 1 medium beet, roasted and peeled
- 1/4 cup tahini
- 2 tablespoons olive oil
- 2 tablespoons lemon juice
- 1 clove garlic
- Salt to taste

Directions:
1. Blend all ingredients in a food processor until smooth.
2. Adjust seasoning as needed.
3. Serve with crackers or vegetable sticks.

Nutritional Information: 230 calories, 8g protein, 23g carbohydrates, 13g fat, 6g fiber, 0mg cholesterol, 310mg sodium, 290mg potassium.

Classic Hummus

Yield: 4 servings | **Prep time:** 10 minutes
Ingredients:
- 1 can (15 oz) chickpeas, drained and rinsed
- 1/4 cup tahini
- 2 tablespoons olive oil
- 2 tablespoons lemon juice
- 1 clove garlic
- Salt to taste
- Water as needed

Directions:
1. Combine chickpeas, tahini, olive oil, lemon juice, garlic, and salt in a food processor. Blend until smooth, adding water as needed for consistency.
2. Taste and adjust seasoning.
3. Serve with vegetables, pita bread, or as a spread.

Nutritional Information: 220 calories, 7g protein, 20g carbohydrates, 14g fat, 5g fiber, 0mg cholesterol, 300mg sodium, 250mg potassium.

Cilantro Lime Vinaigrette

Yield: 4 servings | **Prep time:** 5 minutes |
Ingredients:
- 1/2 cup fresh cilantro
- 1/4 cup lime juice
- 1/3 cup olive oil
- 1 garlic clove
- 1 teaspoon agave syrup
- Salt and pepper to taste

Directions:
1. Blend cilantro, lime juice, olive oil, garlic, and agave until smooth.
2. Season with salt and pepper.
3. Drizzle over salads or use as a marinade.

Nutritional Information: 220 calories, 0g protein, 3g carbohydrates, 24g fat, 0g fiber, 0mg cholesterol, 10mg sodium, 50mg potassium.

Cashew Sour Cream

Yield: 4 servings | **Prep time:** 10 minutes (plus soaking time) | **Cook time:** 0 minutes
Ingredients:
- 1 cup raw cashews, soaked for 4 hours
- 1/4 cup water
- 2 tablespoons lemon juice
- 1 tablespoon apple cider vinegar
- Salt to taste

Directions:
1. Drain and rinse cashews. Blend with water, lemon juice, and vinegar until smooth.
2. Season with salt. Chill before serving.
3. Serve with tacos, chili, or baked potatoes.

Nutritional Information: 180 calories, 5g protein, 10g carbohydrates, 14g fat, 1g fiber, 0mg cholesterol, 5mg sodium, 200mg potassium.

Guacamole

Yield: 4 servings | **Prep time:** 10 minutes
Ingredients:
- 3 ripe avocados, peeled and pitted
- Juice of 1 lime
- 1/4 cup finely chopped onion
- 1/4 cup chopped cilantro
- 2 Roma tomatoes, diced
- 1 garlic clove, minced
- Salt and pepper to taste

Directions:
1. Mash avocados in a bowl. Stir in lime juice.
2. Mix in onion, cilantro, tomatoes, and garlic. Season with salt and pepper.
3. Serve with tortilla chips or as a topping.

Nutritional Information: 250 calories, 3g protein, 15g carbohydrates, 22g fat, 10g fiber, 0mg cholesterol, 10mg sodium, 700mg potassium.

Vegan Caesar Dressing

Yield: 4 servings | **Prep time:** 5 minutes
Ingredients:
- 1/2 cup raw cashews, soaked and drained
- 1/4 cup water
- 2 tablespoons lemon juice
- 1 tablespoon Dijon mustard
- 1 tablespoon capers
- 1 garlic clove
- Salt and pepper to taste

Directions:
1. Blend all ingredients until smooth, adding more water if necessary.
2. Season with salt and pepper.
3. Serve over romaine lettuce or mixed greens.

Nutritional Information: 140 calories, 4g protein, 8g carbohydrates, 11g fat, 1g fiber, 0mg cholesterol, 150mg sodium, 200mg potassium.

Almond Dip

Yield: 4 servings | **Prep time:** 10 minutes
Ingredients:
- 1 cup raw almonds, soaked overnight and drained
- 1/4 cup water
- 2 tablespoons lemon juice
- 1 garlic clove
- Salt to taste
- 2 tablespoons chopped chives

Directions:
1. Blend almonds, water, lemon juice, and garlic until smooth.
2. Stir in chives. Season with salt.
3. Serve with vegetable sticks or crackers.

Nutritional Information: 220 calories, 8g protein, 10g carbohydrates, 18g fat, 4g fiber, 0mg cholesterol, 10mg sodium, 300mg potassium.

Beetroot and Walnut Dip

Yield: 4 servings | **Prep time:** 10 minutes
Ingredients:
- 2 medium beetroots, cooked and peeled
- 1/2 cup walnuts
- 2 tablespoons lemon juice
- 1 garlic clove
- Salt and pepper to taste
- Water as needed

Directions:
1. Blend beetroots, walnuts, lemon juice, and garlic until smooth. Add water if necessary.
2. Season with salt and pepper.
3. Serve chilled with crackers or vegetable sticks.

Nutritional Information: 150 calories, 4g protein, 12g carbohydrates, 10g fat, 3g fiber, 0mg cholesterol, 150mg sodium, 350mg potassium.

Avocado Lime Dressing

Yield: 4 servings | **Prep time:** 5 minutes
Ingredients:
- 1 ripe avocado
- Juice of 2 limes
- 1/4 cup olive oil
- 1 garlic clove
- Salt and pepper to taste
- Water as needed for desired consistency

Directions:
1. Blend avocado, lime juice, olive oil, and garlic until smooth, adding water as needed.
2. Season with salt and pepper.
3. Drizzle over salads or bowls.

Nutritional Information: 230 calories, 2g protein, 8g carbohydrates, 22g fat, 6g fiber, 0mg cholesterol, 10mg sodium, 400mg potassium.

Vegan Cream Cheese

Yield: 4 servings | **Prep time:** 10 minutes (plus soaking time)
Ingredients:
- 1 cup raw cashews, soaked overnight
- 2 tablespoons lemon juice
- 1 tablespoon nutritional yeast
- 1 garlic clove
- Salt to taste
- Water as needed for consistency

Directions:
1. Blend cashews, lemon juice, nutritional yeast, and garlic until smooth, adding water as needed.
2. Season with salt.
3. Chill before serving on bagels or toast.

Nutritional Information: 180 calories, 6g protein, 10g carbohydrates, 14g fat, 1g fiber, 0mg cholesterol, 5mg sodium, 200mg potassium.

Baba Ganoush

Yield: 4 servings | **Prep time:** 15 minutes |
Cook time: 45 minutes (for roasting eggplant)
Ingredients:
- 2 large eggplants
- 3 tablespoons tahini
- 2 garlic cloves, minced
- Juice of 1 lemon
- 2 tablespoons olive oil
- Salt and smoked paprika to taste
- Chopped parsley for garnish

Directions:
1. Roast eggplants at 400°F (200°C) until tender. Cool and peel.
2. Blend eggplant, tahini, garlic, lemon juice, and olive oil until smooth.
3. Season with salt and smoked paprika. Garnish with parsley.

Nutritional Information: 180 calories, 5g protein, 20g carbohydrates, 10g fat, 9g fiber, 0mg cholesterol, 300mg sodium, 600mg potassium.

Smoky Chipotle Aioli

Yield: 4 servings | **Prep time:** 5 minutes
Ingredients:
- 1/2 cup vegan mayonnaise
- 1 chipotle pepper in adobo sauce, minced
- 1 garlic clove, minced
- Juice of 1/2 lime
- Salt to taste

Directions:
1. Combine vegan mayonnaise, chipotle pepper, garlic, and lime juice in a bowl.
2. Mix until smooth. Season with salt.
3. Refrigerate for at least 30 minutes before serving to enhance flavors.

Nutritional Information: 200 calories, 0g protein, 2g carbohydrates, 22g fat, 0g fiber, 0mg cholesterol, 350mg sodium, 10mg potassium.

Conclusion

Congratulations on reaching the end of "Plant-Based Cookbook for Beginners." By now, you've equipped yourself with an extensive collection of recipes that cater to a wide array of everyday meals, from the simplest smoothies to the most comforting dinners. Each recipe has been crafted to ensure that you have the tools to bring variety, nutrition, and excitement to your table, every day of the week.

As you've progressed through the book, you've also learned how to efficiently prepare your meals, making the plant-based lifestyle not just an aspiration but a practical, stress-free reality. The techniques and tips provided are designed to streamline your cooking routine, reducing the time and effort required to prepare healthy, delicious plant-based meals.

The journey through plant-based cooking is one of discovery, learning, and, most importantly, enjoyment. You've now laid the foundation for a fulfilling lifestyle that not only benefits your health but also the planet. Remember, the variety of meals at your disposal ensures that your diet remains exciting and diverse, making it easier to sustain in the long run.

Embrace the no-stress cooking routine you've developed, and continue to explore the boundless possibilities that plant-based cooking offers. Your adventure in the kitchen has just begun, and with the skills and recipes you've acquired, you're well-equipped to make every meal a testament to the joys of plant-based eating. Here's to many more delicious, healthful meals ahead!

SHARE YOUR EXPERIENCE AND MAKE A DIFFERENCE

By sharing your journey to wellness, you can inspire others to lead healthier, happier lives. Let's spread the wisdom of plant-based cooking together.
Imagine being the catalyst for someone else's transformation, even if you didn't get credit for it.
How amazing would that be?
Please help inspire others by leaving a review for my book.

Thank you from the depths of my heart.
With gratitude, Ellie.

The Dirty Dozen and Clean Fifteen

As you embark on your plant-based journey, understanding which fruits and vegetables are most and least contaminated with pesticides can help you make informed choices about what to buy organic and where you might save money with conventionally grown produce. This knowledge is encapsulated in two lists known as "The Dirty Dozen" and "The Clean Fifteen," updated annually by the Environmental Working Group (EWG).

The Dirty Dozen refers to the twelve types of produce that are most heavily contaminated with pesticides. These are the fruits and vegetables that, when possible, you should consider buying organic to reduce your exposure to harmful chemicals. The Dirty Dozen typically includes items such as strawberries, spinach, kale, nectarines, apples, and tomatoes.

The Clean Fifteen, on the other hand, lists the fifteen types of produce that are least likely to hold pesticide residues. These are safer to purchase non-organic if you're looking to prioritize your budget while still making healthy choices. The Clean Fifteen often features avocados, sweet corn, pineapples, onions, and papayas among its ranks.

Here are a few tips for navigating these lists In your daily life:

Prioritize Organic for Dirty Dozen: Whenever possible, opt for organic versions of the Dirty Dozen to minimize your pesticide intake.
Save with Clean Fifteen: Feel more comfortable choosing conventionally grown items from the Clean Fifteen to help manage your grocery budget without significantly compromising on safety.
Wash Produce Thoroughly: Regardless of whether you're eating from the Dirty Dozen or the Clean Fifteen, always diligently wash your fruits and vegetables under running water to remove any residues or dirt.

By keeping the Dirty Dozen and Clean Fifteen in mind, you can make smarter choices that align with both your health goals and your budget. This approach allows you to enjoy the wide variety of plant-based foods available, with greater peace of mind about reducing your exposure to pesticides.

Clean

1. Avocados
2. Sweet corn
3. Pineapple
4. Onions
5. Papaya
6. Sweet peas (frozen)
7. Asparagus
8. Honeydew melon
9. Kiwi
10. Cabbage
11. Watermelon
12. Mushrooms
13. Mangoes
14. Sweet Potatoes
15. Carrots

Dirty

1. Strawberries
2. Spinach
3. Kale, collard & mustard greens
4. Grapes
5. Peaches
6. Pears
7. Nectarines
8. Apples
9. Bell & hot Peppers
10. Cherries
11. Blueberries
12. Green Beans

Alphabet Recipes Index

Made in the USA
Monee, IL
04 January 2025

76075691R00063